Unstuff Your Life!

Kick the Clutter Habit
and Completely Organize
Your Life for Good

Andrew J. Mellen
aka VirgoMan®

AVERY

a member of Penguin Group (USA) Inc.

New York

AVERY

Published by the Penguin Group

Penguin Group (USA) Inc., 375 Hudson Street, New York, New York 10014, USA · Penguin Group (Canada), 90 Eglinton Avenue East, Suite 700, Toronto, Ontario M4P 2Y3, Canada (a division of Pearson Penguin Canada Inc.) · Penguin Books Ltd, 80 Strand, London WC2R 0RL, England · Penguin Ireland, 25 St Stephen's Green, Dublin 2, Ireland (a division of Penguin Books Ltd) · Penguin Group (Australia), 250 Camberwell Road, Camberwell, Victoria 3124, Australia (a division of Pearson Australia Group Pty Ltd) · Penguin Books India Pvt Ltd, 11 Community Centre, Panchsheel Park, New Delhi–110 017, India · Penguin Group (NZ), 67 Apollo Drive, Rosedale, North Shore 0632, New Zealand (a division of Pearson New Zealand Ltd) · Penguin Books (South Africa) (Pty) Ltd, 24 Sturdee Avenue, Rosebank, Johannesburg 2196, South Africa

Penguin Books Ltd, Registered Offices: 80 Strand, London WC2R 0RL, England

Most Avery books are available at special quantity discounts for bulk purchase for sales promotions, premiums, fund-raising, and educational needs. Special books or book excerpts also can be created to fit specific needs. For details, write Penguin Group (USA) Inc. Special Markets, 375 Hudson Street, New York, NY 10014.

Library of Congress Cataloging-in-Publication Data

Mellen, Andrew J.
Unstuff your life! : Kick the clutter habit and completely organize your life for good / Andrew J. Mellen.
p.   cm.
Includes bibliographical references and index.
ISBN 978-1-58333-389-1
1. House cleaning.   2. Orderliness.   3. Storage in the home.   I. Title.
TX324.M45   2010   2010012956
648'.5—dc22

Printed in the United States of America
1   3   5   7   9   10   8   6   4   2

BOOK DESIGN BY NICOLE LAROCHE

For my mother, Frances Mellen;
my father, Jordon Mellen;
and my maternal grandmother, Bess Osborne—
who, each in his or her own way,
taught me about Like with Like
and putting my things away.

I wasn't the neatest kid, so
I guess it finally took.

Contents

Introduction

We are what we repeatedly do. Excellence, then, is not an act, but a habit.

ARISTOTLE

G entle reader; less-than-gentle reader; kind, clumsy, unfocused, slightly desperate reader . . . this book is for you. Welcome to my world. I hope soon it will also be your world. Or your version of my world. That would be even better.

And what exactly happens in my world? As an author, educator, professional organizer, and president of VirgoMan (www.virgoman.com), I travel around the country, working with individual clients and companies throughout the United States, helping them become more efficient, effective, and clutter-free. My clients vary widely in life experience and economic background and come from all walks of life. They run the gamut from award-winning authors, designers, and filmmakers to stay-at-home moms, carpooling dads, and harried executives. They also include small businesses and corporations ranging from production companies and publishing houses to tiny not-for-profit organizations and places of worship. What they all have in common is too much to do and not enough time to get it all done, and absolutely no idea of what to do with *all that stuff*!

I've led and facilitated seminars and workshops across the country, from house parties to hotel conference rooms, spreading the gospel of VirgoMan and unstuffing one's life through a delightfully nonsectarian evangelism. I've appeared in print (*O, The Oprah Magazine*; Oprah's book, *Dream Big!*; *In-Style* magazine, among others) and on radio and TV (NPR; *Oprah and Friends*; *The Satellite Sisters*; DIY's *Wasted Spaces*; HGTV's *Hot Trends*). Like the Johnny Appleseed of stuff, I cross the country spreading the seeds of organization and liberation at every opportunity. Strangers are fascinated by my line of work and it seems every conversation eventually touches on my simple yet comprehensive plan for kicking the clutter habit and completely transforming one's life. Whether I've been chatting with people or writing an article, however, time constraints or word-count restrictions have limited the volume of information I could share at one time. Until now.

Within this book, my enthusiastic editor and publisher have allowed me the room to finally spread out, sharing the step-by-step process I offer to clients and workshop attendees across the country—with greater detail and more instruction and commentary than I can necessarily include in a 1,500-word article, a thirty-minute TV show, or even a daylong seminar.

These simple steps, none of which are complicated, all of which have proved helpful to someone, guarantee success in getting organized. And I hope that number of people will now include you.

From entering and exiting your home with your keys and your bag and your wallet always in tow, to facing the challenges of large-scale spaces such as attics, basements, and garages—we cover it all in these pages. So whether you want to get a handle on your kitchen, your car, or your closet, you'll find exact methods and complete directions right here. I've avoided general living areas such as bedrooms or bathrooms or family rooms—the principles and techniques laid out for typical clutter hot spots are easily translatable to those spaces. Once you've mastered these techniques and applied them in your most challenging problem areas, you'll be able to apply them throughout your home. From your nightstand or entertainment center to your medicine cabinet, you'll easily eliminate expired medicine, unplayable videotapes or board games missing parts, broken emery boards and tweezers that no longer tweeze—until each room, each drawer, each space is neat, clean, and clutter-free.

Simply stated, after you finish reading and working through this book, you will always know where anything and everything is in your home or office or car. Vehicle registration? Got it. Spare keys? You bet. Social Security card? No question. Aunt Betty's famous piecrust recipe? Your tax bill? Without a doubt, you will have it in your hand before you break a sweat.

And you will never again find yourself drowning in stuff—whether it's papers, sporting goods, magazines, collectibles, or clothing. Through a series of activities and exercises you will replace your currently ineffective habits with powerfully successful habits, freeing up hundreds if not thousands of previously wasted hours. My clients know that I avoid absolutes when speaking with them, but I promise you that *always* and *never* are about to come true for you.

The ideas and directions laid out in this book form a road map to freedom from clutter. It may be hard to read that and not get a little excited and feel some skepticism creeping in as well. That's fine. These steps have been field-tested during years of working with clients in their homes and offices, so I feel confident that they will work for you, too.

They are exacting and precise without being rigid. Almost everything here is open to exploration, if not necessarily debate. I seldom ask you to do something without explaining why. I never liked it when my mom told me, "'Cause I'm the mom—that's why!" So I'll avoid doing that with you. You'll see in the chapters ahead that there is plenty of room to customize your approach and the appearance of your spaces.

I've worked hard to provide complete instructions and information so that you may release any resistance to change that crops up when I suggest a new way of doing things. Because, after all, if your previous attempts at getting organized had been so successful, you wouldn't be reading this book, would you? So trust me to give you good, orderly direction and I'll trust you to make it fit your lifestyle and budget.

You may get the urge to ask why you can't just do *some* things the way you've always done them, whether that's sorting the mail or folding the laundry. No doubt you may experience some relief from a piecemeal approach— but by consistently applying these techniques across the board, you are guaranteed to experience powerful and significant relief in every place you've ever been stuck on stuff anywhere in your life.

So before playing devil's advocate and touting minor miracles of successfully finding the insurance policy buried in a pile of catalogs, I will ask again, "If your way of finding and organizing things was working so well, would you really have picked up this book? And wouldn't you already know where your car keys are . . . every time you reached for them?"

While I'll frequently use the word "work" to describe our efforts together, I encourage you to think of this as training. Imagine yourself an Olympic athlete (maybe you are), training for the race of your life. With one major difference. Winning isn't based on beating anyone to the finish line, so there's no need to be intimidated. You don't have to change overnight, and you don't have to be perfect. That's a promise.

We could also think of this as a gift you're giving yourself. Each chapter offers a concise and manageable focus of study and care. There is ample time to learn and master these techniques, and each set of skills is broken down into easy-to-accomplish project-sized pieces. By the time you reach the end of each chapter, you will have achieved new mastery over another problem area. So whether you read only one or two chapters or tear through the entire book, each step along the way will bring you closer to regaining control over your things, your day, your life. That's the prize to keep your eyes on.

I've been asked, "What if I stop and start this process? What happens then?"

While I'd prefer you to enjoy the cumulative and consecutive success of building on each chapter's accomplishments, as I stated, there's no race to the finish line, and you may certainly take a break (or breaks). Because each chapter is its own unit of study, you can't lose the skills learned previously. There is a natural rhythm that you'll develop as you move from chapter to chapter, but a pause here and there won't dismantle what you've already incorporated.

So if you want or need a break, by all means, take one. Just don't stay away too long!

Likewise, I've been asked, "What if I don't want to start with chapter one and I want to start somewhere else? It's the basement that's making me crazy!"

I understand. You're feeling particularly jammed up or stymied, and you've selected this book because you're seeking some powerful and immediate help with a significant problem in your life, and there's no time to waste. To you I reply, please do start with chapter one and chapter two. You've waited this long to clean out your basement, a few more days won't make that much difference. In the first two chapters, this book carefully leads you through a discussion and exploration of your particular relationship with stuff, and teaches you the most fundamental skills first. Together, chapter one and chapter two lay the proper foundation for the work you'll face in subsequent chapters.

If you read and work through nothing else beyond chapter one and chapter two, you'll possess a basic working knowledge of the techniques we build on in the remaining chapters. Please do read the remaining chapters! But if you'd like to read and work through chapter one and chapter two, and *then* move on to chapter six (Auxiliary Spaces: Basements, Attics, Garages), go for it. I hope that is a compromise you can live with. Give me the first two chapters to teach you the fundamentals, and I'll give you the confidence and satisfaction of knowing that the building blocks of organization are well within your grasp.

I also recommend that you read each chapter through first without worrying about having to *do* anything. Read as if you were reading an article or short story, not studying homework or grasping for a life vest. Then return to the beginning and work your way through the chapter again, completing whatever exercises and tasks are assigned. That way, if you do skip around, picking and choosing, you'll be doing so from an informed point of view.

And that informed point of view is key to so much of what we'll do together as we work through this book. I'll hope to guide you toward making clear and informed decisions about whatever you're trying to accomplish. The distance between being prepared and being hasty is not that far in time allotted but vast in results achieved.

As you get in touch with or reawaken to the choices you've made historically around any number of issues, whether that's money and bills or tools or toys or clothes or food or dishes or (insert confounding item here), you'll begin to recognize that you often got into trouble the minute you stopped paying attention to what you were doing in the moment, and began thinking or feeling about something else while continuing to do the thing you had been doing before you shifted gears. So, remember: no multitasking. Leave that to the professionals. One task, one time.

If you're panicking now, thinking you don't have enough time to do one thing at a time, I'm here to remind you that you don't have enough time *not* to. Getting organized is not about doing more, it's about doing less. That is why more people "forget" who phoned or where the lid to the face cream is. *You can't forget what you never knew.* If you were walking around the house looking for the ringing telephone with the top to the face cream in your hand, were you actually paying enough attention to what you were doing to then be able to forget where you set that lid down as you reached for the phone? Exactly.

A key to this work's effectiveness is to move deliberately (one might say "slowly" if that wouldn't rekindle said panic above) and to take on only one area at a time, allowing enough time for new habits to develop, and then to build from there. Researchers say that it takes twenty-one to thirty days to build a new habit, so I think we should err on the side of caution and allow a full thirty days for new habits to become established and rooted. Better to have too much time to perfect something than not enough.

That means you can transform your life in as little as sixty days. Perhaps you're thinking once again, "But I'm in desperate shape, I need help *now* and I can't wait for things to change gradually!" To you I say: perfect, you're in the perfect place. Remember this feeling of desperation. It's the last time you need to feel this unsteady and out of control—and avoiding this feeling again can be powerful motivation *if* you actually remember it. So take a moment and study it. Are your palms a bit clammy? Is your breathing shallow and labored or deep and steady? Are you itchy? Hungry? Angry? Distracted? Ready to toss this book across the room? Note it all.

And here's some relief. That feeling of swirling, unformed impending doom is a great fiction, the product of our unique and remarkable imaginations. Through stories we tell ourselves over and over again—perhaps even unconsciously at this point—we create and re-create these states of panic. Unless a nuclear holocaust is pending, there's little about being late and disorganized that merits this degree of unease. Now, you may be an adrenaline junkie who really doesn't *want* to be organized; you may secretly crave the rush of panic, and if so, then perhaps you should set this book aside. It may not be the right time for you to read this book. It will ruin your buzz. You'll never be able to rush around the house, frantically searching for your keys or your purse or your cell phone or your living will again without hearing my voice or, even better, your own voice reminding you, "This isn't brain surgery; no one is lying open on the table. There is enough time to find or accomplish this."

There is a pervasive, tremendous lie we collectively tell ourselves and reinforce each day—namely, that there is *not* enough time to accomplish what is really important to us. But there is enough time . . . for what is truly important. Anyone who's cared for a sick or dying friend or loved one knows that time shifts when the illusory veil of immortality is removed. The bills get paid, food gets prepared and eaten, but superfluous phone calls are not returned. Sales go unattended. The things that are really important find a way of insisting on receiving if not one's complete attention, certainly adequate attention. And the baloney (or bull$#!%, if you prefer) falls away. Tim McGraw had a very popular song out, "Live Like You Were Dying." And, of course, we *are* dying. I hope not in some immediate tragic way, but slowly, each day we age. And we can never know when our last day will come. So if we can hold that in our beings without feeling maudlin about it, we will gain clarity that our time really *is* limited and that what is important *is* what we really want to spend our time doing.

That's what this book is all about.

I don't think paying bills and filing papers and cleaning out the junk drawer is or should be that important. The messes that surround you are keeping you from what is important. So I'm suggesting that you commit enough time to break some old bad habits, replace them with some new useful habits, and then get on with the rest of your life. Once you've trained yourself to do things consistently, you'll never have to waste a precious moment of your day looking for your house keys or wondering where the phone bill is as they're turning off your service or riffling through the same clothes over and over again in search of the one clean shirt you actually enjoy wearing that flatters you.

It seems antithetical, I know, to spend this time once to never have to spend it again. But there is no free lunch. As with so many other things, either you're going to pay up front or you're going to pay on the back end for being disorganized, and unfortunately, when you pay on the way out it's always more expensive than if you had simply paid at the beginning. Here's an illustration: the trousers you bought on sale and financed may have been discounted when you charged them, but six months later when the finance charges are added up, did you really save 20 percent off their cost, or did you end up paying 30 percent more than the full retail purchase price? There you have it. It's just a little math.

The time you spend now learning simple and easy ways of organizing your life will lay a foundation for uncomplicated and productive time in the future. Not "someday," that mythical land where time stands still and you're an avid scrapbooker, baking ten dozen cookies for the church bazaar, sewing your children's clothes, and finally learning to fly-fish on the Colorado River. That day doesn't exist. Even for Martha Stewart. It's useful to remember that she has staff. And since you probably don't, it's time to surrender "someday." *"Someday" doesn't exist.* But today does. So welcome to it. Grab it, seize it, cherish it, and make it your own. Let's begin!

1 You Are Not Your Stuff

> We don't think our way to right action; we act our way to right thinking.
> **WILLIAM JAMES**

> When I let go of what I am, I become what I might be.
> **LAO-TZU**

> Happiness is a how; not a what.
> **HERMANN HESSE**

n the beginning, God created man. And then, apparently right after that, She must have created stuff. Because it's everywhere. You can hardly move without tripping over stuff. And since stuff is probably not going away, we need to get right with stuff. Because otherwise, stuff will never be right with us.

Please get a pen or pencil and a simple notebook. We're going to do a little writing. I suggest that whatever you use as a notebook, you keep it handy and use it only for this work. I don't suggest you do this in your personal journal or on a series of Post-it notes. You'll probably want to refer back to this work at some later date, and it should be cohesive and somehow bound together.

There are no right or wrong answers to the following questions. They are not intended to humiliate you or to expose your faults or foibles. They're intended to start the conversation about where stuff lives in your life. If we want to unstuff your life, we need to know what needs unstuffing. You won't be graded on your answers, because this isn't a test—it's an exploration. Take your time, write out your answers (rather than answering them verbally), and tell the truth. To yourself. Because you're the only person who's going to be reading this. We're not looking for pretty; we're looking for honest. So resist answering them as if this were an ideal world and this is how you wish you felt. Or answering them as if you had already finished this book and have your stuff well under control.

1. Do you often feel stuck?
2. How often do you feel overwhelmed?
3. Do you feel that there's something else you should be doing but can't ever seem to get to it?
4. Are there things you keep telling yourself you'll do as soon as some other things are finished?
5. Do you ever finish those other things and actually get to the things you've put off?
6. Do you ever feel caught up, as if everything on your to-do list has been checked off?
7. Do you ever complain of being bored, or of having too much time on your hands?
8. If so, how do you address that? What do you do to fill that time?
9. Do you stop what you're doing when anyone calls and shift all your attention to them?
10. Do you do this whether it's an emergency or just an everyday call?
11. Do you always agree to do a favor for someone, whether it's convenient for you or not?
12. If so, do you ever feel put-upon or get resentful as a result?
13. Do you think that saying no makes you a bad or selfish person?
14. Is there ever an appropriate time to say no? When?
15. Do you get resentful if people say no to you?
16. Do you take "no" personally—do you sometimes think they might have said yes to someone else under similar circumstances?

17. What's the difference between an excuse and an explanation?

18. Do you think you're often offering valid explanations for things and not making excuses?

19. Have you ever had a disagreement with someone over this interpretation?

20. Does your stuff seem to have a life of its own?

21. Do you set something down and swear it moves sometime during the night?

22. How often during a week do you misplace something you need—keys, wallet, cell phone?

23. Are you mostly upbeat, except when you think about your stuff?

24. Or did you used to be, and now you just feel beaten down?

25. Do you have piles of papers around but swear you can find anything in them?

26. Have you ever freaked out—becoming panicky or unreasonably upset—when someone moved your stuff?

27. Have you ever lost something that was important to you because someone confused it for trash?

28. If that has happened, do you feel partly responsible or are you the victim of someone else's mistake?

29. Do you get nervous when the phone rings?

30. Do you screen your calls?

31. Has stuff made living in your home challenging?

32. Does your stuff seem to force you into smaller and smaller living spaces?

33. Do you sleep to one side of your bed because you have a pile of stuff next to you?

34. Do you sometimes have difficulty breathing?

35. Do you spend more time looking for things than doing the things you love?

36. Is looking for things threatening to overtake your passions?

37. Are you often just a few minutes late to get somewhere?

38. Do you tell yourself that being late is not a big deal?

39. Do you think that the people you love are more important than stuff?

40. If someone looked only at your behavior, would they objectively see that?

41. When you're feeling blue, do you think that shopping will get you out of your funk?

42. Does the act of buying something give you a warm and fuzzy feeling?

43. Have you ever said, "I'd die without _____?"

44. If you've said the previous sentence, were you talking about a person or a thing?

45. Do you often speak in absolutes (such as "I always . . ." or "I never . . .")?

46. Do you have stories about most of the things you own?

47. Do you like to tell them to your friends and family? How about strangers? Anyone who'll listen?

48. Do they find the stories as fascinating as you do?

49. Do you think you spend more time talking about stuff or about things you've done or plan to do?

Wow. Congratulations. That's a lot of questions. Thanks for taking the time to answer them all. Did you answer them all? If you didn't, please go back and do so. And yes, I am serious.

As you review your answers, make note of any patterns that are revealed—about your relationship with things, about your relationship with time, and about your relationships with people. These questions, again, are not designed to shame you or to hurt you in any way. They're here to help us identify where you're stuck on stuff and where stuff is stuck on you. I've often seen that lightbulb go on behind clients' eyes when they first recognize that what they thought they were spending their days doing was not in fact what they were actually doing. Or it was getting done, but with a heap of resentment or resistance or avoidable delays.

So use the information gathered from your answers to clarify whether you are in fact spending your time doing the things you think you're doing *and* that these are the things you want to be doing. If, instead, you discover that you are caught in a cycle of activities and tasks that may be necessary but are also consistently pushing their way ahead of things that matter more, in the following pages you'll learn how to reverse that process and put the necessary tasks back in their proper place.

If you find that you spend more time with things than with people and that doesn't please you, here too you will learn how to manage your possessions so that you are not spending valuable time interacting with them when you could be enjoying the company of friends and family.

Half-Measures, Staying on the Hook, and Perfectionism

I don't have rules about much. But I am sure that half measures are useless. Actually, they're worse than useless; they undermine our ability to accomplish anything of significance in our lives. So if you're someone who has a history of enthusiastic beginnings and rapid losses of interest or picking and choosing how you'll participate in something, constantly evaluating your commitment and efforts, I'm strongly suggesting you let that go for the rest of our time together. This is voluntary—no one showed up at your door and said, "Read this book and get your act together" . . . did they?

If they didn't, then this is something you think is worth doing. So I'm going to support you in doing it fully. What's laid out before you is a feast of tools and tips and questions and suggestions to help you *unstuff your life.* Whatever that means to you. And whatever that does mean to you, I want you to do it completely. Not three-fourths of the way, not seven-eighths of the way—all the way. You won't know what could have been possible if you let yourself off the hook.

And believe me, I've heard all the excuses . . . I mean explanations. You're tired; you've got chores to do; you've tried this before and it didn't work;

so-and-so tried this before and their best friend told them that it didn't work; you recently read a study that said this could never work; you're too busy; you're not smart enough; you're too smart—you'll figure out all the angles (there are no angles); you're too fat, too thin, too tall, too short, too old, not old enough; someone's on their way over; someone's just about to leave; you're just about to leave; you've got somewhere else to be or to get to; you'll do it "later"; you don't see the point . . . The list goes on.

As a reformed perfectionist, I also understand the corollary notion that if you can't do something perfectly, there's no point in attempting it at all. Which I know today is baloney. Of course there's a point in doing something imperfectly. And more important, there's a big difference between imperfectly and incompletely. You can get a perfect score on a math test, but if you're looking to get a perfect score on life, you may need to redefine what perfect looks like. First of all, life doesn't always add up, and second, unlike a math test, no one's grading you on life (except maybe God, depending on how you define God—but I'd like to think She grades on a curve, anyway).

So let's shift our thinking about how we evaluate our efforts and use a model in which effort expended equals results achieved. That way we can get off the thankless merry-go-round of "everything has to be perfect the first time or it's a waste of time." And we now know that if we are diligent, if we don't let ourselves off the hook, if we apply ourselves 100 percent, then we are guaranteed to receive a 100 percent return on the experience. And when that experience is *unstuffing your life*, of turning chaos into order and moving from confusion to organization, no wholehearted effort is wasted. The outcome may not be perfect, and if so, you're free to try again. *Hmm,* so maybe with enough earnest attempts you actually can get a perfect score on life?

If you still haven't answered all those questions, please go back and do that now. Believe me, I can sit here longer than you can. So just do it and get it over with. Besides, what's coming next is so great that you'll be bummed to miss it and of course it won't make a lick of sense if you haven't answered every single one of those questions!

What We're Going to Cover in This Chapter

☐ What Stuff Is and What Stuff Isn't
☐ You Are Not Your Stuff
☐ If I'm Not My Stuff, What Am I?
☐ Your Core Values
☐ Aligning with Your Core Values
☐ The Stuff Behind the Stuff
☐ The Promise

What Stuff Is and What Stuff Isn't

All this talk about stuff, and what exactly *is* stuff?

Stuff (noun):
Miscellaneous unspecified objects, as in "the trunk is full of stuff."

Indeed it is. And may still be. I love that definition. Stuff is the vaguest of vague objects. Not only is it miscellaneous, it's also unspecified. How perfect is that? So now that we know what stuff is, let's talk about what stuff isn't.

Stuff isn't people. Stuff isn't animals—companion, barnyard, or wild. And it isn't plants. Stuff is nothing that's alive, so let's add that to our definition above.

Miscellaneous *inanimate* unspecified objects.

That's what we've got piling up around us and dragging behind us, and that's the subject of this book. The accumulation of so many individual specified things that they have now morphed and blurred into a mass of miscellaneous inanimate unspecified objects. That makes the next part easier.

You Are Not Your Stuff

As we now know, stuff doesn't breathe. So at least in this instance, you're off the hook. You are not your stuff.

Radical, isn't it? You are not your stuff. Madison Avenue might have you believing otherwise. They'd argue that you are completely your stuff. That you're nothing if you're *not* your stuff. That's a rather bleak outlook, and surprisingly pervasive. But we know better.

Say it out loud with me: "I am not my stuff."

Cool. How'd that sound? Convincing? Say it again.

"I am not my stuff." Louder. "I am not my stuff." Louder still. "I am not my stuff!"

Now go to the window, open it, lean out, and shout, "I'm mad as hell, and I'm not going to take it anymore!"

Just kidding!

Please don't do that. But I appreciate your willingness to consider it. You're a good sport.

On one level, I'd like to think we could all identify where our sweaters or our computers or our music collections end and we begin. But many people cannot distinguish between themselves and the objects that surround them. The stereo system, the television, the dishes, the clothes, the car. They may know that they are not literally a machine for amplifying sound, but somewhere, in some subtle or not-so-subtle way, the lines get blurred. They start to feel like the sports car *is* an extension of themselves. While not exactly flesh and blood, it's an expression of their thoughtfulness, their talent, their success, their discernment, and taste. Maybe even the best parts of themselves. And suddenly we find we are defining ourselves in part by what we own.

The solution for this is not the elimination of objects. It's not their fault. And I'm not suggesting that you get rid of everything you've worked very hard to accumulate. I'm suggesting that in our hurry to gather more and more things around us, we become confused as to what has purpose in our lives and what provides self-definition, or self-reflection, or even distraction.

Think for a few moments about how you or someone you know talks about the things that surround them. Have you ever said or heard someone say, "Man, I love my (new) _____?"

When's the wedding?

How about, "Oh my God! Where has this been? I don't know how I've lived without this _____ for all these years! This is going to change my life!"

We usually leave it at that, that the implied change we're speaking of is assumed to be "for the better," even though it's unspoken.

But how often is the addition of stuff, of some thing, actually the agent of transforming one's life, particularly for the better? Maybe the invention of the modern washing machine. Or the wheel. But an iPhone? Tickle Me Elmo? A remote-control ceiling fan? Really? That might be setting the bar a bit too low.

Computers have certainly made writing this book easier, but I do know exactly how I lived before one. I used a typewriter. And before that, sheets of paper and lots of pens and pencils. I think I also played a lot more tennis and rode my bike more often. So let's try to distinguish between comfortable, convenient, and life-altering. Hyperbole can be fun, and certainly dramatic, but particularly when it comes to unstuffing your life, we're going to want to accurately describe the scale of an event and its impact on our behavior and our choices.

As a teenager, I collected record albums. I loved music. I still do. The point is that I was surrounded by record albums. Collecting them gave me an identity. And allowed me a place to get lost. I owned albums I never listened to because I liked the cover art, or because I thought a particular artist or record was a good addition to my collection. Especially if you were impressed by the breadth of my musical tastes. I lugged those albums all over the Midwest for years. Milk crate after milk crate.

And books—same story. Books I had read and would never read again. Books I found at thrift stores, on the street—who could leave a copy of *Catcher in the Rye* or *To Kill a Mockingbird* lying on the ground, looking so forlorn? It's a classic. It deserves a home. Mine. And I hoped that when you visited me, you'd think me well read and treat me accordingly.

Since I was a little disorganized back then, you may not have noticed that I had multiple copies of *Catcher in the Rye,* since they weren't sorted or stored in any kind of order, just randomly shoved onto shelves somewhere. If I actually needed to find a book, I'd search through hundreds of them, trying to remember something distinct about the spine or cover to narrow it down for me. *Catcher,* in particular, benefited from that burgundy cover with yellow print. Not every book was that easily identifiable.

Most of those books are now gone. There are used-book stores all over the greater Detroit and Chicago areas that became the recipients of my purged collection. Today I buy books that interest me and that I'm committed to reading. I sometimes swap books with friends. And I spend a decent amount of time in public libraries—reading and borrowing books I very much want to read but do not feel compelled to own.

There are plenty of books that we should purchase. Books we use for work. Books we study and need to write in. I'd like to think this book is one of those books. Cookbooks, books for pleasure, favorite books that have become too dog-eared—all worth purchasing. But there are also times when borrowing or swapping with a friend or the public library is a viable alternative. So this is a perfect example of shifting our thinking toward experience and away from possession. If the reading of the book is the primary goal, we can carefully consider the best way to accomplish that—which may or may not include adding another possession to our lives.

All of those albums are now gone, too. Some have been replaced with their CD or MP3 equivalents, but only the ones I still listen to. I let them go long before I started helping others unstuff their lives. And the experience of getting rid of them was bittersweet, to be sure. I loved those albums, I had a great deal invested in them, and certainly the money was in some ways the least of it. They were, I thought (as our sports-car driver thinks about his car), an extension of me—a visible, easily readable piece of me out in the world. I know now today that that's slightly off the mark. That while others may have in fact been judging me on my taste in music, I was much more invested in my own judgment of myself.

I am not my stuff.

You are not your stuff.

We are not our stuff.

Now, I'd like to say that what we think of ourselves is the most important thing, which I believe is true, and that nobody else really cares what kind of cars we drive, or whose name is on our clothing, or what we're reading or listening to, which is not true. Some people do care. They may even care more than they should or more than is appropriate or more than is even healthy. We can't control them. We can control only ourselves.

So instead of projecting into our friend's or neighbor's mind, which can't be very comfortable, let's just say that, going forward, what other people think of us is none of our business. Unless they make it our business by sharing it with us. So until they do, and given that few of us, if any, can actually read minds, let's take all that energy and funnel it through our imaginations into much more fun and productive pursuits.

If I'm Not My Stuff, What Am I?

Have you ever fought with someone you cared about over a thing? Something misplaced, or borrowed and not returned, or returned soiled. Or damaged. Did they seem genuinely sorry? Was that enough? While it's not acceptable for someone to lose or destroy your belongings, accidents happen. As a result, you may decide that you'll never lend out anything ever again. You might take it a step further and decide to never have anyone in your house again, either. Because even under your watchful eye, accidents may happen there, too.

Rather than holding on to things tighter in an attempt to control their permanence, could you decide instead to loosen your grip even more? To recognize or even entertain the idea that all things are impermanent, even you? To shift your relationship with things toward one of appreciation while they're intact, and celebration when they break or fail? This may influence you to lend out only the Honda and keep the Rolls Royce in the garage—that's a fine compromise. But how important do you want to make any one thing, really?

What is worth ending a relationship over? You can usually get another thing, even something as special as a Donna Karan cashmere sweater that was on sale for so little money it's both thrilling and embarrassing to mention. It's a little harder to replace the friend you've known since kindergarten.

So if we think of ourselves as guardians of these things, as stewards responsible for the care and maintenance of these objects, but not their God, then we can be appropriately vigilant and also softer when something about their condition or even existence shifts. We can feel sad or disappointed or relieved, and still not feel called to *do* anything other than feel. That sounds liberating to me.

Notable Note

As much as you may think you own anything, when you leave this planet, wherever you're headed next, the stuff you've surrounded yourself with is staying right here and will be redistributed for someone else's use. Unless your kids, friends, or other heirs have always hated a particular object, and then it's just going in the trash. How about that for an image? Sobering, eh? Take a moment and imagine the thing you are most attached to. See it. Feel it. Hold it. And now imagine it broken and in the trash. Wow. If that's its inevitable fate, can we get right with that? Accept it? Wills and codicils aside, once we're gone we'll have no control over what will happen next to our belongings. As we've no doubt heard so many times before, the lesson is to enjoy them now. And then let them go.

Your Core Values

What is important to you? This is not a rhetorical question.

Your core values lie at the very center of who you are. If you've ever heard anyone mention their moral compass, core values provide direction for that compass. When what you do and what you value are in sync, your life is in balance and the direction and purpose of your life are easy to articulate and pursue.

Once you know your core values, you can eliminate activities that don't align with them, such as accumulating things that don't really serve you or support you in achieving your goals. Such as spending time on activities that distract you from accomplishing the things you're passionate about, or paid to do. Or doing things you are passionate about but not adequately compensated for, and then feeling like a martyr or growing resentful. We may at any time experience acting in opposition to our core values for any number of reasons—feeling that we "should" do something we know isn't right, or doing something we're "expected" to do, when we feel pressured or when we feel we have no choice, or even without thinking, because it's something we've always done.

What follows are some questions and a list of values. The values list is not exhaustive, but it's comprehensive. If something is missing from it, feel free to write it in. As a favor to me, I'd appreciate an e-mail with any additions so I can update my own lists used in workshops and with clients.

There are, once again, no universally right or preferred answers. The right answers are the truthful answers for you. If you value something that you judge as unappealing or wrong or stupid, either shift your feeling or shift your values. Circle fifteen words to begin with, from the list below, that most strongly express the ideas you value.

Abundance	Charity	Courage
Accountability	Clarity	Creativity
Achievement	Cleverness	Dedication
Adventure	Collaboration	Dependability
Ambition	Commitment	Dignity
Candor	Community support	Diversity
Caring	Competition	Effectiveness
Casualness	Contribution	Efficiency
Challenge	Cooperation	Empathy

Energy	Inner harmony	Reliability
Entrepreneurship	Innovation	Resilience
Environmental concern	Integrity	Respect
Equality	Intimacy	Responsibility
Ethics	Joy	Responsiveness
Excellence	Justice	Safety
Excitement	Kindness	Security
Fairness	Leadership	Self-control
Faith	Learning	Self-esteem
Fame	Listening	Service
Family	Location	Simplicity
Financial growth	Love	Spirituality
Financial security	Loyalty	Stability
Flexibility	Mutual respect	Stewardship
Freedom	Obedience	Strength
Friendship	Open communication	Success
Fulfillment	Openness	Support
Fun	Order	Survival
Generosity	Originality	Teachability
Grace	Passion	Teamwork
Growth	Peace	Tolerance
Happiness	Persistence	Transparency
Health	Power	Trust
Honesty	Profitability	Trustworthiness
Honor	Prosperity	Truth
Hope	Purposefulness	Wealth
Humility	Quality	Wholeness
Humor	Receptivity	Willingness
Independence	Recognition	Wisdom
Informal	Relationships	

Great. Now, a few exercises. Please write your answers to these questions in your notebook.

1. Imagine yourself at the end of your life—there's no pain or drama (this isn't an acting class!), just the culmination of a long, well-lived life. Looking back, what are the three most resonant and meaningful memories that you have? And what are the three most important lessons that you've learned? What makes each of them so significant? Imagine you're going to share this information with the person you love most so they might benefit from your experiences.

2. Think of someone you deeply respect and admire. Write down five qualities that they possess that most define them for you. Give examples of those qualities in action.

3. Think of a mentor or someone who has influenced your thinking and choices in a fundamental way. Write down five qualities that they possess that most define them for you. Give examples of those qualities in action.

4. Describe a time when you were particularly proud of how you participated in something, when you felt you were your best self. List the qualities that you exhibited.

5. What do you want to be remembered for?

6. If resources and access were not obstacles, what would you choose to do with your life?

7. What do you love to do, what makes you the happiest, what are you most passionate about?

8. What do you want to accomplish in the world?

9. What do you want to give back to the world?

Excellent. Now, of the first fifteen words you selected, and of everything else you've written above, what are your top five values? What are the five qualities that you cannot imagine living without, that's how essential they are to who and how you want to be. Write them either here or in your notebook.

These values are at the very center of who you are. And that's most definitely not stuff.

Now that you know what's important to you and have a clearer understanding of what you value, it's finally time to put those analytical skills to use on something practical. Return to your answers for the first set of questions in this chapter and evaluate your responses, looking for where your core values are reflected in those answers. Write next to your answers each core value that you see reflected there. If you see none of your core values in your answer, put a zero there, and write what you do see reflected there instead, whether that's fear, resentment, reticence, resistance, envy—just note it.

Once more I'll remind you that you have nothing to fear from the truth—you're doing private work and your frank assessment of your behavior will only help to clear the way for the kind of change you desire. If you value love and kindness and find that you're mostly scared and resentful, how do you get from here to there? What are the choices you need to make to shift your conscious or unconscious stance from one of resistance to one of receptivity? How do you let things go that you don't value or don't serve you to make room for and embrace the things that you do value and will serve you?

There are no universal answers to the above questions. What I believe are universal tools for discovering the answers are open-mindedness, willingness, honesty, and quiet reflection. You don't need to become a monk to sit still long enough to hear something beneath the constant chatter of your mind. Five minutes of doing seemingly nothing besides sitting still and reflecting on the questions above (as well as others that may start to come to you once you begin this process) can quiet your thoughts down enough to reveal some answers. Let's try it now.

Get a timer or something similar that will make a sound when it goes off. You'll set it for five minutes. Focus on your answers to the first questions, your core values, and the questions of how to bring your behavior into alignment with your core values. Ask, almost in a prayer, for the ability to find what you have been responsible for in the past or present and what you can change for the better, now and in the future. If it helps you, you may dim the lights, but do not sit in the dark.

If you find yourself starting to judge yourself or calling yourself names for any of the places where your behavior is not yet in alignment, or even for doing this exercise, recognize that. And then, rather than tightening up or resisting it, just look at it. As if it were someone else who was judging himself or herself. Approach the tension or judgment with a degree of curiosity rather than disappointment or anger and you should be able to refocus on the questions before you.

It may be that the entire five minutes are filled with just judging and looking, with just spinning around mentally with only brief glimpses of the questions. That's fine. The goal is simply to begin or resume a process of sitting still and reflecting. With patience, you will learn both what you have been doing that runs counter to your core values and ways to do something different to yield different results. When the timer goes off, write down anything that seems noteworthy from your quiet time. Do this for thirty days consecutively and you will be amazed at the clarity you obtain around your behavior and effective ways to shift it in your favor.

Set the timer now.

The Stuff Behind the Stuff

Some of the mental "noise" or distractions mentioned in the last section may occur in the form of stories. We tell ourselves stories all day. Some out loud, and some as chatter, running just in the background, barely audible to our subconscious. We make up new reasons or reinforce established reasons why something should be done, or why something shouldn't be done. Why if it *is* done, it should be done a particular way. We spend a lot of time trying to figure out what something means—whether that's guessing at the motivations behind someone's behavior or evaluating and assigning value to stuff.

Let's set the analysis of others' behavior aside for now. What I want to focus on are the stories we tell ourselves about our stuff. I call these stories, "the stuff behind the stuff."

I'm not suggesting that these stories are lies, although some may be untrue or at least not based on fact. What I am suggesting is that we often take an object and weave a narrative around it, until that story becomes bound up in that object. Any interaction with that object means also interacting with the story. So much so that the story almost stands guard over the object, the story acting as the first line of defense. You have to get through the story to get to the object.

This complicated relationship between story and object is why so many people struggle with any part of getting organized, particularly that first step. If often doesn't matter what the objective is—whether it's finding a proper home for the object or sifting through piles of stuff to possibly purge some surplus items. Often the story has so much power over folks that they stand immobile in the face of it—it's become an effective barrier to any change, even at times to simply putting something away.

So getting to and through the stuff behind the stuff is key to this process. Your grandfather's top hat is still going to be your grandfather's top hat. And if the story is that your grandfather wore that top hat at his wedding to your grandmother, that's not going to change, either. What is, I hope, going to change is the imperative that story places on your grandfather's top hat: "You must keep me. I'm eighty-five years old, and that wedding was the reason you're here today. You'd be a terrible grandchild if you got rid of me."

We think nothing of discarding a gum wrapper once we've taken out the piece of gum and put it in our mouths. At a core level, that top hat is no different from the gum wrapper. They both exist, they both served a purpose, they both might have no more purpose to serve *in our lives* at this time. You must know, of course, that that top hat is not your grandfather. That bears repeating. That top hat is not your grandfather. It's just an article of his clothing. So I'm not suggesting that you get rid of your grandfather. You might be hearing that. In fact, the story, the stuff behind the stuff, might actively be telling you that. "Hey! He's suggesting you toss your grandfather in the trash, or send him off to Goodwill. Your grandfather would never do that to you. You ungrateful brat. Put me down!"

But if you're done with the hat, if that hat, practically speaking, is a burden—if it's taking up room that you need for something you do use, such as one of your own hats or bags, or if it makes you sad to look at it, or if it's disintegrating and literally falling apart on your closet floor and could never be worn again by anyone, let alone your grandfather, then we can celebrate your grandparents' wedding. We can appreciate the history woven into that hat, and we can reverently and respectfully let go of the hat. Don't turn everything you own into a ball and chain. Actual balls and chains will be enough. Let the hat be just a hat. And if you're done with the hat, then you are empowered to release the hat back to the universe for its next chapter, a chapter that may not include you.

The Promise

I can't promise you that if you're single, by the time you finish working through this book you'll be happily married. If marriage even interests you. I can't promise you that your boss will start treating you better or that you'll finally get along with the guy or gal in the next cubicle or that you'll always get a good parking space.

What I can promise you is this: If you are diligent about this work, if you are consistent and alert and apply yourself, when you are finished with this book, you will have more time on your hands than you ever thought possible. You will do less, and you will accomplish more.

You will always be able to find anything—in your home or office, kitchen or car—within thirty seconds. You will never be late because you misplaced your car keys. You may be late because of traffic, but we can't control everything.

You will finally have the time to do the things you love to do. Or to discover the things you love. Or to rediscover them.

If you don't have to waste another minute looking for something you were certain you just saw but now can't seem to find, that's one more minute you have to write a love letter. Or the great American novel. Or to bake some brownies. Or to bathe your daughter. Or to visit your mother. Or to solve global warming. Now imagine what you can do with another hour, or hours, or days, or weeks. Exactly.

I can't tell you what to do with that time once you get it. That's another book. Or at least a conversation over a cup of tea. What I can do is guide you through a precise process that will enable you to *unstuff your life* of everything that doesn't serve you and shine a light on everything that does. How's that sound instead?

Now, so we don't waste another minute discussing theories or waxing philosophical—let's get you cracking on this new way of life. I want to launch you into the book with whatever messy mix of enthusiasm and skepticism and inertia and hope you're currently brewing and help you change your life.

Deep breath. And here we go.

2 | Keys • Wallet • Purse • Mail

I can't find my car keys in the morning.
Trying to get out of my house is a nightmare.
Where's my wallet? Where are my keys? I have
to go find a missing person!

ANTHONY LAPAGLIA, ACTOR
("WITHOUT A TRACE")

Beware of the door with too many keys.
PORTUGUESE PROVERB

As silly as this may sound, I suggest you begin this next section on the first day of a month. We're going to be spending the next thirty or so days learning and practicing new behaviors with the goal being to build new habits during those days. It will be much easier to keep track of where you're at if you line up the beginning of this chapter with the first day of the month. Why make this more difficult than it needs to be?

If that seems too long to wait, choose an interval of five—start on the fifth or tenth or fifteenth, etc., and write down your start date here (and on a calendar) so that you can easily keep track of where you are in this process.

I started this course on: _5-5-13_

Avoid starting on the thirtieth . . . you can wait a day or two to begin at the beginning of the month. Just like starting a diet, live it up for a day or two. Make a good and disorganized mess of your house. It's all going to change in a few days, anyway. Why not indulge yourself in some "bad" behavior for a few more days? This little binge can only make you that much more uncomfortable and ready to do something new. So go for it. See you back here then. Just don't misplace this book—you're going to need it!

A Few More Suggestions

Great. Welcome back. This chapter, as with each chapter that follows, is initially to be read in one sitting. Additionally, to lay a proper foundation, to build new habits and anchor them well into your life, you need to have chapter one read and the initial exercises completed within the first two days. That is not the case with subsequent chapters. But remember, we're trying to establish new habits, and we need to allow enough time for these new behaviors to hatch into habits. Once the exercises have been completed, you may read the chapter over and over again during the month—that's actually encouraged. But the first reading and the exercises need to be done within the first two days. Sorry, there's no wiggle room here.

You are also encouraged to write in this book. Along with your notebook, you should consider this a workbook. It's a fun read, certainly, but it is even more of a workbook, so don't be shy about claiming it as a tool. Underline, highlight, or flag key phrases and paragraphs that grab your attention so you can easily find them later.

What We're Going to Cover in This Chapter

- ☐ Day One
- ☐ One Home for Everything and Like with Like
- ☐ A Home for Keys
- ☐ Wallet • Purse
- ☐ Mail's Home

- ☐ Processing Old or Accumulated Mail and Establishing a Mail Routine
- ☐ Living the Work and Maintaining the System

Day One

Congratulations are now in order. By this point, we've successfully navigated several large conversations and explorations. You've investigated and charted (I like maps and thinking of this process in a concrete way as a clear journey) where you begin and your stuff ends. I hope you have a slightly lighter grip on your belongings and can feel a shift in how you relate to your physical environment and the things that surround you. You might—I hesitate to say should—be asking yourself questions when you interact with your possessions, really looking at what you are attached to, what your relationship with an object is, and what function it serves rather than clutching things unconsciously, chasing elusive comfort. Or living in a fantasy of "someday," when a currently useless item will suddenly spring into useful purpose.

In the introduction and in chapter one I've talked to you with no distinction between home and office—possessions are possessions. As we move into more detailed instructions, if only for ease of illustration, I'm going to refer to things as they are found in one's home. For those of you whose homes may be in great shape but whose offices are drowning in paper or other clutter and disorganization, you'll allow me this indulgence and extrapolate from my language the principles I'm discussing and apply them to your situation. I think it will be too confusing to switch back and forth from referring to the home to referring to the office repeatedly, just for the sake of inclusivity. Focus on the directions, outlines, and solutions offered on how to manage each thing—as that information crosses location. Your keys will have their home in either a home *or* an office, or a home *and* an office. The guiding principles of organization, One Home for Everything and Like with Like, know no boundaries and are not site-specific.

One Home for Everything and Like with Like

Let's talk about coming and going. You are on your way out of the house (or office!). You are or are not late. You do or do not know where your keys are. They might be in your purse, they might be lying on a surface somewhere, or they might be in the pocket of the last garment you were wearing. They might still be dangling from the lock of the front door. Most likely, they are not in their "home." And that is where the problem begins.

No (bad) pun intended, One Home for Everything and Like with Like are the keys to the entire process of getting and staying organized. I could almost say, "Reread that last sentence and then close the book; you're finished"—that's how significant these concepts are. They are the foundation and the bedrock, the Rosetta stone and the Stone of Canopus, the . . . Whatever the most important things are, that is what One Home for Everything and Like with Like are.

If everything you own has one home and only one home, it can only ever be two places . . . out being used or back in its home, awaiting its next use. This is so simple a concept that it's easy to see why many people might overlook or discount its significance in the process of getting organized.

Between One Home for Everything and Like with Like, almost anyone can improve his or her relationship with stuff. If you do nothing more than determine where each item lives and group similar items together, you will greatly improve your current situation. I strive for excellence, so "good enough" is not good enough for me. But it may be for you. I won't judge you. If you can now always put your hands on the letter opener or the scissors, if you never misplace your keys again, I'll consider you a success. If, however, you want more out of life than crumbs—please keep reading.

Everything has a home. You have a home. Your friends have homes. Your books have a home. And most certainly your keys and your wallet or your purse, too, have homes. Your wallet may have a different home in your house than my wallet does in mine. There is no absolute home for each object across locations, such as always the top-right drawer in the dresser in the bedroom. You might not have a dresser (or a bedroom). There will be only one right home for each object in each location—meaning wherever it makes the most sense for each object to "live" is its home.

Now, I'm aware that keys and other inanimate objects don't actually breathe and so technically don't "live" anywhere. Indulge me. This is an essential piece of language, and one that will shift how you interact with every single object that crosses your path going forward. Resist the urge to feel morally superior to me and my silly word choices, because once you accept that everything has a home and lives only in that one place, you will always, *always,* be able to find it in its home.

A Home for Keys

Find the home for your keys. Mine hang on a hook just inside my front door. The first thing I do when I walk in the front door is hang up my keys. The first thing. I may set down some heavy packages right inside the front door, but I don't walk into the kitchen or some other room, unload the packages, and then return to the front door. That's not how you build a consistent new behavior. Perhaps in several months you *could* rush to the washroom and then, afterward, return to the front door and hang up your keys. But for now, practice walking through the door and immediately placing the keys in their home. This needs to become second nature to you.

"What if the phone is ringing? What if it's an emergency? I don't want to miss the call because I had to stop and hang up my stupid keys!" Excellent question—as you look for an exception and a way out of new behavior.

This line of thinking and these questions are going to attempt to undermine you and prevent you from changing. They are natural. Counterproductive but natural. Don't fear them. I don't.

For any number of reasons, we each resist change. It's okay; it seems to be part of the human condition. It's worth noting that as creatures of habit, we would often prefer ineffective familiarity to efficient unfamiliarity if it means not having to change. Even change for the better.

Accept that you're going to need to argue with me, hunt for a loophole, and resist changing your behavior *even* when that change is beneficial and what you say you desire. It's almost absurd, isn't it? You want to know where your keys are, and you also want to not change not knowing where they are. Welcome to human frailty.

So argue with me. I can take it. I've done this countless times. You are not unique, and you are not the exception. Take some comfort from that as well. I'm not a bully, and I'm pretty certain I'm right about this, so I can wait for you to run through your excuses and flop, exhausted, into agreement. Or acquiescence. I'll settle for compliance if not enthusiasm. See, I'm easy.

Go find the home for your keys. Whether a hook inside your front door or a decorative bowl or container on a table just inside your front door. It needs to be one of these kinds of choices. It needs to be on a hook or in a container, not just lying on the table but in a vessel that is now identified as the proper home for your keys.

Specificity is very important here. The vagueness of just setting the keys down *near* the front door won't work. Vague is not your friend in these matters. So select something—it can be a cereal bowl; it doesn't need to be crystal. Don't get hung up on the container. Get hung up on the location. When I visit my mom's house, I actually use a cereal bowl. I set it on her kitchen counter, just inside the front door, and that's where I deposit my keys. It's not that pretty, but it works. You, of course, can have pretty *and* functional; pretty is just not that important to me at my mom's house, as I'm only visiting. At my little place in the country, I have a very decorative rice bowl from India just inside the front door—there, pretty *is* important to me.

Perhaps the most important points in all this is for this new home to be:

1. Someplace visible
2. Someplace you can easily get to
3. Someplace *just* inside the door

That way, the keys will always be the last things you pick up on your way out, and therefore also the first things to find their way home when you enter your house.

I'll wait here while you go and find your keys and establish their new home. Go. Now.

Great. Keys have a home.

Write down here where your keys' new home is.

Keys live here: closet myside

Wallet • Purse

Now for the wallet and/or purse. I'm using the word "purse," but if you carry a backpack or book bag and it functions as your carryall container, this applies to those kinds of totes as well. And if you carry your wallet in your purse, focus on the instructions for the purse's location only—we'll assume that your wallet's home will be inside your purse.

When you walk in the front door, you'll put your keys in their home. What are you going to do with your bag? Where is the best place for it to live? We don't want it following you around the house like a lost puppy from room to room. So think about what makes sense for you.

I have another decorative rice bowl on my dresser. This is always my next stop when I get home, when I'm in for the night. I empty my pockets into it. Change, paper money, wallet—all gets dumped into it. I separate all my receipts and anything else that's found its way into my pockets during the day—business cards, gum wrappers, Post-its—and take them into my office to be dealt with later. The trash—i.e., gum wrappers and such—

immediately gets discarded. There's no need to carry trash any farther into the house.

When the money and wallet are isolated in their dish, I'm free to leave the room. As mentioned, I walk down the hall to the office and deposit the remainder of my pocket contents into yet another decorative bowl and then leave that room, unless I planned to spend some time in there anyway.

So that works for those of us who carry wallets in our pockets. For those of us who carry a pocketbook or purse, we still have these questions: Where does it live? Where will you always be able to find the purse (visible), and where can it live so that it isn't distracting or unsightly or constantly underfoot? Is there a chair in your entryway that no one ever sits in, even to put on or take off shoes? Is there a hook or shelf inside the coat closet that makes sense? What about a small table or chair in your bedroom? Do you have a small desklike surface in the kitchen? This would not be my favorite choice, but it might be yours.

So let's figure this out. What makes sense to you? Where will you always know where your purse is? Walk through the house and find that spot. Commit to it, as much as you can, in this moment. I'll be right here.

Great. So this is now where your bag lives.

Bag lives here: _____Closet my side_____

Wallet lives here: _____

If you go to get something out of it, you then return it to its proper home when that errand is complete. You don't defer and say to yourself, "Oh, I know where its home is now; I'll put it back there *later*." "Later" is like a junior version of "someday." If you want to know where the bag is at all times, take the time to go put the bag back in its home. It's surprisingly simple. And just note how insidious that voice is that will seduce you into not following through. That voice is not your friend. It promises this secret cache of time that you'll have by *not* returning your purse to its home. It's a lie. You'll spend all that secret cache of time and then some searching for your purse if you succumb to the voice's siren call. I've witnessed this over and over again.

A friend calls.

Friend: Hey, do you have so-and-so's number?
You: I do; it's in my address book in my purse. I'll go get it.

You set the phone down and go fetch your purse.

You: I've got it. You want the cell or the house?
Friend: Give me both.

You do.

Friend: Great, thanks.
You: You're welcome. Hey, how's the . . .
Friend: Fine. Sorry, I don't mean to be short, but I've gotta run. I need to call so-and-so and then get to the store before they close. I'll call you later.
You: Sure. Talk with you later. Bye-bye.
Friend: Bye.

And now you want to think about the call or so-and-so who she's phoning right now with the number that you just gave her or picking up the dry cleaning or something. And that's fine. Think about it as you're returning your purse to its home. Don't get up from the conversation and wander away, leaving the bag behind. Complete the task—which was fetching the bag, retrieving the number, sharing it, and returning the bag to its home. If every task has a beginning and an end, don't walk away until you're finished. This will prove handy in other circumstances as well.

So now the keys and your bag, whatever bag you carry, have homes. Excellent.

A NOTE ABOUT BAGS

We have only *one* bag going at a time. That bag is your primary bag—your purse, book bag, backpack, briefcase, etc. You may also have a dedicated gym bag with your workout clothes or yoga mat inside, or a diaper bag or other specialized bag that you occasionally carry with you. If you convert one of these kinds of bags into an all-purpose bag for a particular outing, remember to empty it of all "extra" items when you get home, such as your cell phone, wallet, keys, or whatever—when you are finished, it should once again contain only its dedicated items.

Likewise, if you carry different purses for different occasions, you'll want to *completely* empty your purse out when you swap bags. You may want another decorative container in which to store the surplus contents of your bag if you're swapping out from, for example, a large tote-like bag to an evening clutch. After you transfer whatever is essential for your next outing, what will you do with all of the items no longer traveling with you that were so important just hours ago? They need a home, too. Enter the decorative bowl. Or basket. Or shoe box. Again, don't get hung up on aesthetics. I'm all for pretty. It's just that function needs to lead the way, with pretty picking up the slack.

The point is, if you have a standard set of things that leave your house with you most days, keep them all together so you can easily load back up before heading out for the day. You don't want to be frantically searching for your lip balm any more that you want to be looking for your keys. Ditto for your address book or business cards. So keep them all together somewhere that is visible and discreet and that makes sense to you. Someplace where you will always know to look for these items. One Home for Everything. As functional as I tend to be, I wouldn't vote for a shoe box on your coffee table. I'd prefer a sweet basket in your bedroom or office. Everyone else doesn't need to know where this container is or what it's for, just you.

So for those of you who *do* swap bags, find a container for your daily items, and find this container a home. Now.

Bag-contents container lives here: _closet_____

Now, along with the keys and your bag, your daily items for your bag also have a home. Perfect.

Mail's Home

When you bring the mail in, you guessed it, it needs a home until you're ready to sort and process the mail. Bowl, basket, box, bag . . . it doesn't matter. Just be consistent. It's a good thing to keep this container either just inside the front door or inside your office or workspace. If that space can be located only in your kitchen, then you really need to consider where this container will live. We don't want to surrender good counter space to a basket of mail.

Where is the mail's home? Think carefully—where does it make the most sense for the mail to live? Ideally, this location will have a trash can nearby or accessible. An office would be the best place for the mail. If you don't have an office, where do you typically pay bills and answer correspondence? If that has been the dining-room table, unless you also have a hutch or other piece of furniture in the same room where you can store the incoming and processed mail along with the mail supplies (stamps, envelopes, etc.) *behind closed doors,* you'll need to reconsider this. If you actually have a dining room in your house that contains an actual dining-room table, that table is not where your mail (or Christmas presents or recycling) should live. It's where you should be eating dinner. If you live alone and don't ever entertain and also have a dining-room table in your dining room, you are an exception to the above. You may place a basket in the center of the table and deposit the mail into it. For everyone else, find the mail's home now.

I'm absolutely serious. Consider carefully where the mail is now going to live in your home; set the book down and go to this new home for the mail. Establish the new vessel that will receive the mail, and when it is placed, head out into the house in search of any stacks of mail currently lying around. Bring them all together and deposit them into the mail's new home. Do not dawdle, and don't get distracted. Don't stop for a snack—there'll be time for that later. This is simply a search-and-rescue mission. We are not concerned with what the mail comprises right now, we're merely gathering it, so do not start sorting through it. Do not. In a bit we will discuss how to sort and process the mail in an efficient and expedient way. For now, we just want all the mail to finally be together, in perfect Like with Like harmony.

This rule, Like with Like, is the second cornerstone in kicking the clutter habit and ensuring that we'll always be able to find anything in an instant. If you take nothing else away from this book, these two tools alone (One Home for Everything and Like with Like) will transform your relationship with objects. But believe me, there is plenty more on these pages that will prove useful as we continue. So go and gather the mail now, please. When you've completed this task, please return to me and the book.

Excellent.

Mail lives here: ___basket in hall___

So now the mail is all together in a bag or basket or whatever. Good. Finally, those random piles of envelopes, catalogs, magazines, and solicitations are reunited in one location. Kind of like their farewell tour. As there will never again be this volume of unopened mail scattered around your house. That's got to feel like a bit of a relief. Savor this moment. You've just done something quite significant.

Moment's over.

Processing Old or Accumulated Mail and Establishing a Mail Routine

This is how you will handle the mail, starting tomorrow. You will bring the mail into the house, and you will immediately take it to its home. You are not to fish through the mail, hunting for fun things, when you bring the mail in. Sorry. If you do not have the time to sort the mail when you bring it in, deposit the mail in its home until you *are* ready to sort the mail, and then keep walking. You'll soon learn what adequate time for the mail looks like and feels like. You could receive lots of mail or not much at all. Either way, you will need to learn to budget adequate time to sort and open the mail in one sitting.

You'll want a basket/bin/container for each of the following categories, along with a shredder and a recycling bin.

Catalogs
Junk Mail
Bills
Asks
Invitations and Events (time-sensitive)
Read and File (including personal correspondence)
Action Items (finite tasks)
Magazines and Periodicals

We're now going to sort and process this accumulation of mail. These are the same procedures you'll follow each and every time you open the mail. You will, I hope, never have the volume of mail that you are about to sort through, and that's something to celebrate. Don't pout, and don't feel sorry for yourself or tell yourself that you're stupid or anything else that's negative about having to sort the mail in such a deliberate and mechanical way. Who cares? All we really want is a consistent and replicable way of handling the mail. Why it's never been done like this before or what that means about your character is really just noise. There's no need to get lost in a nasty conversation. Today we're building a new skill. Focus on that.

This is how we begin, by sorting the mail into its corresponding baskets.

CATALOGS

Immediately search through the stacks and remove every single catalog. This is because they are large and easy to find. Pull them all out. Unless you are currently shopping for something, toss them directly into the recycling bin. If you don't want to receive a particular catalog any longer, you can harvest the last page, which contains your address label and customer code/ID and inevitably their toll-free number as well, and start a file to get yourself off their mailing list. If you are shopping for something, retain those catalogs only. These few catalogs are placed in the catalog basket, and any harvested back pages may now go into the action items basket.

There is no reason to retain more than the most current issue of any vendor's catalog. Each catalog has an issue number or name, such as "late summer," etc., so find the most current issue and recycle the rest. If you've flagged a particular item for purchase in an earlier catalog, make sure that item is still available in the new issue, then recycle the older one.

On to junk mail.

JUNK MAIL

Same thing. Sort through the remaining stack and remove every single piece of unsolicited mail. Credit card offers and anything that smacks of a potential for identity theft gets shredded. The rest gets tossed or recycled. Shred it now. I'll wait.

Good. Note that we haven't actually opened a single piece of mail yet. This will prove a significant time-saver when you're doing this on a regular basis and not working through an accumulated stack of mail.

What's left is specific mail you have some relationship to. Before opening any of it, let's sort what remains.

TYPES OF USEFUL MAIL

Bills: We know what those are. You've requested a service or created a financial commitment and are now being asked to pay for that. Seems fair.

Asks: You support various charitable organizations and/or friends of yours do, and they sent you a request for a contribution.

Invitations and Events: Little Ashley's bat mitzvah, Ralph and Sabina's twenty-fifth wedding anniversary, Susan and Becky's commitment ceremony, your six-month dental checkup, and so on.

Read and File: Letters from friends, greeting cards, diplomas, etc.

Action Items: Time-sensitive requests that need your response and participation for them to be complete (for example, the field-trip notice requiring your signature for your kid's trip to Washington, D.C., or a request from the insurance company for clarification on a pending claim).

Magazines and Periodicals: Journals and other printed material, usually containing topical information that you subscribe to or that arrives on a regular schedule.

Now that we've identified the different types of mail, please sort yours into the above categories. Note the mail still remains unopened. Let's attend to Bills first.

Bills

Open each envelope now. Discard the envelope the bill arrived in. We don't open the mail and then reinsert the opened mail back into the envelope. That is a waste of time. Likewise, toss any stuffing or junk that comes in the envelope besides the bill (or invoice) itself and the return envelope. Any invitations for "gifts" or other offers go immediately into the trash or recycling. If you pay bills electronically, you may also toss the return envelope. If your bill has multiple pages, please staple those pages together in the upper left hand corner. When this category is complete you should have a neat stack of the bills, either without or with their return envelopes attached to them, with the flap enclosing the bill, secured with a paper clip. We'll turn our attention to Asks next.

Asks

We do the same thing here. Open the mail and toss everything that isn't necessary. If the executive director or your friend wrote a personal note on the letter, retain the letter as a tickler. If not, toss everything besides the donation slip and the return envelope. The carefully crafted plea for support is unnecessary. You're either going to support this group or not based on your relationship with this group or your relationship with your friend. You don't need to spend time having your heartstrings tugged if you're already prepared to support them (apologies to development directors everywhere).

Do you have a giving plan? I do. I have a group of charities that I support annually, and once a year I sit down, review the list, and write out those checks. I always instruct these charities to suppress mailings to me—I don't want to see my contribution used to solicit a donation I'm already committed to giving, which seems wasteful and redundant. Therefore, this basket in my home contains little besides my printed-out spreadsheet of charities and amounts committed. The only exceptions being any asks I receive from friends soliciting my support for causes that are important to them. Depending on the friend and the cause, I consider these as they arrive. Until I write a check, they will remain in this basket.

Invitations and Events

You don't have to attend any event you don't want to attend. You may choose to be a sport and accept an invitation you'd otherwise decline because it's hosted by a close friend or family member who has attended one of yours.

Save the invitation and directions and RSVP card/envelope, and toss any tissue paper, glitter hearts, etc. As above, do not stick the invitation back in the envelope it came in. That should be in the trash. If you need the return address for your address book, tear that flap off and put it in a basket of contacts. This is a basket (or other container) where you will deposit business cards, return addresses, and other contact information to update your contact list or address book. We'll discuss this in greater detail in chapter four. For now, if you don't already have something like this, grab a container and drop any addresses you want to save into it.

The invitations and events basket is also where we keep the reminder cards from the dentist, the doctor, the vet, and so on. If you need to show up at a particular date and time, it belongs in this basket.

Read and File

These are items that you need or want to save. They include bank statements, receipts or other documentation of any capital improvements you make to your home (if you own your own home), insurance policies, and love letters. On page 378 of this book (and on the website) you'll find a handy grid of what to keep and for how long.

Contrary to popular legend, I am a sentimentalist. I have love letters that are older than your children in my files. What I don't have are birthday or holiday cards that were sent to me with nothing more personal inside than:

Happy Birthday!

XO
Bobby

While I appreciate Bobby's thoughtfulness, in all seriousness, I got the message and that's what the card was sent to do: communicate a thought or a feeling. Think about it, if we held on to every thought or feeling that came our way, we'd be drowning in them. Look around. Are you drowning in thoughts or feelings right now?

If Bobby wrote me a heartfelt message or letter, then that might be something worth saving to look back on in my golden years. A preprinted holiday card from my accountant accomplished its mission—it let me know that he was thinking of me at a particular time of the year. Got it. Acknowledged it. Recycled it.

You're not a bad person for releasing these kinds of items. You're not. And it's not uncommon or unusual to throw these kinds of things away. You might be the best baker this side of the Mississippi or a crack Sudoku player, but you would not be exceptional in discarding these things—most of us do it.

You might also want to examine at this time if you have expectations about others and greeting cards you've sent. Do you grow resentful if other folks toss your greeting cards? Are you holding them hostage over a birthday card? If you can let them off the hook, it will be that much easier for you to let yourself off the hook as well.

One thing to consider in all this is the rise of electronic greeting cards, or e-cards. As an alternative to paper cards, they have both advantages and disadvantages. We'll talk in greater length about sentimental objects and their hold on us in chapter eight: Mementos • Sentimental Objects • Gifts • Collections.

Action Items

If you are someone who procrastinates—and if you are, please don't berate yourself for it—this basket is going to be very useful to you. Everything that has a deadline for completion besides bills belongs in this basket. As mentioned, the permission slip that you need to sign off on, the tax return that needs to be mailed—these are the things that belong here. Any task or problem that won't be completed without your doing something belongs here. Those catalogs you want to stop receiving—their back pages go here, since you won't get off their lists until you call and notify them. The possibly fraudulent charge on your recent credit card statement—that lives here too until you contact the card issuer and get your proper credit. Health insurance or other reimbursement forms wait here to be sent in for payment.

The difference between an action item and an invitation or event item is as follows: invitations and events are voluntary—they'll still happen whether you show up or not; action items will not be resolved without your active participation. For example, a wedding, concert, or even a doctor's appointment will still happen if you are not in attendance (unless, of course, it's *your* wedding). If you miss an appointment, the doctor will just see another patient sooner. Your child *will not* board the bus for Washington, however, *unless* and *until* you have signed that permission slip and returned it to her teacher. That's the distinction.

There's no harm in having a lot of things in your action item basket. The only risk is that you will load it up with so many tasks that you become overwhelmed by the volume of pending things to do. If that should happen, increase the time allotted for processing the mail to allow enough time to address more action items. Particularly now, when first processing a large volume of mail, you may discover a lot of items that need your attention. Once you've moved through this historic glut, the number of action items should resume a more manageable flow. If you are unsure of how to categorize a piece of mail, err on the side of placing it in the action items basket. That way it's sure to get addressed sooner than later. Just think of how productive you're about to become!

Magazines and Periodicals

As you travel from the mail's home after you have sorted everything, you should drop off any magazines or periodicals that you subscribe to. They, too, should have a home somewhere in your house.

Think about it. Besides the bathroom, where else do you like to read? In the den, in the bed, in the hammock out back? Where are you likely to settle in for a little periodical perusal? If you commute to work on a bus or a train, and that is really the time you catch up on reading, perhaps a basket or magazine rack near your coats (or purse) would be a great place to keep the magazines, so you see them and are reminded to grab one on your way out the door.

You'll decide what makes the most sense. It should be someplace where you'll see them but not trip over them or create clutter by having them spill over onto a surface, either a table or the floor.

Magazines, like catalogs, come with some frequency and regularity. Be honest about how much back reading you will or can do. Unless there is a very specific article you've flagged in a back issue, a good rule of thumb is to keep only three issues prior to the one you're now holding in your hand, and it shouldn't matter whether it's a weekly or monthly title. So if you've got issues back further than that, unless you're housebound and recovering from surgery (God forbid), chances are you'll never be able to get caught up.

If any resistance to letting back issues go is colored by how much money is invested in those magazines lying around, there are two things to do:

1. Get honest with yourself. You've probably blown more money on something else with less good intentions. Forgiveness is useful here. There's no benefit to shaming or blaming ourselves for past decisions—accept the choices made and let the rest of the conversation go.

2. Suspend your subscription or donate the balance of it to a local hospital or somewhere that has a waiting room in need of reading material. You could also drop off those back issues there as well.

If what you're stuck on is the "time" lie, about all the time that's mysteriously going to appear in which you'll be reading those back issues, it's time (no pun intended) to release that story, too. You don't have a time machine—you're living the same twenty-four hours we all are. You can barely make it through your day with all the current things there are to do; when is "someday" finally going to arrive? The answer is, of course, never. Today is it.

And any magazine that you don't read at all should be discontinued immediately. Regardless of why you began subscribing in the first place, it's now time to cancel.

On that note, let's find the home for the magazines. Go now. Come back quickly. I want to wrap this up and get you prepared for the next chapter.

Magazines live here:_____

Great.

The magazines are in their home. All is almost right with the world.

MAIL SORTING

When you bring in the mail tomorrow, and each day after, you now know where the container lives that you'll deposit the mail into. This container will always contain all the unopened mail, with possibly the back pages of several catalogs (awaiting transfer to the action items container), until you're ready to sort the mail.

It's possible that with very little mail arriving each day, sorting will not require much time. Even so, you might want to set a stopwatch or timer when you sort the mail on the first few days, to gauge how long it takes to do the sorting. Likewise if you're returning from a trip or the mail has otherwise been accumulating—it's useful to know how long things can take.

We want to start thinking in terms of a time budget, just like a money budget. The less guessing we do, the better. Numbers can't hurt us. By extension, we can't have too much information about how long things take to accomplish, since we don't want to create time debt. Remember "someday"?

So keep a log. The illustration below will start you off. If after a week or so you can see that this activity is not where the bulk of your mail time is being spent, you can relax your monitoring of this task. If, on the other hand, you receive a substantial amount of mail, re-create the following format in your notebook and use it for the next thirty days to track your time.

Mail Sorting Log

I began sorting the mail on: _____/_____/_____

Start Time: _____ End Time: _____ Total Time: _____

Start Time: _____ End Time: _____ Total Time: _____

Start Time: _____ End Time: _____ Total Time: _____

MAIL PROCESSING

The mail's being sorted and you're learning to distinguish among differ-ent kinds of mail. The mail is ceasing to be a mess, an amorphous pile of things that only wants something from you and offers little in return. You're also learning how long all that takes. Excellent. Now we need to figure out when exactly you'll interact with the mail—meaning complete the action items, respond to the invitations, and pay the bills.

This can be done every few days or once a week. I do this once a week, but that might be too long for you to wait at this early stage in your development. Find the time in your schedule every three days to have a fifteen- to twenty-minute mail appointment, and add it to your calendar. Now, I mean.

Get your calendar and commit to these fifteen- to twenty-minute sessions. It's best to stagger them between daytime and evenings since some action items may need to be accomplished during business hours. When you are finished you should have a series of appointments with yourself scheduled for the next thirty days. No need to go out any further than that at this time. Because once you get going, you may discover that you've allowed for more time than you need. Or it may not be enough.

If the former is true, if you're blowing through this phase of the mail, then adjust your calendar to reflect the need for less time. Don't just do it mentally. Return to your scheduled mail appointments and alter them manually. If the latter is true, if you're finding that after twenty minutes you still have tons to do, you either need to increase your budgeted time allotted for these tasks, or you may want to enlist help, either paid or provided by another family mem-ber or friend. If you're running a home-based business, it may be time to get some part-time assistance or a volunteer or an intern. Pay attention. Refer back to your log. How long is it taking you to sort the mail before you even begin to respond to it? Also note that in the beginning, as you're possibly playing catch-up on a larger-than-average pile of mail, everything will take longer. For many folks, once a pattern is established of sorting and processing the mail, these durations will decrease.

As you did above, use the following log as a guideline to record how long it's taking you to process the mail. Unlike sorting, however, continue to record these times for each processing session for the full thirty days, regardless of results. Use your notebook to keep track of these times, and add any notes to further clarify your process. For example, if it takes you only a few minutes to write out checks and pay bills and much longer to attack your action items, make a note so that the next time you're doing action items, you adjust your schedule accordingly.

Mail Processing Log

I began processing the mail on: _____ / _____ / _____

Start Time: _____ End Time: _____ Total Time: _____

Start Time: _____ End Time: _____ Total Time: _____

Start Time: _____ End Time: _____ Total Time: _____

Living the Work and Maintaining the System

This is what the next thirty days will look like.

- You will come and go from your house, placing your keys and your wallet or purse in their proper homes.
- You will swap the full contents of your bag every time you change bags.
- You will deposit the mail into its home until you're ready to sort it.
- You'll deliver any new magazines to their home, recycling the oldest issue.
- You will sort the mail.
- You will keep your appointments to process and answer the mail, adjusting them according to your logs.
- You will log your mail sorting and processing times.

And that's it. That's all you have to do. For me and for this process. Obviously you'll need to continue going to work or meeting your other obligations.

But you are not to start digging into the junk drawer in the kitchen after a few days of success. You are not to attempt to clean out the garage with all your enthusiastic fierceness. There will be time for all of that.

Right now, focus on the tasks at hand. Do them consistently, and do them to the best of your ability. Don't judge them, and don't negotiate with them. No corner cutting, no creative juggling, and no procrastinating. If you tell yourself you'll do it tomorrow, gently and firmly remind yourself that you have a commitment to do it today. The conversation doesn't need to be any longer than that. No convoluted schemes or grandiose promises.

Ditto for trying to impress the teacher with your deep understanding of this process. Remember, this isn't nuclear fission, it's the mail. I'm impressed if you're impressed. And it should take only thirty days of consistent behavior to really see what you are capable of. Good luck!

3 Kitchen • Pantry

> In department stores, so much kitchen equipment is bought indiscriminately by people who just come in for men's underwear.
>
> **JULIA CHILD**

> If you can organize your kitchen, you can organize your life.
>
> **LOUIS PARRISH**

Welcome back! By now you've gotten control over the mail and you haven't misplaced your keys once since working through the last chapter. You rock!

Before we dig into the kitchen, let's remember our ground rule laid out in the last chapter—this chapter's initial read should be completed in one day.

When you begin working, you'll find that some of the exercises in this chapter may take more than one day to complete. But none of them should take more than two days, and I'm confident that you will find two days in a row to dedicate to completing them. It is important that you choose two consecutive days—both practically and psychologically. Once you begin the process of emptying cupboards and drawers and sorting, there will be substantial piles of things lying around. Navigating the space around these piles may be awkward physically, and living with these piles any longer than necessary may sap your energy and enthusiasm for finishing the project.

The good news is that after you've completed them, you likely won't have to repeat them for a long time to come, perhaps forever.

What We're Going to Cover in This Chapter

☐ What a Kitchen Is and Isn't
☐ What's Happening in Your Kitchen?
☐ One Home for Everything and Like with Like
☐ Structural Elements of a Kitchen
☐ Breathing • Visualization
☐ Sorting, Purging, and (Re)Arranging
☐ The Sad, the Lonely, and the Mismatched
☐ Reloading the Storage
☐ Appliances
☐ Maintaining the System

What a Kitchen Is and Isn't

Kitchen (noun):
A room equipped for preparing and cooking food; any room used for the storage and preparation of foods and containing the following equipment: sink or other device for dishwashing, stove or other device for cooking, refrigerator or other device for cold storage of food, cabinets or shelves for storage of equipment and utensils, and counter or table for food preparation.

So in turning our attention to the kitchen, I'd like you to think food shop, as in wood shop but with different tools. This is a room to prepare food—unless you don't prepare food. We'll address that separately. Assuming you do prepare food, is your kitchen currently set up to support that activity? Either way, when you're finished with this chapter, you'll possess a functional, accessible kitchen where any kind of food preparation and cooking is easy and as fun as you find cooking to be.

There is much talk these days in shelter and home-improvement magazines about the kitchen being the hub of one's home. And I'm all for that when it comes to the kitchen being a gathering place, a return to the hearth, and a warm place to visit while food is prepared.

The kitchen is not the hub of the house if you're thinking "war room" or "command central" or "Houston, we have a problem."

Rather, the kitchen is a workroom. This doesn't mean devoid of character or drab or uninspired—why is it that things that involve habitual tasks are so often viewed as tedious or dull or chores? Let that go. Your kitchen can reflect as much of you as you desire—it should also foremost be a room that functions well and serves its purpose without unnecessary complications.

What's Happening in Your Kitchen?

Get your notebook and take a few minutes to write down the different activities you currently perform in the kitchen. Please omit any that involve you and another person without clothing and in prolonged bodily contact.

Great. Of the activities you just wrote down, how many would you do in another space if you had other functional spaces in your home? Circle them. We'll come back to these later—and find you more appropriate locations for them to be accomplished. For now we want to remove them from the kitchen so we can streamline the kitchen's contents and purpose.

That leaves us with which remaining activities? Review them now.

These are the things that your kitchen needs to accommodate. Not that this can't change, but for now let's be mindful of what you want to do in the kitchen and how the kitchen can be arranged and organized to best support these activities.

To reiterate, the kitchen is the room where raw supplies and tools are stored specifically for the preparation of tasty, nutritious meals. Even if all you ever do is hire caterers and "assemble" meals from prepared foods purchased somewhere else, it is still a room that is dedicated to food and its preparation and distribution.

I think it's great if your kids are nearby doing homework while you cook. Or if your partner/spouse/roommate is paying bills from the bar as you slice and dice (or microwave a frozen meal). Or if you're watching the Food Network and incorporating tips and recipes into your day. All good. But the homework doesn't live in the kitchen. Neither does the checkbook. And unless you have a surplus of counter space, it would be a shame to have a chunk of it dominated by a television, even a sleek flat-panel LCD.

One Home for Everything and Like with Like

As we move through the home, knowing where things live (One Home for Everything) and having them living with all their brothers and sisters (Like with Like) is going to simplify your life significantly. We're about to rip apart your kitchen, so remembering these governing principles is going to be useful when you start to reassemble your drawers and cabinets.

Over and over again, I've seen cabinets and drawers previously exploding with things suddenly become more than adequate storage simply by applying these two basic concepts when assigning homes to everything in your kitchen. So before you lament your particular lack of storage, wait and see what One Home for Everything and Like with Like can do to solve some of your storage challenges.

Structural Elements of a Kitchen

COUNTERTOPS

These are probably the largest surfaces in your kitchen, possibly larger or longer than your kitchen table, if you have room inside your kitchen for a table.

Countertops exist as shining, gleaming potential in every kitchen. For example, a large expanse of uninterrupted countertop is essential for rolling out pastry dough. Imagine how difficult that would be if there were obstacles strewn in your path.

While the only things that live on my countertops are a crock filled with utensils, a basket with fresh produce, and a sentimental (and functional) spoon rest, these are just some of the things I've seen on other people's counters:

Answering machine

Ashtray/lighter/cigarettes/incense

Blender

Bread box

Cake plate (with or without a
    domed lid)

Canister set, or derivatives
    (for tea, coffee, sugar, etc.)

CD player

Cell phone charger station

Clean dishes

Clock radio

Coffeemaker (drip or espresso)

Compost container

Computer

Cookie jar

Cutting board

Decorative cruets

Dirty dishes

Dish soap container

Egg (or other) timer

Food processor

Food-storage containers (empty
    or full)

Fruit bowl/basket/container
    (including a banana hook)

Hand soap or lotion
    dispensers

iPod docking station

Lazy Susan (laden with any number
    of essential items)

Knife block

Magnifying glass

Mail (opened or unopened, or ready
    to be mailed)

Microwave

Napkin holder

Oils and vinegars or other bottled
    ingredients

Paper towel holder

Pet food

Plants (living or dead)

Postage stamps

Radio

Random kitcheny or non-kitcheny
    decorations

Recipe card file

Recycling

Root vegetable bowl/basket/
   container

Salt and pepper mills or shakers

Spice rack

Sponges

Spoon rest

Stand mixer

Telephone

Things to be returned to stores

Things purchased and unopened,
   either in or out of shopping bags

Toaster

Trivets

TV

Utensils

Vacuum sealer

Vitamins or other pills

Wraps, plastic bags, aluminum foil

There are certainly many more items that could be populating your countertops at this very minute. That's fine. For today.

Let's go into the kitchen now (if you're not already in there). Bring a pen, your notebook, and your camera with you. Before you touch anything, take pictures of the kitchen as it currently is. *Do not* move a thing.

When you're done taking pictures, put down the camera and pick up the pen and begin writing down everything, all the items currently living on your countertops. We don't need to record that there are five wooden spoons or thirty-seven pens, in or out of a vessel—*wooden spoons* or *pens* plural will suffice as a single item.

Since I'm not there to support and police you, we must employ the honor system. *Do not* omit anything, even if you're telling yourself right now, "Oh, well, that was just on its way to the linen closet" or "I'm taking that back to the store on my way to class in the morning. . . . I just can't find the receipt right now."

This is the insidious nature of denial. We minimize the things that contradict our established view of ourselves. Either by promising (again) to finally complete a long-delayed task or by glossing over anything that might make us look "bad" or that we believe *would* make us look bad in someone's eyes *if* they knew the whole truth.

No one is judging you—well, they may be, but who cares? If it really mattered to you, you'd have made different choices by now, anyway. It's worth noting that we often care only what people think of us just enough to punish ourselves with it, not enough to actually do anything about it.

So tell the truth, at least to yourself. If there are piles of papers or other things you consider "in process" that are currently lying on your counter, note them. You can't develop new habits until you cop to the old ones. What would there be to change if you were already doing everything efficiently?

Finish writing down the things that are currently living on your counters.

If there are more that twenty things living on your countertops, pay attention. Don't abuse yourself, just note it—you have a lot of things on your countertops.

Now I'd like you to study these things, really look at them, and think about the last time you used each of them. Can you remember the last time? Do you make toast often? Are you a daily smoothie drinker? Do you take your vitamins regularly? See if you can find a timer, then set it. Give yourself three minutes to explore the counter's contents and their frequency of use. Go.

> ● **Notable Note** ●
>
> Purchases still in bags (either coming in or going out) should not be lying on your counters. If the kitchen is their final destination, the items should be integrated into the appropriate drawer or cupboard. If they are destined for some other room, how did they end up in the kitchen? Likewise, if they're awaiting a return to their store of origin, there needs to be an established location, ideally near an exit door, where all returns gather until loaded back into a vehicle for transport home. Of course, with the correct store receipt!

Great. Now let's address two things. What have you not been able to do because there is clutter on your countertops? The tasks you defer doing because clearing space seems like too big of a hassle. So you either find some other surface to use for this purpose or just don't do it at all. Write down the things you would do if you had the room.

And what do you *really* need to have on the countertops? Forget about storage space right now—let's pretend that whatever you didn't want on your counters could find a home inside a cupboard. What do you use every day that you would not want to have to get out of a cabinet? Not out of laziness, but practically speaking. Some items, like a cactus, would obviously not fare well behind a closed door.

Refer back to your list of countertop items and circle the essential items—things you feel you must have on your countertops. Are there things not on this list that you would have on your countertops if there was room? Add them to your list.

Excellent. Now physically gather these essential items together and set them aside. When we're done, these are the only things that will live on your counters. Everything else that didn't make the cut should also be gathered together into a separate group.

Congratulations. In completing these two actions, you have just successfully sorted something.

The items in the group that will no longer be living on your counters fall into one of the following categories.

1. Things that are leaving your house
2. Things that need new homes in other rooms
3. Things that need new homes behind closed cabinet doors

Since we're on a roll, let's sort them into one of the three groups above. First get yourself a large container, such as a box or a basket or a tub—something with stiff sides and bottom. Right now. Great. Now identify everything that you're done with, that's leaving the house, and put each of these things into this container—this has just become your thrift-store donation container. You can keep this nearby while we do this work—ultimately, you'll want to find a permanent home for this container or containers, as some version of it is going to remain in your home. At any time on any given day, you may decide that something needs to leave your home for good, and until it does, its new home will be this container. I find that either just inside the garage or just near a doorway to the outside is a great place to permanently locate the thrift-store container.

Now collect everything that is headed for another room and place those items at the entrance of the kitchen so you can take them to their new homes the next time you exit the room. If they are heading to a new home in the kitchen, just set them aside. They will join their sisters and brothers some-place very soon.

Breathing • Visualization

I understand that this is a potentially challenging project, or series of proj-ects. I realize that your heart might be racing now. You may be muttering under your breath or out loud to yourself that this is impossible or pointless or exhausting, or that you think I'm too demanding and this is fine for a per-fectionist like me but too much work or too much "something" for someone like you.

I get it. It's okay. Breathe. We're not attempting to solve world hunger or some incurable disease. No one is holding a loved one hostage, threatening to hurt him if you don't do this or if you do it poorly or bail on it halfway through. So you can soften your shoulders right now, breathe, and release the tension in them. They are never really supposed to be up around your ears. Let them fall.

Some of us, along with breathing shallowly, may also retreat to home-improvement magazines or reality TV shows, where the renovation and cleanup have already occurred. We fantasize about these other kitchens, not without a touch of envy, where other people get to live. We tell ourselves, again, that it's fine for someone else, but we'll never have that kind of kitchen. And then we start to list the reasons why.

We're done with those negative lists. That's what the exercises in this book offer you. There are no *good* reasons for your kitchen to be anything *other* than the room you want it to be. So stop the lists. You aren't exceptional or unique, at least not in this case, no matter how hard you fight to tell yourself why only *you* can't put things away, or only *you* have to live with X, Y, or Z. It's a lie. Stop making excuses for yourself, and stop letting yourself wiggle out of responsibility for the way things look. There may be circumstances operating in your life beyond your control, but it is the rare individual indeed who can't put the can opener back into a drawer when she is through with it.

And I'm completely serious now, if your life *is* that threatened or compromised that putting the can opener away creates some sort of dangerous situation for you, put this book down right now and get out of the house and get some help. Call the police, get to a friend's house, get to a shelter, go somewhere. You have bigger problems than clutter. I mean it—*go!*

For everyone else, reading this book will not cause you to suddenly blink and discover that you now have granite countertops and gleaming stainless-steel appliances and exotic wood cabinets. For you to accomplish what you want in the kitchen, none of those things are necessary. Pretty, sure. But necessary? Not for a minute. Your kitchen just needs to be neat and orderly and clean. And that is not beyond anyone!

For many of us, food is a way that love was shown to us, and it continues

Notable Note

If you have an older kitchen and/or an awkward floor plan, think creatively to solve these challenges. Will rearranging any of the appliances help the flow? Maybe the fridge and range could be swapped? Are there any cabinets that block your view or impede access to other areas of the kitchen? Could these be relocated or removed with little finishing work required? Would a cart on wheels or a freestanding cabinet or hutch provide additional storage? Is there an adjacent room that could easily house seldom-used appliances or serving pieces, or become a pantry? Zoom out far enough to shift your perspective of these design flaws and they will cease to be problems and become challenges—from this new vantage point you will find workable solutions for many of them.

to be a way for us to demonstrate our love for our family and friends. It is an offering of care and nourishment, both physical and spiritual. Without getting too "woo-woo," let's take this time to hold that vision gently in our hands. Let it rest in our outstretched palms. There's no need to grab or clutch it, just let it lie there, content.

Your kitchen can become a room where you express your love for yourself and others through food in a simple and direct and sustainable way. Think of the kitchen in the film *Babette's Feast* but on a scale that works for you. If you're ambitious and accomplished in the kitchen, you can prepare complicated multiple-course meals. And if you're satisfied with tasty and nourishing less-complex fare, your kitchen can support you in that effort as well. Whether you're inspired by the culinary encyclopedia *Larousse Gastronomique* or an Eggo toaster waffle, your kitchen can be the room that makes it possible.

Now sit down for a minute. And really breathe. Think about your dream kitchen. Think about the meals you'll make for those you love. Or even just like. Think about waking up in the morning, walking into the kitchen, pouring or making yourself a delicious cup of tea or coffee, or a glass of juice. It's peaceful in this room. Things are put away, and there's room to breathe. Room to plan and room to spread out. Your knives are sharp, your dishes clean. Imagine how it would feel to have this room be the room of your kitchen dreams.

You know where everything is. You have the tools you need. You don't have to get clutter out of your way every time you want to prepare something; you have just what you need, just where you need it. The broken appliances, the tools with missing or incomplete parts, are gone. Your kitchen is a model of efficiency for *you*; it's been organized by you to serve you. You are strong and capable and efficient and effective when you are in the kitchen preparing food. You move through the kitchen easily. It is a pleasure to be in this room, even if it's just to heat up a bag of microwave popcorn. You're smiling. Good. Now let's create this room for you.

CABINETS

Besides countertops, the other major structural element of most kitchens is the cabinets. These come in as many different configurations as there are kitchens. You may have any combination of drawers, bins, shelves, doors, and cubbies. You may hate your cabinets, love your cabinets, be indifferent to your cabinets. They may be laid out in the most organic, flowy, smartest way possible, or they may be seemingly plopped into place by an absent-minded contractor who had never boiled water in his life. Short of renovating your kitchen (which is another book), we're going to stretch and utilize your current cabinet configuration to provide you with the most useful and clever storage possible without having to do anything besides shift what's contained in each of them. Because in the kitchen, getting organized is an inside job!

WORKSTATIONS

For those of us who have never had the privilege of working in food service, this may be a new way of thinking about your kitchen and of particular interest to you. For those of us who have worked in food service before, this may prove to be a somewhat nostalgic trip down memory lane. It may also prove to be something that made sense in a professional kitchen but that we never thought to apply on a smaller scale to our home kitchens.

In every commercial kitchen, there are dedicated work zones or stations. While the specificity of stations in a commercial kitchen would be overkill in most residential kitchens (i.e., individual stations for salads, desserts, sauces, grilling, deep-frying, etc.), the general concept is useful for us as a guide.

Don't be misled, either, if you're a big fan of the Food Network or other channels' cooking shows. When you're inside Paula Deen's or Ina Garten's or Tyler Florence's "home" kitchen, you are in a kitchen large enough to comfortably fit a film crew in addition to the professional chef who is filming television in her or his home—they have more space than most of us, and perhaps even more significantly, they have prep and cleanup staff.

So for now, let's focus on the main zones you'll want to consider in your own kitchen. They are:

Preparation

Cooking and Baking

Beverages

Food Storage/Pantry

Tableware

Cleanup

It doesn't matter how large or small your kitchen is, some variation of these zones is possible in any size space. If you're thinking, "There's no way to distinguish these kinds of zones in my little space," you may want to explore why inside your tiny apartment, where you seldom cook, you feel compelled to keep service for twelve and have a pro-size stand mixer. Just asking.

KITCHENETTES AND MINI-KITCHENS

All kidding aside, if you have a kitchenette or a small or even tiny galley kitchen, these rules can still be applied to your spaces. Just reduce everything. If you entertain a lot, first of all, hats off to you—it's no small feat to pull that off when your space is so limited! The thing to work out is where everything will live. Maybe the space is so small that all tableware is relocated to a bureau or buffet wherever you eat—the dining room or dining/living room. That can include plates and cups and glasses, as well as silverware and napkins and place mats. And that frees up more space for actual cooking tools and supplies in the kitchen.

That also applies for seasonal serving items or appliances. See if there's room in a coat closet or somewhere else to relocate items you use maybe once or twice a year.

Whenever possible in small kitchens, consider all of the vertical space available. If you're tall, this might be something you already do; if not, look around. Can you hang a pot rack from a wall or the ceiling? How about a utility bar for utensils across a backsplash wall or on the face of the exhaust hood? What about a magnetic strip for your knives mounted to the wall or the side of a cabinet? Likewise, a hanger for your paper or cloth towels.

Without creating a chaotic jumble of things, think of how you might keep everything you need organized and within reach. In small spaces particularly, a lot of things stuck all over the walls can blur into a visually noisy mess, so choose carefully. Take adequate time to reflect on how you cook, the tools you use often, and where you use them to determine what to place or hang where. And if you look around the room and still can't find anything because your eyes won't focus for all the visual activity, consider how you can edit what is out in the open and what could live behind doors or drawers.

PREPARATION

- Knives, scissors, other cutting or chopping tools
- Steels, stones, other sharpening devices
- Graters, zesters, peelers, rasps
- Spoons, spatulas, scrapers, other mixing utensils
- Cutting boards
- Graded measuring devices
- Mixing bowls
- Strainers, colanders, cheesecloth
- Herbs, spices (or with Cooking and Baking)
- Small and handheld appliances
- Squeeze bottles for sauces
- Cookbooks, recipes

This is where you'll prepare foods, and most likely where you'll spend the bulk of your time, so this should be the largest dedicated space. I consider prep to be everything right up until you apply some form of heat or refrigeration to the food or arrange it for serving. So your chopping and slicing, cleaning and seasoning all takes place here. It's important to make sure that all the tools and ingredients you'd need for prep work are in or near this area. Ideally, this area is built around an ample bit of clear surface—I'd recommend at least thirty-six inches of uninterrupted countertop space and would prefer forty-two inches whenever possible.

The storage below or near this area should include your knives and other cutting/coring/chopping tools, mixing bowls, ramekins, or other vessels for your *mise en place* (pronounced MEEZ-ahn-plahs, and literally translated as "putting in place"), spices and marinades, cutting boards, etc. This is where these items want to live.

In my kitchen, I have a four-drawer base cabinet directly below this surface area. And this is how the drawers break down.

Top Drawer: This is dedicated to cutting tools—all the knives, graters, scissors, and cleavers live here. I have an in-the-drawer knife block that holds the bulk of them, with the fine-toothed Microplane (my favorite tool!) and other graters alongside the block. I put these things in the top drawer because they are the tools I use most frequently.

Second Drawer: The drawer directly below the cutting drawer houses additional prep tools—everything from a mushroom brush, sushi rollers, small spatulas and spreaders, a nutcracker, and a garlic press to melon ballers, basters, zesters, peelers, and funnels. There's also an ice bat in there. It tickles me. I've used it twice. If I was pressed for space, this would be the first thing to go.

Third Drawer: This drawer is the baking drawer. It contains cheese-cloth, cookie cutters, graded measuring cups and spoons (the larger measuring cups have their own space on a shelf opposite this area), pastry knife, pastry brushes, pastry bag and tips, and pie weights.

Bottom Drawer: This drawer contains wax papers, aluminum foil, plastic wraps, and plastic storage bags in assorted sizes.

Diagonally opposite this base cabinet is a six-foot-long stainless-steel counter unit from a retired diner—I got two of them from a local auction. They flank my range. On the upper shelf are all my small appliances—the food processor, blender, hand mixer, and immersion blender, and all their exchangeable parts corralled inside one basket. This is also where the rolling pin lives. And the slow cooker.

The lower shelf houses all the mixing bowls (stainless, copper, ceramic, glass, plastic), measuring cups, strainers, and colanders that I use. Kitty-corner to these two cabinets is a bookcase, where I store my cookbooks.

COOKBOOKS AND RECIPES

Cookbooks are an exception to my rule of Like with Like—these are the books that don't live with other books, but they do all live together. I have a bookcase where I keep all my cookbooks, arranged either by celebrity chef (alphabetical order), genre (desserts, baking, slow cookers), or cuisine (ethnic, seasonal). I have to look in only one place to find any cookbook I want before I start to prep.

I suggest you find a cupboard shelf or bookcase or some area that you can dedicate to the storing of your cookbooks. Like everything else we're discussing, do not fetishize your cookbooks. If you have some that you have never used, it's fine to release them. The Internet is a wonderful resource when it comes to recipes, so let go knowing that if you really need to find that recipe for lemongrass crème brûlée, it's probably only a few clicks away.

For pictures of my kitchen, you can visit the book's website, www .unstuffyourlife.net—that way you'll have a visual to go along with these descriptions. Just follow the link to kitchen design.

COOKING AND BAKING

- Pots and pans, griddles, woks
- Utensils (for turning, stirring, and mixing ingredients)
- Pot holders, trivets
- Oils and vinegars
- Herbs, spices (or with Preparation)
- Cookie sheets, cooling racks
- Pie weights, pastry bags
- Cake pans, muffin pans, pie plates, ramekins

This is where the heat comes in. You've done your prep work, and now the fire happens. It's nice, whenever possible, to have adequate surface area around the heat source as well. Most kitchen designers agree that eighteen inches on either side is the minimum. See what you can do to clear that much surface on at least one side of your range or cooktop. That way you can have all your *mise en place* containers on one side, and a landing place for any hot dishes or utensils you're using as well.

As I mentioned, the only things I have on my countertop are a large crock containing all my cooking utensils (whisks, spatulas, wooden and metal spoons, tongs, ladles), a basket of produce, a salt cellar and pepper mill, and a spoon rest that belonged to my late father. The crock, salt and pepper, and spoon rest live directly next to the range. While the spoon rest is not really my taste, it still makes me smile whenever I see it and certainly anytime I use it. This spoon rest was in my dad's kitchen when he lived in Santa Fe (it's decorated with red chili peppers!), and he brought it back to Michigan with him when he decided that the Southwest was not for him. It also represents the perfect marriage of sentiment and function in one object. It allows me to have my dad in my kitchen with me (sentiment), and it fills a consistent need—I rest spoons and other tools on it every time I cook (function).

I store all the pots and pans in the cabinet to the left of the range. I'm a lefty, which is significant only in that I have laid out my kitchen for my convenience. So should you. If you're always reaching for the tongs with your left hand, as I am, it makes sense to store them to the left of where you will be standing when you need them. This sounds simple, but few people think about how they use their kitchen rather than what fits or what looks good.

You're not, most likely, living in a show house, so it doesn't make any sense to live as if you're on display or constantly expecting to be judged by company. And perhaps what would be more impressive is a well-laid-out kitchen that they could imagine themselves cooking in rather than a sterile space that looks off-limits and for sale. Friends and family love to cook in my kitchen because it's easy to find everything and it's easy to use. And easy to clean, so I don't need to hover over them, wiping up behind them until they begin to feel self-conscious.

I store the skillets and frying pans together, the pots together, the roasting pan and griddle together, and the Dutch oven together with the cast-iron stockpots. Cookie sheets and cake pans and pie plates are kept together. Covered casserole dishes are kept with the uncovered casserole dishes. Like with Like.

I'm lucky to have enough room to not need to stack things, so getting them in and out is easy. This won't be true for everyone. If you keep your pots with your pots and your pans with your pans, you'll at least make finding the right size vessel easier, and you won't be constantly unpacking drawers or cabinets, searching for the three-quart pot and always coming up with the wok.

It would be good to have all the cooking oils, sauces, and spices used for cooking nearby as well, either in drawers or on a lazy Susan inside a cabinet. It is not a good idea to store them near the heat, as that weakens their potency, so avoid stacking them on a ledge behind your range or in an upper cabinet directly next to the exhaust fan and over the range or cooktop. The utensils used to mix and move the food around over the fire should also be nearby— again, in a crock on the counter, hanging from the range hood, or in an adjacent drawer. Likewise, hot pads or insulated gloves. And if you use a cookbook holder, moving it from the prep area to the cooking area should be accounted for as well.

Notable Note

DRAWERS OR DOORS

I find drawers to be the best use of space in a kitchen. It's simpler to just open a drawer rather than having to open one or two doors and then possibly get down on your hands and knees to start rooting around for something. I realize we're not redesigning your kitchen, but if you are planning a remodel soon, consider base cabinets with drawers.

The next best thing to drawers are pull-out shelves inside base cabinets with doors. If you are not planning a remodel and can afford to retrofit your kitchen, consider this option. While you'll lose a bit of interior space to the new hardware, the convenience of having everything roll out more than makes up for the inches lost. Many companies offer some "after market" version that makes conversion very easy regardless of who originally made your cabinets.

BEVERAGES

- Wine, beer, liquor, mixers, soft drinks, juices
- Teas, teapots, tea cozies, tea balls, and strainers
- Coffee, coffee grinder and maker, filters
- Corkscrew, bottle opener, corks
- Ice buckets, coolers, tongs
- Specialized stemware, glasses, mugs
- Cocktail shakers, strainers, stirrers
- Cocktail napkins, coasters

Regardless of whether you have a bar in your home, you can still have an area dedicated specifically to storing and possibly also serving beverages. If you are a serious collector of wine, you have special needs around controlling temperature, light exposure, and other factors, so I'll trust that you have arranged for your investment to be properly stored. If that's in your cellar and you have an elaborate wine room where you invite people to taste your wines, then you would store all related wine items together in that cellar.

If you are a casual consumer of wine, keeping it stored with the other beverages is fine. Just keep it out of direct light, as cool as possible (not stored on the top of a fridge or other appliance or near a vent), on its side (keeping the cork moist, thus minimizing premature exposure to oxygen), and not exposed to unnecessary vibration. Ideally, some form of wine rack (of any design or price point) or even speed racks (found in commercial bars for storing bottles) will keep your wines neat and condensed within your beverage area. Speed racks are excellent alternatives as well for storing other beverages, from hard alcohol to shaved-ice syrup.

All other bulk beverages, from mineral waters to mixers, should be stored here. If you have an under-the-counter fridge or refrigerated drawers, the best place to create a beverage center would be near these appliances. Conversely, if you have the room, install a small fridge near where you already store beverages to keep them chilled and ready to serve. All beverage-related tools will live here, too—stirrers, shakers, corkscrews, wine keys, bottle openers. Bar napkins, swizzle sticks, and specific glassware for cocktails or wine also could be stored here—or with other glasses in the kitchen proper. Likewise mugs—here or with other glasses and cups stored elsewhere in the kitchen. Either option is acceptable; space and proximity to serving and convenience can inform this choice. Coasters could also go here—or they could live on the surfaces you're interested in protecting.

FOOD STORAGE • PANTRY

- Pastas, cereals, grains
- Canned vegetables, dried vegetables, beans
- Canned fruits, dried fruits
- Canned meats and fish—tuna, ham, chicken, smoked seafood
- Prepared sauces, marinades, stocks
- Prepared soups
- Boxed meals (mac and cheese, Tuna/Hamburger Helper)
- Bulk ingredients
- Snacks, chips, crackers

This is where dry goods, canned goods, and packaged goods all live. I keep them all organized by subtype here as well: pastas and grains, cereals, canned vegetables, canned fruits, canned meats, prepared sauces and marinades, and so on. It's much easier to find what I'm looking for when I'm starting to cook if I find the rice in the same place each time and don't need to hunt through the tomato sauce and canned pineapple to find it. Likewise, dried fruit all lives in the same area—raisins, currants, cherries, cranberries, figs, dates, etc.

I store my flours in the fridge to keep them fresher longer. I keep the seeds and nuts in the freezer for the same reason—the oils in them will get rancid faster when exposed to fluctuating temperatures.

TABLEWARE

- Flatware
- Dishes, glasses
- Serving pieces (platters, bowls, plates, gravy boats, specialty pieces)
- Serving utensils (salad tongs, carving knives, etc.)
- Napkins
- Place mats, tablecloths, trivets
- Candlesticks, vases, decorative items for the table

Like with Like informs our choices here, too. We're about to leave the kitchen (at least the cooking area) and are heading to the eating area. So everything you will use to serve the food should be located here together, including serving utensils, larger platters, and dishes. That way you can select the appropriate vessels, then fill them and bring them to the table. Additionally, this will be where you store the textiles and other things you use to dress up and protect your table, such as napkins, place mats and tablecloths, vases, and decorative trivets.

CLEANUP (INCLUDING STORAGE)

- Plastic ziplock bags (assorted sizes)
- Plastic, paper, and foil wrap
- Resealable and other storage containers
- Vacuum sealer and supplies
- Jars with lids
- Soaps, sponges, brushes
- Trash can and trash bags
- Recycling
- Composting

The meal is finished, and it's time to clean up. We're recycling what we can, composting vegetable and other degradable waste, discarding trash, and storing leftovers for a later date, either in the fridge or in the freezer. We want to have each item we need for this task near one another, sort of like a *mise en place* in reverse. As we disassemble the foods and store them, it is much easier to have all the possible containers close by rather than having to leave the room in search of a stray plastic bowl and its lid.

Sorting, Purging, and (Re)Arranging

We have covered a tremendous amount of theoretical ground in this chapter. We even did a little sorting of our countertop items—all excellent as a foundation. And so the real work begins.

Now that we've mapped out how you might arrange your kitchen into specific zones that allow for the simple and logical grouping of like items and tools together, let's start to put this into practice. If you're not currently in the kitchen, pick up your book and head into the kitchen.

Earlier in the chapter, we eliminated everything from the countertops that wasn't kitchen-related. Those items are either in a container destined for a thrift store or outside the room, waiting to be taken to a new home in your house.

What remains on your counters right now is everything you believe still belongs in your kitchen. Now clear these items off, too. Clear every surface in your kitchen. Just for now. If you need to have your toaster on the counter, we'll replace it when we're finished. You have several options in doing this—you may use your kitchen or dining-room table, you may set up a card or banquet table, or you may use the floor.

As you're doing this, if you haven't already, you should be separating out *anything* that is broken that you have not repaired in six months. If you haven't replaced it, it is clear that you don't need it, because you've gone half a year without it. Place it either in the trash or in the recycling bin now.

Please, do not debate with me, silently or otherwise, about this. Trust me, you don't need it. You haven't used it, and you haven't missed it. Or if you have missed it, you've found some working alternative, so it's still no longer necessary.

The items that still work and that you still use should be grouped according to our zones:

Preparation

Cooking and Baking

Beverages

Food Storage • Pantry

Tableware

Cleanup

This is the basis for what's coming next.

Now open the doors of your cabinets and start to gather like items with one another, and group them with the items that you've already sorted. Pay attention and keep your eyes open for redundancy and duplication. We'll come back to this in fuller detail in a few minutes; for now it's enough to recognize overlap and excess.

Gather all the cookbooks and recipe files and scraps of paper and put them all together. We'll find a proper home for these in a bit.

I know this is going to look chaotic and scary. It's fine. It's the first step in identifying what you own, what you need, what really makes sense for you, and where you'll end up storing it so you can easily put your hands on it when you need it or want it. And given all the places we've yet to travel to in your home, the kitchen should be relatively painless when it comes to this kind of sorting.

As we did before with the countertop contents, as you empty cupboards and drawers you may discover things that don't belong in your kitchen at all. Whenever you come across one of these items, place it near the exit or the door of the kitchen so you can take it "home" the next time you head out into the rest of the house. If you're uncertain where its home may be, set it aside in another large container, and as we move to other parts of your house, we'll discover its proper home.

The Sad, the Lonely, and the Mismatched

Isolate broken, mismatched, and orphaned things immediately—pots without handles (that originally had handles), plastic or other storage containers without lids or bottoms, hand mixers missing a blade, damaged plastic utensils, etc. The same goes for tools that you have *never* used—like the pineapple corer that Secret Santa gave you three Christmases ago. Any broken tools, sad melted spoons, ice-cream scoops missing the swipey part that forces out the ice cream from the scoop . . . anything that is missing a part or damaged beyond full use is now to be discarded. Broken things do not get sent to the thrift store; they end up, unfortunately, in the trash. A broken wooden spoon will not be useful for someone else if it's so damaged that you can no longer use it, either. In this one example, if you have a fireplace or woodstove, you could burn the spoon as kindling. Otherwise, what you're looking at is trash.

Don't torture yourself about this. Just note it. You're not wasteful or a bad environmentalist for discarding broken items responsibly. Anything that *does* still have life in it should of course be repurposed by you or a friend or a stranger through someplace such as a local thrift store. Trash is trash. What I hope you will take away from this experience is an awareness that once you bring something home, whether a stray dog, a lover, or a spatula, you are now its steward. So choose wisely. This is a useful lesson.

Calling yourself names for something ending up in landfill as you navigate this process is not serving anyone. Chances are the result of that kind of shaming talk will have you either clinging to things that serve no purpose in your life or resenting yourself for trashing the planet. Be a conscious steward. Many things can be broken down into recyclable parts, and for those things that can't be, they will end up in the trash. If you pay attention, this should have to happen only once. I'm not being dismissive when I ask that you please let that be enough comfort to you as you work through this part of this process.

I realize that the costs of waste are significant. I also feel that you must be as responsible as you can be and then forgive yourself for past mistakes. Growth occurs for us when we start to make different choices about accumulating and hoarding things rather than hiding out and feeling crappy about ourselves while doing *nothing* to change our behavior. If you don't want to have to eventually throw something away when it breaks, don't bring it home in the first place. That is the simplest way to resolve this dilemma. One thing you can definitely do to positively affect the environment is to wean yourself away from using disposable paper towels and make the switch to washable cloth towels exclusively.

Continue sorting. Each pot with the other pots. All the lids for these pots should be with the pots as well. If the pot is supposed to have a lid, find it now. Put all the wine keys and corkscrews together. All the small appliances. All the mixing bowls. All the dish towels. The oven mitts and hot pads. All the wraps and bags. All the food items—canned veggies with canned veggies, canned fish with canned fish, dried beans and grains, ditto.

Do the same thing with all the drawers—open each one and empty its contents into the growing piles of things surrounding you. Like with Like. That's all this exercise is about. It's like a giant three-dimensional game of Concentration.

When all this is done, when every space inside a drawer or cabinet is empty, take stock. This is what you own, what you are the steward of, what you've accumulated. How does that feel? Are you feeling abundant, as though you have enough of everything? Do you feel wasteful, as though you have too much stuff and don't understand where it all came from? Do you feel sad or disappointed that you actually have less than you thought and are surprised at how so little could take up so much space? Sit with whatever it is for a few moments. Set the timer again, this time for two minutes, which should be enough time to consider your feelings before we begin the next step.

When the timer goes off, start moving deliberately and slowly through each area, from pots to pans to baking to serving, and pull out everything that you are certain you don't need, haven't used, don't know what it's used for, and add it to the thrift-store container. (There might be more than one by now!) It's leaving your life. Resist the urge to set things aside for specific people.

If there are a few items you could give away—perhaps a friend just mentioned needing to replace her blender and you have three of them—then sure, earmark it for her and set it aside. But as a rule, this practice of "saving X for so-and-so" will trick you into feeling that you're just being a good friend/neighbor/steward while you're actually procrastinating. Be clear: the beginning of the task is the identification of something obsolete. The end of the task is when it's no longer in your possession. So remember that right now it doesn't matter how you feel about any of this—it matters only that you finish.

> ### Notable Note
>
> Staying hydrated, snacking, and taking little breaks during this sorting process is acceptable, and often helpful, in remaining focused and on track. If you're going crazy looking for the stray pot lid, break it up by gathering all the mugs together. If you haven't eaten and you're energy is crashing, make a sandwich or grab a slice of cheese or some other protein. This is hard work, and you want to stay alert and attentive from beginning to end. If you feel yourself slipping or getting distracted, re-group, refuel, and forge on.

Now is also the time to get serious about how much storage you have and the volume of things you need to store. You can't keep three sets of pots and pans in a modest kitchen. Who needs three sets of pots and pans, anyway? Even if you keep kosher, that's only two. Choose your favorites and let the others go. Continue using this process of elimination as you sift through items in each area.

If you inherited your grandmother's china and you don't like the pattern and you already have dishes, it's okay to let them go. It doesn't make you a bad child or ungrateful or heartless. Really, it doesn't. They are only dishes, ultimately, regardless of what you (or anyone else) tells you.

If you have duplicates of certain items, select the better one or your favorite one and let the dupes go. If you feel stymied and need a way into this process, ask yourself the following questions:

1. Is _____ something I currently and/or frequently use?
2. Is _____ beautiful? Do I enjoy looking at it?
3. Does _____ serve a practical purpose in my kitchen?

If you can answer no to any of the above questions, the item needs to leave. I realize it may be difficult to accept what I'm about to say: we are not living for posterity. Having a pizza stone is useless if you don't eat carbs, no matter

---

Notable Note

A WORD ABOUT JUNK

Let's not have a junk drawer that contains all sorts of random things, some of which are clearly trash. I have a dedicated folder containing all my delivery menus, rather than randomly shoving them into this drawer. If you use rubber bands and twist ties, keep them neatly organized in snack-size ziplock bags rather than scattered throughout the drawer. Matches, a pen or pencil, some Post-its, a pad of paper, batteries for the timer—none of these are junk. Resist the urge to shove useless receipts in here, or spent batteries, or the one earring that's missing its mate, or a commemorative key chain, etc.

This drawer should *not* be a catchall for anything you can't figure out what to do with. If an item is that confusing to identify, it probably *is* junk and belongs in the trash. If it's not, you most likely have similar items elsewhere. Find them and store them all together.

how cool you might think it is. Likewise, a food processor you never use, just so someone will think you've got skills when they visit. That's not a good enough reason to hold on to something. Particularly if the food processor is hogging valuable space that could be used for your blender or toaster or espresso machine.

You're not doing this for me; you're doing this for yourself. Really be honest with yourself about how you live, how you want to live, and how you don't want to live. If you're tired of living in a fantasy of "someday" and ready to live your life as it actually is and, even more important, how you want it to be, chuck the stuff that's holding you back. Thinking clearly, we can see how letting these things go can't possibly affect your life negatively, since some of these things have never seen the light of day or been out of their boxes—how can you miss something you've never used?

Practically speaking, toss out all herbs and spices that have expired, but keep a list of all of them so you can easily replace them at the store. But think this phase all the way through. If you cooked Indian food only once and you just tossed out the cardamom seeds, you probably don't need to replace them until you're ready to make aloo gobi again. Likewise, oils—they get rancid after a while. Examine the label and see what you can find out about the current life expectancy of your oils, nuts, and seeds. Things that contain fats will go bad eventually. That time may have already come and gone. Be informed and thoughtful about ingredients you need to have on hand, and what you may need to pick up when an infrequently used recipe calls for it.

Reloading the Storage

So now we've purged. What remains all works. Pots and pans have lids, as do food-storage containers. Appliances have all their parts. Their wires are intact and not frayed. Groceries are organized into their categories as well. We have everything laid out in groupings according to our zones:

Preparation

Cooking and Baking

Beverages

Food Storage • Pantry

Tableware

Cleanup

Before putting a single item away, wash and wipe down the interiors of every cabinet and drawer. Really.

Now, as we start to put things away, we're going to load the zones with all the tools necessary for the tasks of each zone. Concentrate items near where they will be used. Store heavier objects down low, where getting them out will be easier. Store pots and pans in a base cabinet near the range or cooktop. Likewise, if you bake often, put all your cookie sheets and muffin pans together and near the oven. Dishes go together, as do glasses—typically near the sink or dishwasher so that putting them away is convenient after they've been cleaned from use. When putting food back in the cupboard or pantry, load unopened packages in the rear and opened packages in the front for easy access. Group all the spices together, snacks together, juices together, breakfast cereals together, pastas together, and so on.

When you begin loading things back into the cupboards, pay attention to the space each family of items takes up. If you find that you have too many boxes of instant pudding and other dessert mixes to put next to the boxes of tea, reconsider which cabinet you're using. This is your kitchen— bend it to serve you. If there is a larger cupboard that would easily house all your dishes but it's not exactly next to the sink, it's more important to have everything living together according to type, rather than spreading things out across several locations just so some items are more conveniently housed. Always use Like with Like to guide you when confronted with situations such as the above.

Use the blanks below to identify where each zone will be located in your kitchen. List the cabinets and other structural elements within each area so that you'll end up with a comprehensive list of where to find each kind of item without hunting or opening every cupboard door.

Preparation lives here: _____

Cooking and Baking live here: _____

Beverages live here: _____

Food Storage • Pantry lives here: _____

Tableware lives here: _____

Cleanup lives here: _____

Whenever possible, do not stack things on top of one another inside cupboards. Bowls that naturally nest inside one another are one thing, but stacking all the pots inside one another when the bottom stockpot is the one you use every day doesn't make much sense. Make choices based on accessibility and convenience as you arrange the contents of each zone within your kitchen. Reload the drawers and shelves to support you in efficiently preparing whatever it is you're cooking, whether it's a pot of chili or a five-course meal.

Once you're finished and everything is back in a cupboard or a drawer, look around at what's left. The only things remaining out and unaccounted for should be the things you still want living on your countertops.

With the doors and drawers all still open, scan each space to see if there is anywhere you might store any of the items that are still out and destined for the countertop. Could the vitamins live near the sink in an upper cabinet or in a drawer by the fridge? Do you really make toast every day, or could the toaster live on the top shelf in the base cabinet next to the stove? Don't do it just to please me—do it because it makes sense to you.

And if it doesn't, if having the vitamins on a staggered tower below the paper towels is where you want them, then that's where they should live.

Now, with all the drawers and doors still open, take some pictures. Then close the doors and drawers and take a few more. Job well done.

Appliances

REFRIGERATOR • FREEZER • WINE COOLER

Even I have a few things on my fridge door, such as magnets and a few photos. Nothing that prohibits me from opening or closing the door, however. And all are secured well enough that opening and closing the door doesn't cause them each to shift. That may be a useful guide when it comes to decorating yours.

Turning our attention to the interior of your fridge and freezer, you should arrange it in the same way we've arranged your food storage and pantry. Keep all the condiments together, jams, eggs and dairy, beverages, meats and cold cuts, flours. I have a few shelves just dedicated to leftovers, enabling anyone to find what they need with a minimum of fuss. I was always yelled at as a child to keep the fridge door closed—know what you're looking for before you open the door. It's much easier to do that when each shelf or bin has its own category!

My grandmother used to keep a red pencil near her freezer, and she would carefully label everything that went in with its name (chuck roast, chicken breasts) and its date. That way, she could always use the oldest items first. If you're buying in bulk and portioning out things and then vacuum-sealing them, a label maker or a permanent marker works just as well.

STOVE • RANGE • OVEN • MICROWAVE

My late Aunt Sylvia never—and this is not hyperbole—never used her oven. It was stuffed—again, not hyperbole—with baked goods that others, mostly large agribusiness corporations, prepared, including the Keebler elves, Sara Lee, and Little Debbie. If you wanted a sugary snack, the oven was the place to look.

I think a few things were going on for her there. One, it was a minor act of defiance that not only was she not interested in cooking but she rendered the act of cooking impossible by the sheer volume of packages. Two, she didn't have a pantry, and she had limited cabinet space. And three, she had a tremendous sweet tooth.

I'm all for repurposing things, even appliances. If you don't cook and find you're short on cupboard space, go for it. Of course, I'd suggest you disconnect any source of power to the appliance so you don't end up with flammable wrappers so close to a source of ignition.

Other than that, I think having adequate heat for cooking is what a range is all about. Whether that's induction, gas, or conventional electric is a matter of personal taste and budget. If yours is active, do not clutter the range with anything that might be combustible.

Maintaining the System

So we've sorted through everything, gotten rid of a bunch of stuff, and found smarter places to store what remained. Excellent. How will you maintain this? By remembering that everything has only one home. And now that you've successfully identified everything in the kitchen's home, anything you take out, any tool you use, will either be in your hand, in the sink or dishwasher, or back in its home. It is that simple. Put things back where you found them and they will always be there when you look for them.

This system begins to unravel the minute you defer returning something to its home in favor of doing it "later." Bad habits die hard and this is one of the most stubborn. The seductive, insidious voice you'll hear that suggests you could just set something down on the counter and get back to it in a bit is going to win if you do not remain vigilant. Take comfort in knowing that if you are diligent and deliberate about your efforts, after thirty days of consistently putting things away when you are done with them, it will naturally start to seem wrong to leave something lying around. And that's the best kind of freedom—free your mind and the rest will follow.

If you have family and they have not yet been a part of this process, you need to bring them in now. Everyone needs to know what you know—where each item lives. It is not silly to consider labeling each door or drawer for a while so everyone can easily find what they are looking for.

What you'll begin to understand as you do this work is that much of the result is now alive in your muscle memory. You've had the process of touching every vegetable peeler, every food container, and every cookie sheet, so you have a commitment to replacing things where you found them.

Others don't have that memory—they just have the pleasure of working in a functional and orderly room. So either get those who also use this room to do this work with you or help them out with some labels or other short-cuts to bring them up to speed. Remember that their frustration at not finding what they want when they want it might not be sufficient motivation for them to learn the new system. It might be just enough motivation for them to tear through the pantry, looking for a bag of chips, leaving a trail of smoked almonds, crackers, and sardines in their wake. You can choose to be happy or you can choose to be right—it shouldn't be too difficult to figure out which one will keep your house organized and stress-free.

Finally, let's turn our attention to the tasks that you've been doing in the kitchen that you'd choose to do elsewhere, if there was room. Refer back to your list and take a few minutes to study those activities and figure out where they would best be performed. Laundry room? Home office? Living room? Bedroom? It's okay that there still may not be room for these activities to take place in these newly identified spaces. That will be a goal—to clear those spaces as well. Hiding out in clean and organized spaces will not bring you any closer to

> ### ● Notable Note ●
>
> Learn to sharpen your knives or find someplace that will sharpen them for you. A sharp knife is a happy knife. And a happy knife is a happy cook.

transforming the holdout spaces, so keep this list alive until every task has been properly relocated.

Likewise, let's grab whatever you set aside that didn't belong in the kitchen. It's now time to redistribute those items around the house. Using Like with Like to guide you, begin walking these things to their new homes. Clothes are destined for a closet or a drawer. If you know that some of the items belong in the home office and we haven't gotten there yet, see if you can figure out what they would live alongside; what are they like? If that baffles you, keep them in a container near their future home and we'll get to them in the up-coming chapters. Do this for each item. Even if you have to move things one or two more times until you find the best home for everything, each trip brings you that much closer to mastery of Like with Like and One Home for Everything.

4 Office • Home Office • Paperwork

> Our two greatest problems are gravity and paperwork. We can lick gravity, but sometimes the paperwork is overwhelming.
>
> **DR. WERNHER VON BRAUN**

abba-Dabba-Doo! Your kitchen is working. How great is that?

Now you're ready for the first real foray into Paperland. We now enter and exit our homes and offices with our keys always within reach. The mail is under control. We've seen how the kitchen can look and function without clutter.

Here we'll learn how to deal with paper, including bills and the other mail we began sorting in chapter two. We'll also tackle office supplies, setting up a computer and printer (organizing files and other information stored on your computer will be covered in chapter ten), owner's manuals and instructions, catalogs—all the tools and equipment that are supposed to make running our lives and our homes so much simpler and more manageable.

For the sake of convenience, I'm going to speak about this office space as if it were a room with four walls and a door. If you're attacking an actual office at work, adjust any references to a home to be your company's suite, and if something is not easily translatable in the moment, keep reading, because chances are, it soon will be.

For those of you at home with less space than a full room, let's do the same thing we did in the kitchen—adjust my words to match your space. If I'm calling for a cabinet for office supplies and you have a small desk in the corner of your dining room, perhaps the adjustment would be to get a small basket or box, or an old trunk or suitcase, to substitute as a corral for your office supplies. Work with me to get beyond the limitations of the page by adapting these tips and information to your particular situation. That way, you'll get real results from this work.

Whatever the confines of your office space, this is big stuff. And remember, this can't hurt you—your biggest risk is of getting a paper cut. So let's take a deep breath. Really.

Pause, breathe, and acknowledge what you've accomplished and what you're about to embark upon. Close your eyes, inhale and count to five, exhale and count to five. Repeat twice.

Excellent.

If you haven't already done so, grab your notebook and travel to your office or paper space, or the place where you do paperwork, or would do paperwork if you did paperwork and didn't leave it in a pile on the dining-room table. Or in a shoe box next to (or under) the bed. At least the mail is no longer a part of those piles, right?

How do you envision using this room or area if you could be here without clutter? Whether you have a dedicated room or simply a desk, you can have order and manageable paper flowing through your home. I've converted tiny closets to home offices for clients. I've even set up desks in out-of-the-way hallways or in corners of other rooms. There are many ways to isolate paper in your home and gain control of it, so please don't allow limited space to deny you a healthy relationship with paper, mail, and technology.

Now that we're here in this space, what will you do here? Do you imagine writing the great American novel? Maybe scrapbooking or assembling photo albums? How about paying bills, researching your family tree, writing holiday cards, helping your child with a research paper, or downloading music and burning CDs or DVDs? If you build it, they will come.

What We're Going to Cover in This Chapter

☐ What an Office Is and Isn't

☐ One Home for Everything and Like with Like

☐ What's Happening in Your Office?

☐ Office- and Container-Supply Stores Are Not the Answer

☐ Filing Is the Answer

☐ Superior Filing Tools

☐ Designing and Practicing the Right Way to File

☐ Structural Elements of an Office

☐ Transitioning from an Outside Office to a Home Office

☐ How to Set Up Your Office

☐ Client-Friendly Space

☐ A Time to Gather

☐ Sorting, Purging, and (Re)Arranging

☐ Converted Closets and Other Snug Places

☐ Those Other Activities

☐ How Long Do I Have to Keep This?

☐ To Shred or Not to Shred?

☐ Maintaining the System

What an Office Is and Isn't

Office (noun):
A place of business where professional or clerical duties and activities are performed.

Home office (noun):
A room in a person's home equipped as an office so that the person may work from home.

If a kitchen is a food shop, think of your office, home or otherwise, as a paper and technology shop. This is where you run the business of your business, or your life and your family's lives. It's a serious kind of place, although that doesn't mean glum or drab or without levity. But in some ways, the crispness that we're called upon to achieve here is as close to perfection as we will probably see in any other room. If that makes your heart race, think of it this way: math is one of those disciplines that doesn't function in an "almost" or "approximate" way. We know that two plus two equals four all of the time, not just occasionally. When it comes to bill paying and checkbooks, or even filing, let's stretch our math metaphor to encourage precision and care, ensuring our equations always add up. The consequences of a misplaced lid in the kitchen are much less critical than misfiling your insurance policy or bouncing several checks.

So if you have a tendency or desire to fudge the corners or aim for "pretty good," I'm going to really encourage you to dig in and shoot for excellence here. To tame the paper tiger, you'll be best served if you will call on all your innate fierceness.

This isn't to scare you, because at this point I believe you are completely capable of this kind of clarity and accuracy when it comes to organizing a room. Rather I'm making the point that once this room is in shape, the real work of the room comes alive. And that work invites rigorous consistency.

One Home for Everything and Like with Like

When it comes to paper and technology, One Home for Everything and Like with Like are essential in keeping up with the flow of documents and equipment that inevitably travel through this space. Bills with bills, statements with statements, warranties with warranties. Same with cables, printer paper, folders, paper clips, staples, and pens and pencils. Evaluate what you need to store, find adequate and appropriate storage space, and establish each thing's home. Even if most of your banking is done electronically, we aren't completely a paperless society yet. There will be paper, and without taking the time to identify and institute One Home for Everything, you will create additional work and delays for yourself.

What's Happening in Your Office?

Let's start by writing down in your notebook the different activities that are currently performed in the office.

Good. Of the activities you just listed, how many would be done in another space if you had other functional spaces in your home? Let's identify them now by circling them. We'll find you more appropriate locations for them to be accomplished a little later. For now we want to isolate and remove them from the office so we can streamline the office's contents and purpose.

If you had adequate space, which activities would you do somewhere else? Copy all the non-office tasks to their own list now.

Now you've determined the tasks that actually belong in your office. Rewrite that list on a clean page now.

These are the things that your office needs to accommodate. Not that this can't change, but for now let's be mindful of what you want to do in the office and how the office can be arranged and organized to best support these activities.

To reiterate, an office is a room where the business of our lives happens. If you have someone handling your personal finances for you on-site, if you have staff, or if you are the designated manager of all things business, this is the room that should house the documents and machines that facilitate that work.

I think it's swell if this is the only unclaimed room (or space) in the house, and as such doubles as the den, the library, the dining room, the craft room, or the exercise room. I'm thinking that together we can create a system for all of those activities (and more) to coexist. But to do so, we must ensure that there is adequate storage for papers, supplies, and tools before we begin loading in the sewing machine and treadmill.

Office- and Container-Supply Stores Are Not the Answer

Indeed, they are not. Getting organized, and managing paper in particular, is not an outside job. No amount of file trays or pretty bins or decorative folders or playful labels will bring you any closer to actually being able to put your hands on a document when you need it or want it. You can, of course, use colored folders for specific categories or types of documents. You could have all the files relating to money be green, for example. Or you could use randomly colored folders simply because you'd rather look at colored file folders instead of manila ones. The point is that any of these choices can make it more fun or pretty to be disorganized, but they won't deliver what I think you ultimately want. And that's a filing system that is easy to use and easy to maintain.

The next fad or latest trend in office supplies will not fix what ails you. Which isn't to say that innovations won't make office work easier—good ones always will. But the answer to managing paper more efficiently and effectively lies in less rather than more. Remove every single thing that is nonessential from your relationship with paper and you'll gain control over paper. Anything—any tool, any technique, any methodology—you put between you and filing is what will keep you from immediate access to any document.

I realize that may be disappointing to hear. Or even upsetting. No one likes filing. I don't. It's tedious and repetitive. I can't change that. I could dress it up in clown folders and zany labels and it would still be a drag. Sorry. But the sooner we get over our upset, the sooner we can settle into acceptance and get down to work. Because what we want is the result of a good filing system. We want to know where everything is, and we want to put our hands on it quickly. So that's what we should focus on. I'm not particularly fond of taking out the trash or flossing, either, but I sure like having a house that doesn't stink and healthy gums.

Filing Is the Answer

So what does a good filing system look like, and how simple can we make it, so you'll actually use it?

Filing is not a mysterious thing. Just like sorting in the kitchen, we begin with categories. Then from the categories, we come up with any subcategories that apply, and within those subcategories we gather together all the documents that belong to each of those subcategories. The difference is that instead of workstations and cupboards and drawers, here we have file cabinets and desks and drawers. Otherwise, it's the same process of sorting and organizing.

Start with the file cabinet's or desk's drawers—each category will be assigned its own drawer. Then the subcategories will each have their own folder within that drawer. Finally, the documents within each folder are there because they belong in that particular subcategory.

Once you have this system defined, you'll label your drawers, then create a series of folders that are also clearly labeled, and you'll put the corresponding documents into those folders in chronological order, with the oldest documents in the back and the most recent documents in the front of each folder. The folders within each drawer are arranged in alphabetical order, and here's where you can jazz it up a bit. You can decide whether you want your drawers to go from A to Z or from Z to A, left to right or front to back. How's that? Beyond that, it couldn't be simpler.

The more drawers you have, the farther you can isolate certain kinds of documents from one another. Here's a generic illustration of a filing cabinet's structure.

Drawer (Category)
> **Folder** (Subcategory)
>> Document (Oldest)
>> Document
>> Document (Newest)

Here's a list of the drawers I have in my actual filing system.

Administrative: Personal
Administrative: VirgoMan
Capital and Home Improvements
Client Files I (A to M)
Client Files II (N to Z)
Research: Personal
Research: Professional

And here's what they contain.

ADMINISTRATIVE: PERSONAL

This has everything in it pertaining to the administration of my life, including my medical records, mortgage and deeds, bills and statements, tax returns, insurance policies, résumés. If it is about me, Andrew Mellen, personally, and not my business, this is where it lives. Travel folders also live here, from trips

I've taken that had particular itineraries I want to refer back to. And a folder of maps, including a clear plastic sleeve containing tourist information for the town my house is in—I give this to guests when they visit.

ADMINISTRATIVE: VIRGOMAN

This is where everything about running my business lives. Blank forms for client contracts, informational handouts and flyers, press clippings, correspondence with the Trademark office, my client folders live here, including my copies of client contracts, my contracts with my agent and my publisher. Bills for business expenses live here. My assistant's files are also in here.

CAPITAL AND HOME IMPROVEMENTS

I did a major renovation of my house several years ago. When I bought the house it had a faulty foundation, which had been deliberately concealed from me, so there was a lawsuit between the seller and me. The lawsuit files are in here, along with all the receipts and documentation for the repairs and reconstruction. These will substantiate my capital improvement expenses when I sell the house. I don't keep monthly bills for services here; those are filed under "Administrative: Personal." Just finite billing for specific improvements to the property.

CLIENT FILES I (A TO M)
CLIENT FILES II (N TO Z)

These are documents that belong to the clients themselves. Any bank or credit card statements, tax returns, correspondence between the clients and their vendors or creditors, receipts, they all live in the client's folder in these drawers. If I have their copy of our contract, it would live here.

RESEARCH: PERSONAL

This drawer contains articles and documents that interest me personally. Information and articles about everything from home improvement projects and gardening to health and fitness. Articles on staining concrete floors and types of deer-resistant plants live here. Also, articles on yoga and meditation and a folder of interesting places I've yet to travel to.

The key to this drawer and the drawer below is that these are things that interest me but have no transactional relationship to me—nothing in these drawers has actually happened yet and may never happen. But when I see an interesting article in a magazine or newspaper about inexpensive travel or the latest way to do something I think I might actually do, this is where it lives after I rip it out. It doesn't just lie in a pile on my desk.

I'm in this drawer a fair bit throughout the year. Even so, at least once a year I look through this drawer with an eye specifically to purge obsolete items.

RESEARCH: PROFESSIONAL

This drawer contains articles and documents that interest me professionally. Information about public speaking, business development, marketing techniques, new products for storage, creating franchises—all those and more live here.

I'm in this drawer frequently as well. I schedule a few hours every few weeks to look through here to spark my imagination and creative thinking. If I don't make an actual appointment with myself—if it doesn't make it onto my calendar—it won't happen. I'm likely to book that time with a client or find something else to do with my time. Which is fine. But I need and want a certain amount of time to be proactive in building my business and to think about ways to increase efficiency and enjoyment, too.

Like the drawer above, at least once a year this drawer gets purged of obsolete items.

Using these drawers as examples, here's an illustration of how they further break down.

Administrative: VirgoMan (File Cabinet Drawer)

Domain Registration & Hosting (File Folder)

Domain Registration Request (Oldest documents on bottom)

Registration Certificate

Invoice: 19XX (Five years at a time)

Registration Renewal

Invoice: 20XX (Five years at a time)

Registration Renewal

Invoice: 20XX (Five years at a time)

Here's another:

Administrative: Personal (File Cabinet Drawer)

Medical Records (File Folder)

Test Results (10/11/95) (Oldest document on bottom)

Referral Letter from Primary Care Physician (PCP)

Test Results (2/2/99)

Test Results (3/14/02)

Letter from PCP

Test Results (1/16/05)

Letter from PCP

Test Results (5/17/09)

You can see that organizing the documents themselves is not difficult to do, it just takes time. If you have a home business and an assistant, or responsible children of a certain age, you can enlist them to do this with you or for you, if they are careful and reliable. The *worst* thing that can happen, in regard to filing, is having someone file who is not careful. Once a document is misfiled, it becomes a major hassle to locate it again. You or the person filing can try and retrace your steps, but you may end up having to look through every folder or else wait until you may stumble across it, when looking for something else.

Filing may not be thrilling but it is about as simple a task as can be—and just requires focus and attention to detail to complete it without error.

Superior Filing Tools

I lied a bit earlier when I said I didn't like filing. I actually find it somewhat calming to put on some music and work my way through the To Be Filed box until everything's been put away. When it comes to filing, One Home for Everything and Like with Like are the one-two punch of organization. They ensure that loose papers will never be lying around unfiled for long and that each kind of document will be easy to find among its brothers and sisters.

I recommend two-hole punches and classification or fastener folders for all filing. Each document is punched at the top of the document and secured inside a folder. These folders have metal fasteners at the top of each page or divider, so all documents are secured inside the folder. You'll recognize them as the folders you've seen in doctors' or attorneys' offices with your records in them, although those typically are end tab folders, and for our purposes we'll want top tab folders.

They come in a variety of colors, and as classification folders they are available with one, two, or three interior partitions or dividers. They are called fastener folders when they have no interior dividers, just fasteners on the inside of the front and back covers. Classification folders allow you to classify the contents into subcategories within each folder, using each page within the folder to further isolate different types of documents from each other. Depending on the number of subcategories, you'll determine how many dividers (or pages) you'll need.

For example, let's say you have five different credit card accounts, and you still get paper statements for all five. By using one classification folder with two internal partitions (six possible pages) to file all these statements, each individual account can have its own page within one folder.

The folder would look like this:

Credit Cards 20XX (File Folder)

    American Express 21000 (Page One)

        January bill

        February bill

        March bill

        Etc.

    Bank of America 4339 (Page Two)

        January bill

        February bill

        March bill

        Etc.

    Bank of America 7828 (Page Three)

        January bill

        February bill

        March bill

        Etc.

    Chase Continental 4399 (Page Four)

        January bill

        February bill

        March bill

        Etc.

    Discover 6004 (Page Five)

        January bill

        February bill

        March bill

        Etc.

Each individual page is home to one particular account and that account's statements are arranged in chronological order from the oldest on the bottom to the newest on the top. Now, instead of interacting with one of five folders anytime you need to check a credit card statement, you just have to get one folder out of the drawer and all five accounts are there in one neat folder. Perfection.

Designing and Practicing
the Right Way to File

We're now going to design your filing system. On a separate sheet of paper in your notebook, list the names of drawers (or categories) for your file cabinet. Refer to mine above for guidance.

Great. Now create a page for each of those drawers, and begin to list the folders (or subcategories) that would live inside them. Don't worry about keeping this list in any order, alphabetical or otherwise—for now just write them all down. When you create the actual file folders, you'll load them into the drawers in alphabetical order at that time.

This exercise is *not* busywork. It may seem remedial, but it will focus your thinking and help you to design a useful and manageable filing system. It's also a chance to practice and explore different ways of naming and organizing folders *without* wasting time and money renaming and reprinting labels and folders.

If you currently have some sort of filing system, refer to the folders you already have for your list above. Are your existing folders specific enough? Too specific? Now's the time to shed any old bad habits and develop new ones that support using and maintaining a new system.

While there's no perfect way to name files, these tips should help hone your efforts:

1. Look for what is common and what is unique about the content of each folder.

Like with Like tells us that all the insurance folders should live together, but each policy is distinct. So you could label them Auto Insurance and Health Insurance and Homeowner's Insurance, but what they all have in common is the fact that they are insurance policies. Using what's common unifies them while what's unique distinguishes each from the other:

Insurance: Auto

Insurance: Health

Insurance: Homeowner's

This way we know they all are filed under I for Insurance, and then in alphabetical order from A to Z.

2. Keep folder names simple and structured: Category, year or date (if applicable), subcategory, any additional information.

The fewer the words are and the more specific they are, the better. So, rather than this:

Our Trip to the Grand Canyon with Bob and Sally 20XX

Try this:

Travel: 20XX, Grand Canyon (Bob and Sally)

We begin with the category—Travel. Then the year or date—20XX. Then the destination—Grand Canyon. Finally, any additional information—here, the companions, Bob and Sally.

3. Look for ways to combine Like with Like documents together into one folder.

Rather than a series of individual folders labeled:

Utilities: 20XX: Cable

Utilities: 20XX: Gas and Electric

Utilities: 20XX: Mobile Phone

Utilities: 20XX: Telephone

Utilities: 20XX: Water and Sewer

Use a classification folder that is labeled Utilities: 20XX with internal pages for each separate entity on its own page. See the illustration of the Credit Card 20XX folder on page 101 for a visual refresher.

Once you feel confident that you have a system that makes sense to you and follows the common practices I've laid out, leave the page and enter the actual cabinet to create or rearrange and rename the folders you currently have.

If using fastener folders and a two-hole punch seems tedious or overly involved for you, it may be. Consider, though, that with this system, you will never drop a folder and have its contents scatter across the floor again. The one document you swore you had put into the X folder will never actually be discovered in the Y folder. I have saved clients thousands of dollars and hours of time through always insisting on fastener folders. Nothing can be lost, and the little bit of extra time involved in the actual filing guarantees that you will never inadvertently drop a document in the wrong folder ever again.

If you're still not convinced, then simply use regular file folders and be *very careful* when filing. Filing is not an activity that should ever be multitasked. As repetitive an activity as it may be, it requires your complete attention to avoid the simplest of mistakes. It will give me no pleasure to tell you, "I told you so," should the inevitable result of distracted filing eventually occur.

Structural Elements of an Office

FURNITURE

Desk
Desk chair
Additional chairs and other seating
Filling cabinet/credenza
Bookshelves
Bulletin board/dry erase board
Magazine holder/rack

Fireproof safe or file cabinet

Other: _____

FILE FOLDERS

Three-tab plain folders

Hanging file folders

Fastener and classification folders (my favorites)

Other: _____

PAPER: WHITE, 8½" X 11"

Lined, three-hole punched

Lined, no holes

Unlined, three-hole punched

Unlined, no holes

Unlined, no holes—colored

Unlined, no holes—different sizes (8½"x14", etc.)

Other: _____

OFFICE SUPPLIES

Desktop blotter

Calendar

Letter trays/bins/in and out baskets for sorting

Three-ring binders

Report covers

Pens/pencils

Markers/highlighters

Index cards, in or out of an index card holder

Post-its, or some kind of scratch paper for notes

Staples

Paper clips

Binder clips

Clear tape

Glue/paste/rubber cement/liquid adhesive

Correction fluid/Liquid Paper

Rubber bands

Pushpins/thumbtacks

Other: _____

PRINTED MATERIAL

Books

Magazines

Newspapers

Journals

Catalogs

Other reference/resource materials

Other: _____

PROPER LIGHTING

General illumination

Task

Other: _____

EQUIPMENT AND TECHNOLOGY

Shredder

Computer

Printer/All-in-one (print/scan/fax) machines

Software (installation disks, etc.)

Internet (high-speed, dial-up, wireless "borrowed" from your
neighbor . . .)

Other: _____

CABLES

Ethernet

USB

FireWire

Extension cords

Power strips/surge protectors/battery backup

Other: _____

BLANK MEDIA

CDs

DVDs

Floppy disks

Thumb drives

Other: _____

EXTERNAL HARD DRIVES

FireWire

USB

FireWire/USB combo

SATA

NAS

Other: _____

HANDHELD EQUIPMENT

Three-hole punch

Two-hole punch

Stapler

Staple remover

Scissors

Tape dispenser

Pens/pencils (in some sort of container)

Pencil sharpener

Ruler

Letter opener

Paperclips/binder clips in some sort of dispenser or container

Calculator

Telephone/headset

PDA/smart phone/mobile phone

Paperweights

Batteries (AA, AAA, C, D, 9-volt, etc.)

Other: _____

This is a thorough but perhaps not comprehensive list of all the things that one might have in a home office. Certainly, everyone need not have one of everything listed above.

So look around your office now. Use the above list as a guideline for things you would use but don't have, have and don't use (these you may release—put them directly in the thrift-store container), and have and use. Check off each item that belongs in *your* office. Then use this list and Like with Like to determine where each item or group of items will live.

Transitioning from an Outside Office to a Home Office

With more people working from home, it's important to make the transition from an outside office to a home office as smooth as possible. And working from home, you'll still want your work to be done in a timely and professional fashion.

If you're used to having a staff, you may find it frustrating to have to get your own coffee in the morning. The tonic for that may be that you get to do it in your pajamas. However, friends and colleagues who telecommute stress that after the novelty wears off, they universally agree that dressing for work is imperative. They all confirm that they are more productive and focused when they are wearing trousers and a shirt instead of just boxers or sweatpants. I'll take their word for it.

In addition, if you left your office with boxes of files and office supplies and personal artifacts, incorporating them into your home will take some time and effort. If you have duplicate framed photos of significant people in your life, consider gifting one or harvesting the photo and recycling the frame. Like with Like directs the marrying of office supplies together, with excessive surplus being passed along to others. If you do most of your work online and seldom print documents, how many cases of paper do you really need? Even if they were "free."

How to Set Up Your Office

FURNITURE

The largest and most used piece of furniture in the office will most likely be a desk. So let's place or rearrange that first. It's nice to not have your back to the door of the room. It's not imperative, but if you can avoid it, please do.

You should have a comfortable chair with adequate back and wrist support, one that adjusts up and down—particularly if you plan to spend lots of hours at your desk.

If you have room and use a credenza or a file cabinet (I prefer lateral cabinets) and are in and out of your files often throughout the day, then it's probably a good idea to keep the file cabinet nearby. Likewise, if there's room, have some shelving also. If there's little floor space for freestanding shelving units, consider wall-mounted shelving. For storing reference books and office supplies as well as displaying personal items, adequate shelving is crucial.

ELECTRONICS

Make sure that you have enough electrical outlets and telephone jacks for all your equipment. Make sure that you have power-surge protectors as well. Anything that can be plugged into a surge protector should be—the fewer things directly plugged into the wall, the fewer the opportunities for power surges to short out your equipment, even just blowing lightbulbs in lamps.

For space-saving reasons alone, I suggest a multifunction printer whenever possible. While they may have a larger footprint than a regular printer, as a single machine they certainly take up less space than all the individual machines needed for flatbed copying and scanning and possibly faxing in addition to a stand-alone printer. If color printing is not important to you, I always suggest a black-and-white laser machine over inkjet machines. Laser machines are faster, and the cost per page is much lower. If color is important and cost is a factor, then inkjet it must be. Color laser machines continue to come down in price but typically print slower and are still somewhat expensive to purchase and operate.

The only suggestions I'll make about computers are to get the largest, highest resolution monitor you can afford, and to max out the RAM on your CPU or laptop. Additional RAM is relatively cheap when configuring your computer purchase, and essential to quick multitasking with several applications running at the same time. Unless you're playing a lot of games or editing video, some minor variations on processor speed will probably not be that noticeable. But inadequate RAM will slow you down and frustrate you again and again. Don't be penny-wise and pound-foolish in this instance.

LIGHTING

The right lighting is key. You'll want a desk lamp for task lighting, and secondary lamps and/or overhead lighting fixtures for general lighting. The guideline for good lighting is that there should be enough light available anywhere someone might be sitting and reading—three-way bulbs and dimmers can certainly create a softer mood when you're not working, but there's no reason to struggle with inadequate lighting when you're trying to get some work done.

FILING

A place to put documents and folders on their way into the filing cabinet is essential. As is a scheduled time each day or week when filing takes place. I don't think there's a need to distinguish between never-filed and previously filed documents. If a project requires you to frequently return to a particular folder or two, keeping it handy in a current work area may prove to be a better choice than filing and refiling the folder throughout the day. Either way, there should be a bin or basket established for all documents that are ready to be filed but haven't been yet.

MAIL, REVISITED

We're now going to return to the mail. If you remember, we talked about sorting the mail into the following major categories.

Bills

Asks

Invitations and Events (time-sensitive)

Read and File (including personal correspondence)

Action Items (finite tasks)

Catalogs

Magazines and Periodicals

I'm assuming that you have been managing the mail as detailed in chapter two for at least a month. If the office is *not* where you have been processing the mail, the first thing to do now is make the office the home for the mail. Given that much of what will need to be filed probably arrives through the mail, it makes sense that the mail should be sorted and processed in your office area.

I have no opinion about whether the bins/baskets for the mail are stackable or wicker or wire mesh, whether they're lined or unlined—all I'm concerned with is that the mail is processed consistently as outlined in chapter two. And I think if there is adequate room, you should establish a home for the bins that does not need to be moved or altered on a daily basis. This way you don't need to set up the bins every time you want to process the mail; they're already in place.

OFFICE SUPPLIES

Like with Like informs us that all office supplies live together. When it comes to a home office, that means all the raw or bulk supplies live together, ideally in a container or two clearly labeled as such. I have a stapler, a tape dispenser, a container of pens/pencils/markers with two pairs of scissors inserted (points down), a small dish of paperclips, and a coaster on my desktop. The boxes of paperclips that I replenish my dish with all live together in one box labeled Office Supplies. Rolls of tape for the tape dispenser, binder clips, boxes of staples, etc., also live in this box. Stacks of Post-its live in this box. Everything that would be considered surplus or backup supplies is in this box. So anyone can come from anywhere in the house and find a pad of Post-its or staples, and they have to look in only one place.

In my world, you may have a pair of scissors in the kitchen, but I would draw the line at a stapler. No doubt you may need to cut open a food package in the kitchen, but given that paperwork is located somewhere else, I'd encourage you to go to that place, that home-office place, to fulfill all your stapling needs. Scattered tools mean a greater likelihood of misplacement, running out of supplies, and wasted time rather than convenience.

COMPUTERS AND OTHER ELECTRONICS

I suggest that all computer equipment be located in the office area. Likewise, calculators, printers, scanners, copiers, fax machines, shredders, and so on. If it's considered an office machine, it should live in the office. As should these machines' supplies—toner or ink, paper, shredder lubrication sheets—all of it should live here as well. These supplies should be stored separately but alongside the smaller supplies from the previous section.

There are many websites and even some books written on proper ergonomic computer setup. Utilize them. Make sure that using your computer and other electronic devices does no harm to your health, both short-term and long-term.

I will suggest that aside from a list of frequently dialed fax numbers affixed to the fax machine itself or the number of a reliable service technician, you refrain from sticking notes and other things on your monitor or on any other piece of equipment. Learn to create reminder notes either on your computer or, even better, write them or enter them in your calendar as tasks so they actually get done—after a few days, you will no longer even notice the note or its contents, wherever you stuck it, but you will still be surrounded by clutter.

Software: Ditto

All software should also be stored together. Regardless of whether it arrived with a new machine or you purchased it retail, it should all live together. You can certainly group Like with Like subcategories together, such as the system disks for your computer, or the drivers for your various printers, or games. If you have both Macs and PCs in your home, you may want to have one container for the disks that correspond with each operating system—just in case someone less computer-savvy is looking for a particular disk, they won't inadvertently grab the PC disk for their Mac.

As you gather all the software together from around the house, make sure that you discard the software for any machines or programs that are either obsolete, no longer in your possession, or no longer being used. For example, at this point, few of us would have use for old Windows 2000 restore disks. These can be discarded or possibly donated to a computer lab somewhere or a museum of faded technology.

Data CDs, DVDs, and Floppy Disks

Just like software, above, now is the time to collect old floppy disks, CDs, and DVDs that have data stored on them. Don't confuse these disks with commercially purchased movie DVDs or audio CDs—those should be stored wherever the TV and corresponding players live. For now, we're focusing only on data disks.

Gather these data disks together and review them. Compare data on disks against data on your hard drive, making sure that any files you need or want from these disks is also loaded onto your computer. To avoid creating any more confusion when it comes time to sort these files in chapter ten, make sure that any files you import onto the computer at this time are specifically deposited into your documents folder. You could even create a new folder within your documents folder just for this task and label it, "20XX Doc Import."

Check any backup disks against each other, looking for duplicates as well as making sure you have the most current backups together with the rest of them. While you can almost never be too backed up (just ask anyone whose computer has ever crashed!), multiple copies of multiple copies are just redundant and could prove confusing, should you need to restore data from one of your backups.

Any disks that you're discarding that have personal information on them should be shredded or broken before being tossed. You don't want sensitive materials getting into the wrong hands.

OWNER'S MANUALS

All owner's manuals should be gathered together and stored in either a clear plastic envelope or an accordion folder or two (as volume dictates). The first thing to do is to collect them, from every drawer or cubby or surface where they might currently be. Once you have them all together, like the software above, immediately purge any for equipment that you no longer own. Throw these in the recycling bin.

Of the ones that remain, you can either alphabetize them; group them according to subcategories, such as small kitchen appliances, large appliances, office machines, etc.; or leave them in random order. Whenever you bring a new piece of equipment into the house, you should add its manual to the others.

And anytime a piece of equipment leaves, the manual should be retrieved. If the machine is being recycled, so should the manual. If it's being given away, give away the manual and any spare parts with it at the same time.

CONTACTS CONTAINER

In chapter two, we created or established a container of contacts for any return addresses we might have harvested from incoming mail. I suggest that all random business cards, matchbooks, and other scraps of paper with phone numbers scribbled on them also end up in this container. And that once a week (or at some other regular interval) you make it a point to enter at least some of these contacts into either a paper or a digital address book or contact list.

Whether you are constantly meeting people and bringing home business cards or seldom exchange information with others, it is imperative that whenever you do, you make some sort of identifying notes on the back of the card to remind you of who, where, and why you now have this card in your possession. Something as simple as the following.

Stuart's: Christmas 20XX
Worked w/Steve: Troyan Proj.
Wife: Sally

If you're attending a conference or other event where significant networking may be happening, take a ziplock bag with you and drop all the cards you collect into it whenever you're back in your room. Label the bag with the event and dates and this will help refresh your memory when you begin processing these cards.

Prior to taking my suggestions, many clients have found themselves with stacks of random cards from people they can't remember. This is not only useless but it may even prove counterproductive. You'll never know if someone whom you could have helped or who might have assisted you is now lying in those stacks, a missed opportunity, and their information destined for the trash.

Client-Friendly Space

If you see clients in your home office or in your home, it's important to maintain a professional appearance for your workspace. Food wrappers, leftovers, and other signs of your personal life do not belong here when you're open for business. It's also important to be able to easily put your hands on any files that belong to the client when visiting, or any forms you may need for your work together. This only reinforces the imperative that you must develop a filing system that is easy to use and easy to maintain—and that you do in fact use it.

A Time to Gather

You've already done a junior version of this exercise with just the owner's manuals. Now travel around the house and gather all remaining documents that you think belong in your office area, from wherever they are in the house. The mail is already accounted for, as are the owners' manuals, but there are bound to be other papers lying around. Let's corral them all together into a container of some sort, not worrying too much about their order. Step one is to find them. Step two will be to sort them.

Sorting, Purging, and (Re)Arranging

THINGS TO KEEP, THINGS TO TOSS

Now that we've gotten every stray piece of paper together from the various corners of the house, it's time to sort through them. The following are things that you can toss out immediately. You don't need to wonder or fret about any of them, I promise.

Junk mail

Requests/solicitations/invitations from charities you do not intend to
support

Requests/solicitations/invitations from businesses you do not use or
have no intention of using

Requests/solicitations/invitations for events that you do not plan to
attend

Expired coupons

Expired warranties and service contracts (harvest any key tech support/
manufacturers' contact information first)

Schedules/itineraries that are complete or outdated (keep calendars and
day planners or other documentation of where you were and when if
these trips are a business expense or you like to keep track of your
travels)

Generic account info/privacy statements you've read or don't intend
to read

Greeting cards that do not contain a detailed personal or very special
message

Receipts for any nondeductible expense, particularly for personal-care
and personal food items

Invitations you've received to events that have already happened

Owner's manuals for items you no longer own

Installation manuals for anything that is already installed

Expired insurance policies (after comparing the old to the new to ensure
that coverage is consistent and accurate)

Business cards from anyone whose name you don't recognize

Maps or atlases that are more than three years old

Periodicals and catalogs (three months' worth for periodicals; new catalogs always replace old catalogs)

Articles/clippings that you've not read or referred to in more than two
years (including recipes!)

Duplicates of anything (unless copied for someone—in which case put

them in Action Items, with an envelope addressed to the intended
recipient)

Brochures from tourist destinations (whether you've been there or not,
these are not souvenirs)

Financial/banking documents (confirm with your accountant):

- Statements/canceled checks that are more than seven years old
- Monthly or quarterly statements where the year-end statement reflects all twelve months' transactions
- Canceled checks for personal expenses (save canceled checks
for major purchases and all tax-deductible expenses for either
the life of the product or seven years)
- Unused checks for closed accounts

What remains is now to be filed. Like with Like makes filing go faster,
especially when there is a stockpile of things to file. So begin by grouping like
things together—all your utility bills, bank statements, and credit card statements, and so on. Then further sort them by account number whenever there
are multiple accounts with the same vendor. This way, when you start to pull
out or create folders, all of a certain kind of document is already together,
ready to be filed at the same time.

Always create the folder and hand-write its label before committing yourself to a printed label. You may determine that you need a larger or smaller
folder, or that the nature of the contents has shifted enough to warrant a
change in label.

Continue filing until everything has a home inside either a folder, one of
the mail bins, or the recycling bin. If you need a further reminder about the
how-to of filing, please refer back to the sections on filing on pages 95
through 104. When you are finished, there should no longer be any loose
documents around the house, all the owner's manuals should be in one place,
and your filing cabinet or crates should have accurately labeled and smartly
filled folders arranged within them.

Converted Closets and Other Snug Spaces

As I mentioned above, there are almost no instances when some sort of space to house and manage paperwork can't be found in a home. So don't give up hope. Don't let limited space convince you that disorganization, missed appointments, or even late payments are your destiny. I disagree, and I support you in humming louder than your denial can talk to you.

With that in mind, carefully explore your home and see where you could reasonably establish a workplace for yourself that is large enough to contain all you need to store there and the kind of work you'll do there, and set it up. Is that a corner of the basement or an odd-shaped closet under the stairs? If it's large enough for a chair and a work surface, you can have a fully functioning, if snug, office of your own. And once there, be creative in utilizing every inch of usable space. Consider installing shelves right up to the ceiling. Hang your monitor on the wall. Even your printer can be supported on brackets, taking no space from your desktop.

Keep things in scale. After Like with Like and One Home for Everything, that's the best advice I can give you for working with and in smaller spaces. If you're not self-publishing a one-hundred-page annual report, you don't need to have three cases of paper on hand and six thousand mailing labels ready to be printed. If and when you have a large project coming up, still stock up on only the supplies you need for that project. Only maintain what you actually need to work effectively and not run out of supplies. Let the rest go. And you will have a crisp and tidy space to call your own.

Those Other Activities

Now that you have a functional office or officelike space, it's time to consider those other activities that you isolated at the beginning of the chapter. In this new configuration, what do you have room for? And what would be better relocated to some other room or part of the house?

Consider each activity and each space in your home to find the strongest match. If the office is still the best fit, sizewise and taskwise, then carve out enough space to house whatever equipment and supplies belong to the activity. If instead the den or family room or basement would be preferable, take the grouping of things to its new home. If these items are already contained in a cabinet or basket or bin, that's great. If not, guesstimate the volume of things and get them an appropriate-sized container and label it as necessary. Do this for each activity that has been displaced from your office.

When you get to the new space, do not just dump everything in a corner, but find whatever you've brought with you a proper home. Employ Like with Like liberally in identifying these new homes. Even if the rest of the room is a shambles, create a distinct and orderly location for this one activity and its requisite parts. In so doing, you will lay the foundation for your return to this space with a plan of action. Make it a priority that the next time you visit this space, you will work to bring the rest of the space into alignment with your one new crisp and defined area.

How Long Do I Have to Keep This?

This is one of the questions I'm asked most often. "Is it okay to get rid of _____?" "Do I still have to hold on to _____?" Not knowing what to keep and what can go stops more people in their tracks than almost anything else when it comes to paper. Rather than go into excruciating detail here, I've created a handy list at the back of the book (see pages 378–81), which is also downloadable as a PDF file from the book's website (www.unstuffyourlife.net). Refer to it whenever you have a question. And given that rules and laws may vary from jurisdiction to jurisdiction, *always* check with a tax or legal professional if there's even the hint of doubt. It's always better to err on the side of caution before shredding your last copy of something important. The one thing I will state here definitively is to *never* get rid of your tax returns. Your tax adviser will counsel you on when you can dispose of supporting materials, but never, *never, never* discard your copy of the actual filed return. *Never.*

To Shred or Not to Shred?

Identity theft is a big deal when it happens to you. Until then it's not quite an urban myth, but it may be like a mysterious illness that only your cousin's neighbor's best friend came down with or like those killer bees on their way up from Mexico—a vague threat you feel no urgency to protect yourself from. Believe me, if and when you find out someone's been using your ID to do their Christmas shopping or to purchase a condo in Miami, it'll be a sad, sad day and a colossal pain in the butt as you start to trace when the theft occurred and what the total damage is.

I wish I could say that shredding your documents guarantees you protection from this most personal intrusion and violation, but it doesn't. It goes a long way toward prevention, but sneaky people are always on the alert to discover new ways to beat the system, and we'll have to do our best to keep up with them or not fall too far behind their deviousness. In the meantime, anything, *anything,* that has your name, address, and any account number, suggestion of an account number, or an offer to *establish* an account number should be run through a crosscut shredder. Remember Oliver North and Iran-Contra? The cheapest shredders simply cut your papers into smaller strips of paper that could be painstakingly taped together to re-create the original document. Crosscut shredders turn your paper into a version of confetti that is virtually impossible to piece back together. This is not a time to cut corners or to save a few bucks if the difference is between these two types of machines. Spring for the shredder lubrication sheets as well, to keep your blades sharp and unclogged. The last thing you want is to be in the middle of destruction and find the gears seizing up.

Likewise, any old floppy disks, CDs, etc., that may have confidential information need to be destroyed by running them through a shredder or breaking them so that the device is no longer readable. If you don't know what would render a disk unreadable, shred it. That'll cover you. You won't be able to recycle your shredding once you've also shredded a CD or DVD, so empty the contents of your shredder before changing material to be shredded, isolating nonrecyclables from recyclables each time.

Maintaining the System

I'm a proud member of the clean-desk club, and I'd like to sponsor you for membership as well. If possible, never leave your office with papers lying on your desk. The one exception being a current project that you'll immediately resume working on in the morning. Even if you're a whiz at multitasking, you can still start working on only one project first. That should be the only thing left out. Otherwise, at the end of the day, your work surface should be clean.

You don't have to file everything every night before leaving, but every document you're finished with should be placed in the To Be Filed basket. Any other documents that arrived in the mail should be returned to their baskets if there's still more to be done with them as well. Any cables or other electronic-y thing you've pulled out during the day should find its way home, too.

At the end of the day, even if you're just walking down the hall, you want to go home for the night. So does everything else you've used throughout the day. So put it back where it came from, establish a proper home for anything that came in from the outside during the day, and dispatch anything that is now leaving your home to at least the thrift-store container, if not the trash or recycling, when you're certain the item is no longer useful. Ten to fifteen minutes at the end of the day should be enough time to ensure that everything is back where it belongs. And certainly if you pulled out something during the day for a finite activity, there's no reason to wait until the end of the day to send it home. Build the habit of returning things to their home as soon as you're finished with them, and maintaining order will actually take care of itself.

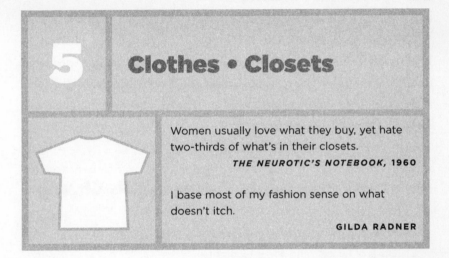

5 Clothes • Closets

Women usually love what they buy, yet hate two-thirds of what's in their closets.

THE NEUROTIC'S NOTEBOOK, 1960

I base most of my fashion sense on what doesn't itch.

GILDA RADNER

So we've conquered, or at least survived, the home office. We now have a system set up in a dedicated area for paying bills; we know how to deal with the mail when it comes in; we have a handle on our magazines, catalogs, and other periodicals; and there's no longer piles of paper scattered in other areas of our home.

Now it gets personal.

I've heard this countless times: "I've got a ton of clothes and nothing to wear." You've got fat clothes, skinny clothes, torn clothes, worn clothes, red clothes, and blue clothes, and even with all that, you can never find that adorable cashmere sweater with the scoop neck when you're looking for it. Well, that, too, is about to change.

Suggestion (or Rule, if You Respond Better to Rules)

If you don't wear it, if you can't wear it, or if you haven't worn it in two years, it's time to shed it. When we get to sorting, we'll tackle and dismantle, once and for all, those stubborn arguments for why the above applies in almost every situation except yours.

What We're Going to Cover in This Chapter

☐ What a Closet Is and Isn't
☐ Kinds of Closets and Their Contents
☐ Structural Elements of a Clothes Closet
☐ Clothes and Proper Storage I
☐ I Currently Wear These Sizes
☐ Clothes That Don't Fit or Work and the People Who Love Them
☐ Clothes and Proper Storage II
☐ Pre-Sorting and Purging
☐ The Emptying of the Closet(s)
☐ Sorting and Purging
☐ Reloading the Closet
☐ Drawers (Mini-Closets on Their Sides)
☐ Overbuying and Buyer's Remorse
☐ Shoes
☐ Maintaining the Clothes Closet
☐ Other Kinds of Closet
☐ Dirty Laundry
☐ Maintaining the System

Things You Will Need for the Work in This Chapter

- A Good Friend
- Seven Containers/Areas Defined on the Floor:
  Keep
  Donate
  Sell
  Trash
  Someplace Else
  Sentimentaland
  The Fence
- Good Lighting
- A Full-length Mirror

What a Closet Is and Isn't

Closet (noun):
A small and enclosed space, a cabinet, or a cupboard in a house or building, used for general storage or for hanging clothes.

Since we're focusing on the hanging-clothes part, let's first agree that there will be no general storage in our clothes closets, except when clearly labeled and absolutely necessary because of space constraints.

A closet is never a hidden room where you can barely open the door, and where to avoid an avalanche of oddities tumbling on your head, you frantically insert another random object and slam the door, narrowly escaping disaster.

That is *not* a closet. That is your next project.

The goal of this chapter is simple: for you to organize your closets so that within thirty seconds of opening the closet door, you can successfully put your hands on whatever you're looking for.

Kinds of Closets and Their Contents

Entry/Mudroom: outerwear, foul-weather gear, sporting goods and equipment, pet items

Presents/Gifts: gifts gathered throughout the year to be given to others, wrapping paper, bows, ribbon

Party: supplies for parties and entertaining, decorations, children's party games

Pantry: bulk foods, serving pieces, smaller appliances, surplus paper products like napkins and paper towels (not office supplies)

Clothes: clothing, shoes, adornment, and accessories

Utility: household maintenance items, cleaning supplies, tools

Linen: towels, bed linens, surplus bathroom supplies, sewing kit

In your home, identify the types and locations of the closets you have. Make a list of them, following the format below.

Type of closet: _____

Location in the home: _____

Contents: _____

Structural Elements of a Clothes Closet

These are the things I'd like to find in any clothes closet. Use this as a shopping list for any items or elements you may be missing.

☐ Good, bright, and ample lighting

☐ An ample supply of wood, padded, or other good-quality hangers (preferably uniform in size and type)

☐ Sturdy rods and shelves that don't bow or cup under weight

☐ Hooks or a hooked hanger for belts

☐ Hooks for robes

☐ Racks or hooked hangers for neckties

☐ Shoe racks/shelves/cubbies that are expandable or already sized for your shoes

☐ A valet hook or pullout rod

☐ Containers, baskets, or bins for small or odd-shaped items

☐ Containers, baskets, or bins for small handbags (purses, clutches, etc.)

☐ Clear shoe boxes for special-occasion shoes

The following are things I wouldn't like to find in any clothes closet.

Dry-cleaning bags discarded and lying on the floor

Old food or food containers

The one remaining shoe of a former pair

Random piles of dirty laundry or baskets of clean, unfolded laundry

Discarded or obsolete telephone equipment

Expired animals—pets or pests

You get the idea.

Clothes and Proper Storage I

If space allows, this is how you will organize your closets.

Items will be sorted by type—all slacks together, shirts together, coats, etc.

Within each type, they're further sorted by color and style—long-sleeved or short-sleeved, by neckline, etc.

All two- and three-piece outfits go together and stay together

All hanging clothes are kept on uniform hangers, so everything hangs at the same level

Robes and nightwear hang on hooks nearest to the door

Handbags and decorative hats go on shelves (cold-weather hats belong with outerwear in coat closets)

Smaller handbags (purses, clutches) will be stored in baskets or bins

Small or odd-shaped items will be corraled in baskets

Scarves should be folded and placed in baskets

Belts belong on hooks or hangers with hooks

Neckties go on racks or hooked hangers

Seasonal shoes go on the floor (snow boots, etc., are stored with outerwear in a coat closet)

Clear shoe boxes on shelves are for special-occasion or fancy shoes

If adequate space for your entire wardrobe is unavailable in one contiguous space, your closets should contain only clothes current to the season.

Twice a year—and it may be worth adding it to your calendar just like daylight saving time—you can rotate your wardrobe to a storage closet or a hanging rack, so the current season's clothes are always front and center.

Notable Note

Some odd and interesting apparel facts:

- More than two-thirds of women are wearing the wrong bra size, which can cause saggy-looking breasts, back pain, and unflattering clothing fit.
- U.S. women's clothing sizes are not held to any specific standard; therefore, manufacturers can use whatever sizing they want to. In the 1940s, the Department of Commerce did a study of women's measurements that measured mostly young, unmarried women without children. This is the basis of the actual numbered sizes that are still used today.
- The average clothing size for an American woman has been quoted many times as a size 14, which is considered a plus size.

I Currently Wear These Sizes

Athletic shoes _____

Belt _____

Blazer/sport coat _____

Blouse _____

Boots _____

Bowling shoes _____

Brassiere _____

Button-down shirt _____

Camisole _____

Coat _____

Dress _____

Dress socks _____

Dress suit _____

Garter _____

Gloves _____

Gown _____

Hat _____

Jacket _____

Jeans _____

Nightwear _____

Shorts _____

Slacks _____

Socks (ankle/crew) _____

Stockings _____

Sweater _____

Tuxedo _____

Shoes _____

Ski boots _____

Tank top _____

T-shirt _____

Underwear _____

Clothes That Don't Fit or Work and the People Who Love Them

THE BARGAIN HUNTER

My client—we'll call her Doris—used to be a size 6, and she wore a size 7½ shoe. Then she had Jesse and Claude. She's now a size 10 to 12, and her foot will never see this side of an 8 again. She has plenty of clothes that fit her. But occasionally she'll see a great Gucci loafer on sale in size 7½, and she can't seem to help herself. Sometimes they even come home with her in different colors, they were such a bargain. She'll tell me, "You don't understand, it's a woman thing," but I think I do understand. I love a bargain as much as the next person, but it's not a bargain if you can't fit into it. It's a bargain for the lady behind you, who still wears a 7½.

THE SIZE KING/QUEEN

If you've struggled with your weight, body image, or eating disorders and your size has fluctuated, you may have several wardrobes competing for your (possibly) limited closet and storage space.

Take a deep breath. And let's speak frankly. When was the last time you actually wore that skirt? Or those trousers? If any article of clothing is more than two sizes away from your current size, it's time to say good-bye.

I have a client, we'll call her Claire, and she has struggled with her size for years. She's been up and down, and she has a wardrobe that reflects this. When I first met her, she had already worked with another organizer who had "redesigned" her closet with expensive hardware that actually reduced the amount of clothing that could be stored in it. While it was lovely in the way it displayed her clothing, in a Manhattan apartment with limited closets it was also a huge waste of prime real estate.

On top of dealing with limited space, there was also Claire's frustration at her unsuccessful attempts to lose weight and a stockpile of clothes in many sizes. Currently, she was stuck somewhere between her heaviest and her ideal weight. I encouraged her to tell me the story of her most recent attempt. After her tearful and heartfelt recounting, we climbed into the story together. I helped Claire to see which parts of the story were factual, and which parts were just stock phrases that she was not aware she was even repeating—that's how ingrained they were in her way of thinking about herself and her size. Phrases such as, "I'm fat; no one's ever going to love me" or "I'll always be alone" or "I can't do anything right," were automatic responses to any discomfort she was feeling.

After a few minutes of this playful, direct dissection, we were both giggling at the blatantly false and at times absurd ways she viewed herself. Several times she started to say some variation of the above, something she had said often without ever really listening to herself, only to catch herself and burst out laughing.

Wiping tears from her face, this time from joy, she marched over to the closet and began tossing out clothes she was saving, just in case she woke up forty pounds heavier. Overnight. The freedom in her voice and laughter as she gathered these plus-plus-size stretch pants and flowing, drapey tops was inspiring. No longer waiting for something "inevitably awful" to happen, Claire was now free to use her closets for her life today.

We also curated her "skinny" clothes, keeping some timeless pieces and letting go of the rest. Most of the things she was holding on to for her descent in size were too random, and while the sizes might have been right, some of the styles were way out of date, even for a retro or "arty" look. We kept the best pieces, and made peace with the fact that if and when Claire gets down in size and needs more clothes, this would be a legitimate reason to shop. And in the meantime, her closet is an accurate reflection of her current size, with room for some movement north or south in the size department.

William, too, had clothes that he just couldn't fit into any longer. In sorting through his closets, we repeatedly came across another pair of "skinny" jeans or a favorite pair of shorts from college. These discoveries were always qualified with "God, I really need to get back to the gym" or "I had those on a few weeks ago and I could almost button them all the way up!" When pushed, William admitted that his gym membership had lapsed seven months ago and that the "few weeks ago" he was referring to was actually a year and a half past.

I'm aware that some of you may be holding on to clothes in smaller sizes in the hope that you will once again fit into them. And I support you in accomplishing your goal. But like Claire and William, you need to be honest with yourself about how diligently you're working on slimming down. And if you are more than two sizes away from those "skinny" jeans, how likely is it that you'll be back in them before the styles change? Only you can answer that. I will say that if you're keeping them as any form of negative encouragement, or as some other shame-based motivational tool, you need to get rid of them immediately. Any victory achieved at that cost is too expensive.

If they are providing positive motivation, I still suggest selecting the best examples and strongest styles, and letting faded or quirky pieces go. Read on for more on this topic.

THE RETRO GOD/GODDESS

Clothes that are out of style should not be difficult to spot. And unless you're a famous artist, fashionista, or other public figure, chances are that you will not be leading a trend by reclaiming some iconic era-specific design. Let them go. And if in twenty years you still look good and need to wear elephant bell-bottom hip-hugger jeans again, you'll buy them at the Gap like everyone else.

ALWAYS A BRIDESMAID

Bridesmaids' dresses, mother-of-the-bride outfits, and other theme clothes are what I like to call "specialty" clothes. These are often the easiest to release, because while you may have enjoyed the event, you may not have liked wearing the outfit in the first place. I know, too, that they may not have been cheap, but that's the price of love and friendship. And you can always get revenge when *you* get married, if you're so inclined. Meanwhile, make a drag queen happy. Get those dresses out of here now.

THE ONLY-IN-YOUR-DREAMS OUTFIT

I fell in love with a pair of bright electric-cobalt-blue, brushed-cotton Cacharel jeans when I was eighteen. I wore them out of the house exactly once. There is no doubt they were beautiful and fit me well. And I was so self-conscious in them that I couldn't relax the entire day. I am not exaggerating when I say that when I walked into a room, everyone looked at me. You couldn't *not* look, that's how bright and shiny they were. I didn't want *that* much attention. They weren't me. Even though I wanted them to be. I'm sure by now they've found a happy home in some aspiring rock star's closet.

THE UNIFORM

I'm not advocating a homogeneous style or look for everyone. You know what you look good in, or at least what you feel comfortable wearing. I wear button-down shirts and khakis or jeans. It simplifies things for me. That way, I don't have a big debate in the morning. If I'm going to someone's office, it's khakis and a dress shirt and lace-up shoes. If we're doing cleaning and sorting at someone's home, it's jeans and maybe a sweatshirt and sneakers. It's a uniform of sorts, and one that I'm comfortable in. I own a few suits, and even a tuxedo. And yes, they all fit me.

For daily wear, a tailored, somewhat limited wardrobe can make getting out of the house that much easier and quicker.

THE NEW ENGLAND "OLD MONEY" LOOK

I'm hard on my clothes. A favorite shirt becomes too worn and gets retired. It's okay that clothes wear out. If you wear them a lot, it's inevitable.

Other than serving as a bizarre badge of Yankee pride, clothes that have worn thin or have holes in them are best relegated to yard work, cleaning the garage, painting, or community service work, such as when you volunteer to plant two thousand bulbs with your neighborhood gardening society. And we need only a few changes of these clothes as well. No need for fourteen sweatshirts with grease stains and holes. Three or four will suffice. The rest become rags or chew toys for a pet.

A CAUTIONARY TALE FROM THE "INTERWEB"

Perhaps you've read the story that has traveled around the Internet maybe fifteen million times about the brother who is cleaning out his sister's dresser after her funeral and discovers a silk teddy or some fancy lingerie. She was saving it for some special day. He implores us to recognize that *today* is that special day. He wants us to cherish the moment, live the day fully, and be here now, because we don't know what tomorrow holds for us. Or, for that matter, if we even get a tomorrow. And you certainly don't want someone writing about you on the Internet after you're dead. As we've already discussed, urban myth, Internet chain letter, or not, "someday" is a fiction.

So by all means, wear the teddy. And when it gets frayed, get a new teddy. Don't get forty-seven new teddies. Because you can wear only one at a time.

POSTCARDS FROM THE EDGE

There are clothes that are special because of where we got them, who gave them to us, who they belonged to, or what we were doing when we wore them. This always makes me think of the play *The Woolgatherer* by William Mastrosimone. I think the title says it all. It doesn't matter whether the sweater was from an old flame, your grandfather, or Sears. Sweaters with holes in them go to someone who can mend them, meaning reweave them, not sew a patch on them. Likewise, suits and other dressy clothes. They should be repaired if possible, and discarded if not. They are not souvenirs. They are clothes.

If you absolutely cannot let a particular piece of clothing go that you also cannot wear, place it in a separate pile that will join its brothers and sisters in a place I call Sentimentaland. More on this later.

Clothes and Proper Storage II

Before we take everything out of the closet, open the door and take a few pictures. While the door is open, pull up a chair, sit down, and study the closet. Does it have everything you need or want it to have? The more time you spend planning now, before we begin the big sort, the less time or money you'll spend later in either physical labor or correcting mistakes.

Take some measurements. Evaluate the space.

- Do you have adequate shelving?
- Are the shelves sturdy and stable?

- How about the rods—are they well secured to the walls? Do they bow in the middle?
- Were all your clothes bunched up with no room around them, or was there adequate space between the items?
- How about shoes? Do you have cubbies for them or a shoe rack? A slanted shelf or two down low? Or are they all just jumbled in a big pile on the floor?

Get out your notebook, begin a new page labeled Closets, and write down your observations, notes, and ideas. Dream big, from a design point of view—we're less focused on finishes right now. Honed granite or porcelain tile, solid walnut or white melamine—these decisions don't matter as much as adequate and appropriate storage for everything you need to contain in the closet in front of you. There'll be plenty of time to dress it up; let's make sure right now it works *as a closet*.

Now review your notes and answers. Is there anything about your closet that you would redesign? Look around online at closet-design sites for additional ideas.

If so, are they simple fixes that you can do by yourself or with a friend, or do they require a contractor's help? Before we start sorting, you should make sure that the space you'll return everything into is a space that works for you. There's no point in sorting and purging if, when it's time to put everything back, there's still clumsy or inadequate space for everything.

For tenants or other people who cannot physically alter the layout or location of the closet, think about what you can do to improve the closet to better serve you. Are there freestanding pieces you can use to transform the closet's interior? Are there too many shelves, and could some be stored elsewhere or doubled up to create more depth between shelves? Work with whatever structural limits exist to creatively transform an awkward closet into a more useful closet.

In thinking about the physical layout and construction of your closet, if you determine that restructuring or replacing components is necessary, draw yourself a plan and start to create a shopping list. If this is a DIY (do-it-yourself) project, make sure you have all of the proper tools and new/improved components on-site *before you go any further*.

Keep in mind that the finished project will look cleaner and crisper if the products, hardware, materials, and appointments go together well. Personal preference and budget may influence whether the look is more utilitarian or decorative, but standard and uniform finishes and design lay a good foundation—simple lines keep the focus on the clothing and other items stored, and quiet any visual jumble.

Equally important is not to fall prey to propaganda. There is seemingly no end to the stream of innovative and new products and gadgets for "organizing." No product will magically produce the same results that you will as you work your way through this book. Don't be seduced or confused by advertising claims that a product will transform your disorganized closet (or office or life) from X to Y for only $19.95. There is no magic device, and you don't need to be rescued. Carefully consider what you need when it comes to clothing storage, and then search the marketplace for the smartest and best products. You may not need to spend a lot of money to get useful and well-constructed components. As with many things, a moderate approach often yields the best results, even in closet transformation.

Compose a list of all the things you need or want to restructure your closet, and this will become your shopping list.

Pre-Sorting and Purging

The time to embark on this next phase is after you've gathered all the supplies, tools, and hardware needed to restructure your closet yourself. And if you're doing a closet makeover and using a company to supply materials and labor, your appointment should be scheduled for today. That way, you can unload the closet for the work crew and take the entire contents into another room to work while they transform your closet for you. Either way, you should be prepared to complete any construction as soon as the closet is empty of its contents.

Things to have on hand as you begin:

A GOOD FRIEND

Only if he or she is objective, committed to the process, and not easily distracted—otherwise, you're better off on your own.

SEVEN CONTAINERS OR AREAS
DEFINED ON THE FLOOR

Keep: These are items that you really love, not items that you loved many years ago or wish to love in many years to come. These are items that fit and flatter you today. These will be laundered, folded or hung up, and put away.

Donate: These are things you are clearly done with, either stylistically or sizewise, that you're willing to give away.

Sell: These are things you are clearly done with, either stylistically or sizewise, that are heading to a local consignment shop or being sold online, either by yourself or by a service that manages online auctions for you.

Trash: These are the unfortunate things you've kept long beyond repair or use, which are being discarded.

Someplace Else: These are the things that should have never been in your closet to begin with, the "general storage" items I mentioned at the top of the chapter. When we're finished with everything else, you'll containerize and label them, and find them appropriate homes.

Sentimentaland: As its name suggests, a mythical land defined by clear plastic tubs containing objects of dubious monetary value but, as the commercial says, ultimately "priceless." These clothes can be further sorted by type—baby, maternity, etc.—or just placed in tubs along with other objects that you don't necessarily use but that are too significant to let go of.

The Fence: As in to be "on the fence," or unable to make a decision. This category is to be used with hyper-vigilance, and only in cases of extreme confusion. It is never to be used as a mask for procrastination or regret, but only in cases of true confoundment. This is not a "get out of jail free" card—use it only as a last resort!

GOOD LIGHTING

This is not a date, and there's nothing romantic about to happen. You need to be able to see, and see clearly. We're looking for rips, holes, stains, and, most important, fit. If the overhead light is out, replace the bulb. If you have only indirect lighting, remove the lampshades from the lamps. Even better, hang up a clip light or two and turn the place into *Close Encounters* . . . When you can actually see what's going on, you'll be more likely to act on it and remain decisive.

FULL-LENGTH MIRROR

Be sure you can see from your head to your toes.

The Emptying of the Closet(s)

This is the moment of truth. As we've done before in other spaces, begin by removing everything from the closet. This is an exercise in trust (me) and in liberation (you). To create a little emotional space, perhaps you can think of this as an inexpensive and exhaustive shopping trip to a store you have always heard about but have never been to. You're about to discover old treasures, fashion mistakes, and everything in between, without ever leaving your home!

Resist the urge to sort as you remove things, exceptions being those things you already know are trash or are being donated. It's important to empty the closet quickly, so you don't want to get distracted by sorting when you're really just unloading.

Once everything is out of the closet, now is the time to do any rebuilding, repairing, or restructuring. If the basic structure of your closet is completely satisfactory, then all you want to do right now is clean it. Take this time to wipe down everything—every surface, every piece of trim—and finish by sweeping, mopping, or vacuuming the floor.

Now that that's done, we can start sorting in earnest.

Sorting and Purging

Clothing with holes, or stains that can't be removed, gets tossed. Resist the urge to turn every piece of clothing that is torn or stained into a rag. The moth-eaten cashmere sweater is sad, but it's not a chamois for you to polish your Bentley. Throw it away.

Clothes that don't fit, including shoes—even really expensive, sexy shoes—go away. If they're in great shape and worth some cash, take them to a consignment shop. If not, a local charity gets them.

> **Notable Note**
>
> It turns out that moth larvae—not moths—are the culprits of fabric disasters.

Clothing that is ripped in unfashionable or inappropriately revealing ways may be something you'll change the oil in or wear as a costume, but it doesn't belong in your closet anymore. Feel free to start a costume bin to store the things you wear only on Halloween or at Burning Man or on "play night." They don't deserve prime closet real estate unless your daily work *requires* specific costumes.

These designations should allow you to move quickly through the worn, the torn, and the obsolete. Anytime you come to a piece of clothing that you're on the fence about, set it aside, and we'll return to it in a bit.

Everything else is subject to the following six questions. If the answer to numbers 1 or 2 is *no*, let it go. If any answer to numbers 3 through 6 is *yes*, let it go.

1. **Have I worn this item in the last year, or in the last two years? No.**

   This item is no longer in your current wardrobe. You may be saving it for any number of reasons, but to wear it isn't one of them. Let it go. The exception is formalwear that *still fits.*

2. **Does this go with anything else I own? No.**

   A kissing cousin to number 6. Although you spent decent money on it, you're not going to build a wardrobe around it. Different from a costume, this is something that is terminally unique. Let it go.

3. **Has this item lost its shape (stretched or shrunk), or has the color faded? Yes.**

   Of all the questions, this one has the least interpretive wiggle room. While the item itself may have evoked some sentimental tug, it's clearly past use. Let it go.

4. **Am I waiting for this trend to come back before I wear it again? Yes.**

   It's not coming back. Not in this form. With the exception of haute couture, when something returns as a style, contemporary designers typically "interpret" the classic fashion elements and either offer the new piece as an homage or as an ironic take on the past. Either way, yours will just look dated. Let it go.

5. **Am I waiting to lose or gain weight before I can fit into this item again? Yes.**

   How many sizes away are you right now? If more than two, again, let it go. You can bargain all you want with yourself; I'm pretty immovable on this point. When all else fails, remember the stories of Claire and William at the beginning of this chapter.

   If you're struggling to put on weight, it might not be clothing that's providing the best motivation. Consult your therapist or other professional on how to move deliberately and consistently forward to your appropriate size and weight. No need to create opportunities to feel bad about yourself in the closet you're in every day. Let it go.

6. **Am I keeping this item because it was an expensive impulse purchase? Yes.**

This is often one of the more difficult conversations I have with clients. The shame and remorse most people experience when confronted with these impulse purchases often freezes them in place. This is how the conversation often goes.

VirgoMan: Are we done with this jacket yet? (or hat or scarf or blouse or . . .)
Client: I don't know.
VM: What's the debate?
Client: It was expensive.
VM: I can see that.

(Pause.)

VM: Do you ever wear it?
Client: Of course not. Never.
VM: How do you feel when you see it?
Client: Stupid. Angry. Stupid.
VM: That can't be fun.
Client: Yeah, it sucks.
VM: Okay. Tell me about your last relationship.
Client: That jerk?
VM: Okay. So you don't hang on to him/her because he/she was expensive, do you?
Client (laughing): Of course not.
VM: So . . . why keep this hanging around just to give yourself something to feel bad about? Let it go.

Client *(with attitude)*: Fine.

VM: Look, don't do it just to make me happy. Do it because it makes sense to you. I don't have to live with it, you do. And it's taking space away from clothes you actually wear.

Client: No, you're right. I just hate it. I hate that I bought it, and I hate that I can't let it go.

VM: I get it. It's okay. It's fortunately, I hope, not the biggest or most expensive mistake you've ever made, so all things considered, it's not such a big deal.

Client: I hear what you're saying, but it still does feel like a big deal.

VM: All right. Then feel it as a big deal and still make the choice to let it go. Give yourself room for the things you love—don't let them be crowded out by the things you feel regret and remorse over.

Client: Oh, this is so hard. *(Pause.)* Why is this so hard? *(Pause.)* Good grief, where's the container for the consignment shop? Put this in it. It's ridiculous, I know. I'm just . . . I'm done, just get it out of here. Oh my God. I need help!

VM *(holding up another garment)*: How about this? Are you ready to let go of this?

Something to think about is how you feel right now—do you identify with this client? Are you agitated just reading this? Study this feeling so you can remember it the next time you're shopping and looking at something you love but don't know what you'd do with once you get it home. That's when this feeling comes in handy. You can appreciate the item—shoes, slacks, belt, whatever—as a beautiful thing. You can appreciate it in the store and then just leave it there for others to admire as well. Then you don't have to come home and feel this way again. Try it the next time you're out shopping. Leaving the lovely item behind likely won't feel worse than the sense of remorse does, and chances are it'll feel a whole lot better.

For me, this is not about winning an argument. It's about advocating for the part of the client they seem less inclined to stand up for in those moments. The part that wants to be on the other side of the struggle, to relax, release, and be done. Unfortunately, there's that other part of most of us that's really committed to protecting some sense of being right. That we must have been right to buy it in the first place, because no one would knowingly do something so wrong, or make such a costly mistake. It's humbling to recognize, that despite our best efforts, we all do some things that are costly and don't serve us. If we've survived this long, we can take some comfort from knowing that it didn't kill us. It's just a piece of fabric. Maybe with a few sequins or bugle beads attached, but it's still just fabric. We can let it go.

Once more, if the item has significant value, you can always return it to the store you purchased it from. If too much time has lapsed, then place it in the sale container and take it to one of the higher-end resale or consignment shops in your area. This often proves to be an excellent way to turn lemons into lemonade.

You should not stop until each item has been sorted into one of the seven piles. Except for bathroom breaks.

THE FENCE

At this point, everything should have been touched once, and a decision about it made. For the few items you were uncertain about, which you've placed in the "fence" pile, now it's do-or-die. Try them on, one at a time. Look yourself over. Flattering? Pouchy? Clingy in any number of wrong ways? Itchy? Anything that doesn't flatter, that doesn't fit well, leaves. For some things, the answer will be immediately visible. For any that look good *and* you're still on the fence about, ask yourself the six questions above. Nothing will remain a mystery after both a fitting and the gauntlet of questions.

CLOTHES-SWAPPING PARTIES: AN ALTERNATIVE TO THRIFT STORES

Although women are more likely to arrange something like this (men—what a missed opportunity!), I often hear of clients or friends attending clothes-swapping parties.

This is the basic idea: a bunch of friends and/or co-workers get together. Food and drink are always welcome components. Everyone brings the clothes they're done with and tosses them into the middle of the room. Each person takes a turn selecting an article of clothing, going around the room until everyone's had a chance to pick something. Repeat until either all the clothes are spoken for or no one wants the items that remain. These are then bagged and donated to a local charity.

Beyond this basic structure, the rules of the game are wide open to alteration—I've heard of swaps that resemble holiday grab bags, where the last to draw has the right to swap with anyone prior, or where cross-negotiations for coveted items are brokered. The key is to have fun and come home with new clothing that you'll actually wear, while eliminating items you were done with.

Reloading the Closet

Once you've cleaned the closet, repaired or improved anything structural that wasn't up to snuff, and determined which clothes you are going to keep, you're now ready to put them back into your closet.

As I mentioned above, the simplest system for finding and keeping clothes organized is to arrange them by category, and within each category by color. For example, on the clothing rod, keep all your jackets together, shirts together, pants together, dresses together, skirts together, and so on. You can clearly delineate categories with labeled rod-divider disks if you get confused by where the trousers end and the blouses begin.

When arranging the clothes within each category, hang clothes by color from either light to dark, starting with white, or corresponding with the order of colors in a rainbow, beginning with white, pink, red, orange, yellow, green, blue, purple, and black.

Also match your hangers to your clothes. Pants should have pant hangers, skirts skirt hangers, jackets and shirts sturdy wooden or padded hangers, and strappy dresses or lingerie notched hangers to hold straps.

If your closet has built-in storage (drawers, shelves, or cubbies) or you are corralling things into baskets or other containers, these too should each be assigned a specific category (e.g., slogan T-shirts, or pajamas, or workout clothes, etc.).

I've learned from several female clients that the best way to store pantyhose is to roll them up to prevent runs, and never store them in wicker or rough baskets without liners.

Drawers (Mini-Closets on Their Sides)

Like your closets, your drawers should be organized by type of clothing stored—ideally containing one kind of item per drawer. Like with Like rules the day here. So store socks with socks and, if space allows, sport socks and shorty socks isolated together, and heavier wool socks or wintry socks living together. Stockings can live alone or be combined with one of the sock categories. Keep T-shirts with T-shirts—if you have a category of dressy T-shirts, those would live distinctly from non-dressy T-shirts; likewise, you may want to separate long-sleeved T-shirts from short-sleeved or cutoff T-shirts. Organize sweaters with sweaters—these, too, can be subdivided further into bulky wool sweaters distinct from lighter cotton sweaters, and cardigans separated from crewnecks separated from V-necks, etc. Keep underwear with underwear and, if space allows, bottoms (panties or boxers or briefs) with bottoms, and tops (undershirts or bras) with tops. Shorts with shorts, swimwear with swimwear . . . You should have the picture by now.

If space is limited, think about what can be logically combined. Underwear can be combined together, with tops and bottoms in the same drawer, although I wouldn't merge sweaters with shorts, since sweaters are cold-weather wear and shorts are for warmer weather. Shorts would do better with trousers/jeans, since they're both bottom clothes.

The most important result of organizing your drawers is that you should be able to see the entire contents of each drawer easily as soon as you open it, as you can for your closets. A drawer should not be a crammed and jumbled mess of clothing needing to be compressed just to get the drawer to close. Items that can be folded should be folded. Neatly. Items that want to be rolled up should be—again, neatly. You want to be able to find exactly what you're looking for in a drawer the same way you can find things inside your closet. It may help to label each drawer (temporarily) with a Post-it or some other signage until you can remember the contents of each drawer.

I tend to load drawers whenever possible from head to toe in descending order. Meaning things that go on the top of your body tend to go toward the top drawers of the dresser, with socks usually in the lowest bottom drawer. I find it easier for folks to remember the contents this way. You do want to take the dimensions of the drawer and the volume of the clothes into consideration as well, however. So if you have larger drawers on top and not so many bras, you might want to adjust your storage to match the drawer capacity, forgoing the head-to-toe strategy.

Overbuying and Buyer's Remorse

These two concepts are related to each other through our relationship with time. The first involves a deferred decision in the store—we've gathered surplus items, such as the same pant in several sizes or colors, or similar tops in different fabrics, figuring we'll sort through them or try them on at home and then just return the ones that we don't like or that don't fit . . . "later," which as we've already discussed is the stepchild of "someday." I cannot count how many times I've come across clothing in clients' homes with tags attached, the sad story told to me about misplaced receipts or too much time elapsing before they made it back to the store.

In all seriousness, this is an advanced shopping concept, not to be casually employed by anyone who has trouble keeping track of paper or time. It's like trying to juggle credit card balances—not for the weak-spirited or flaky. Before you know it you've been levied late fees and over-limit fees, and you'll never know what hit you. This, too, in the novice's hands, will at best result in store credits all over town, and at worst fill your closet and home with unnecessary and unwanted merchandise.

Buyer's remorse is a different experience. You were in love with the item in the store and had no doubt when you swooped though the checkout line that you two were destined for each other. Now that you're home, maybe you're thinking about a commitment you made to yourself or to a partner or spouse about your spending, or feeling self-conscious in some other way, and this is now intruding on your shopping buzz. You're having second, possibly even third, thoughts.

You need to have someplace *outside* of your closet where this item can land. Preferably a hook or rod where it can hang in plain sight. I suggest stuffing the receipt into a prominent pocket or pinning it through a buttonhole so it stays with the garment. This way, you can see it each day until you're sure it's staying or you've decided to return it to the store. If you put this kind of item away, chances are the conversation's over—it's staying put. Which pretty much guarantees some unhappy feelings when the piece surfaces again, never worn.

Shoes

If you remove your shoes at the entrance to your house, provide some sort of shelving or rack for their storage so the entryway remains neat and stray shoes do not become a hazard for the hapless person entering or exiting with packages and their view obscured.

If you wear your shoes in your house, the proper place to store them is on the floor and down low in your closet. Keep the pairs mated, and arrange them in a similar fashion to your hanging clothes—sandals together, athletic shoes together, dress shoes together, high heels together, boots together. Shoe racks are available everywhere these days. You could also build yourself a few low slanted shoe shelves or repurpose some cubby shelves and turn them into an impromptu shoe center.

It may go without saying, but I'm saying it anyway. We don't keep only one shoe of a pair. If after a thorough search you still cannot find a lone shoe's mate, it's time to say so long to the steadfast holdout. No matter how much you loved them as a pair, the solo shoe hits the road for the last time, alone.

Maintaining the Clothes Closet

Once you've done a complete reorganization, if you've been thorough and diligent, even if it takes you a while to complete, you won't ever have to do this again. Hanging clothes in the closet becomes a fun game of Concentration—simply match the incoming items Like with Like, and you'll maintain it without even exerting yourself.

If you're happy with your clothes now, another way to maintain the integrity of your closet and wardrobe is to keep the balance in place. When you buy something new, rather than augmenting, have it replace something old. Now that you've bought those new boiled-wool slippers, do you really need those scuzzy old plastic ones you still have from college?

And if you can't help shopping for new clothes, keep your existing ward-

Notable Note

Full Disclosure: I have a serious linen fetish. I don't collect them like Hummels or Bakelite jewelry, but I am drawn to linen sales as if called by a Siren—the higher the thread count and the deeper the discount, the more seductive to me. I struggle to balance my sense of appropriate consumption with my hedonistic celebration of luxury linens. When a high-end housewares outlet down the street from me was going out of business, I'll confess to buying two king-size sets of 100 percent linen sheets at a fraction of their original price, $39 marked down from more than $400! After multiple washings (they are linen, remember), they are so yummy it feels sinful sleeping on them. So there, now you know.

robe in mind. Buy things that will coordinate with as many of your current clothes as possible. That's the best way to avoid ending up with another "lone wolf" or "only in your dreams" piece.

Designate an area, hook, or chair where you can place any clothes in purgatory—the ones that aren't quite dirty but not quite clean, either. You'd wear them again to run to the market or to scrub the kitchen floor but maybe not for lunch with your mother-in-law. This way, you avoid doing more laundry than you need to, and you won't grab the slightly wrinkled khakis when you're late for casual Fridays.

Finally, rather than having them end up in piles on your floor, take your wire hangers back to the dry cleaner to recycle. If you care to, if uniformity of appearance is important to you, you could transfer your clothes from the wire hangers to your own hangers when you first bring the clothes home from the cleaners.

Other Kinds of Closets

LINEN CLOSETS

As we've discovered already, there are few places "someday" is more evident than in our closets. Closets seem to be the very temples to "someday." And curiously, sometimes more than even clothing, people cling to old sheets and pillowcases and towels as if someday they will be descended on by hordes of out-of-town guests, all in need of a hot shower and a comfy place to rest their heads.

The sweet antidote to this case of the somedays is that, of the many projects outlined in this book, organizing the linen closet is remarkably manageable and easily accomplished, even for the most disorganized among us.

And this is partly because it's one space with ideally only one kind of content—linens. Whether towels, sheets and pillowcases, duvets, pillows, or blankets, it's all just linens. And for the frugal among us, it's also a project that requires few, if any, new purchases. This project should take you, at most, only a few hours, with the results being significant and lasting. Like the clothes closet before this, we'll begin by emptying out the linen closet. Great.

Now clean and wipe down the shelves, the walls, the trim, and the baseboards. Vacuum or sweep the floor. If your shelves are adjustable, now is the time to do so. Likewise, consider installing extra shelves, if called for.

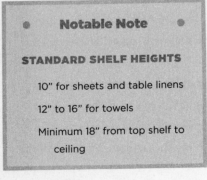

Now sort everything into like piles, and match linens with their siblings—so that the pillowcases and top and bottom sheets of a set are reunited. Do the same thing for suites of towels—if you have bath towels, hand towels, and washcloths that match, they should be gathered into groupings as well.

Then subdivide by room: master bedroom, kids' bedrooms, guest bedroom, master bathroom, kids' bathroom, guest bathroom. You might also want to color-code your linens to help keep everything organized. Assign different-colored linens to different rooms of the house—such as patterns for the kids' rooms, white for the master bedroom and bath, and sage or ecru for the guest room.

The strays should all be laid out as well—not to make them feel bad, but so we can really take stock of what there is and whether we'll be keeping them or not.

If you're saving the Speed Racer sheets from your son's first bed, now is the time to either let them go or at least send them to the container we now know as Sentimentaland. It's possible that you'll need more than one tub or box for Sentimentaland before we're done with your entire house. That's okay. These items all need to live together, and we need to ensure that their contents are consistent. Do not mix general items seeking a home into these meaningful touchstones of life's important moments. Like with Like.

Think of threadbare towels as retired soldiers. If budget dictates that they cannot be replaced at present, you can still assess all of the towels you own to find the ones that have passed their usefulness for absorbing anything less than a major spill on the carpet. Let those go, or repurpose them as rags for cleaning.

Ditto for blankets and quilts—exceptions being handmade heirlooms and hand-me-downs. If the heat were to fail, how many blankets would you really need? Or would you go to a friend's or neighbor's, or to a hotel? It's okay to let some of these go. Shelters and secondhand stores are always ready to accept donations of used linens.

I suggest that smaller and frequently used table linens—napkins, place mats, table runners—live in a sideboard or somewhere closer to the dining table. Infrequently used fancy tablecloths with coordinating napkins could be stored in the same closet where the leaves to the dining table are stored,

---

• Notable Note •

Many of us may have lovely vintage or antique linens—crocheted tablecloths, place mats, delicate linen napkins and tablecloths, etc. Like fine silver, they "tarnish" with age and disuse. This is the dark side of "someday"—that someday there will be an occasion worthy of such finery. But certainly not today. That is a shame.

Get them out and start using them. If inevitably they will end up yellowed and frayed, why not enjoy their journey there? What a missed opportunity to allow them to decay from neglect rather than from vigorous and enthusiastic use.

---

preferably in a coat closet nearby. Fold tablecloths lengthwise and hang them on a wooden suit hanger at either end of the rod inside the closet, and the napkins in a tub or basket above. You'll always know where they are.

Always clean and iron table linens after use, before putting them away. If relocating table linens is not possible, then these linens should also be sorted according to suite, creating small piles of matching tablecloths and napkins and storing them with the other linens. If you're more bohemian in your approach and like a mix-and-match kind of look for your table, at least put all the tablecloths together and all the napkins together. That way, when you're making the table, you have to look in only one place to find everything.

By now, you should also have a growing pile of everything that isn't linen or some kind of textile. Everything. If you store items such as surplus paper products or a sewing kit in the linen closet, that's fine—we'll find a place for those items in the closet when the process is finished.

Once you've sorted each thing into its family pile, it's time to address the strays. Either donate them or keep a few for rags. Only a few. I'd suggest that the rags live in the laundry room or someplace where the cleaning supplies are kept. It's important that the items now identified as rags are no longer mixed in with current and still useful linens.

A good rule of thumb for bed linens and towels is three sets per person, room, or bed. So that there is always a set of sheets on the bed and one in the laundry and one in the closet. If space or resources dictate that you have room for more or less, that's fine as well.

The same holds true for towels—for each person, there should be one on the towel bar and one in the wash and one on the shelf. Add in one set for each potential guest you could host at one time. For example, if you have a three-bedroom home (all occupied) and a pullout sofa in the family room that could possibly sleep two, that would equal ten sets of sheets (three times three plus one for the sleeper sofa) and eleven sets of towels (three times three plus two for the guests).

If space is an issue and a closet can't be dedicated solely to linens, consider a repurposed dresser or armoire to store table linens in the room where they'll be used, such as the dining room. Likewise, extra pillows and blankets could easily live in the guest-room closet. Another option when space is at a pre-mium is rolling up towels and sticking them in a decorative basket in the bathroom or under the sink.

Ideally, the only items that live in the linen closet are concerned with making the bed and bathroom—sheets, pillowcases, shams, towels, blankets, quilts, bedspreads, duvets, and duvet covers. If you are so inclined, sprays and potpourri might find their way here as well. Some people line their shelves with scented acid-free shelf paper. Others will scatter sachets throughout the stacked sheets. Alternatively, an open box of baking soda, activated charcoal, or calcium carbonate in the closet will help keep items smelling fresh.

What doesn't belong in the linen closet is anything that might generate dust—particularly vacuum cleaners. And no shoes or anything that spends time on the ground outside, such as sports equipment.

Once you've determined what's staying, fold everything neatly and as flat as you can, then reload the shelves. If you can, keep each set of sheets or towels in their own stack. This way, you'll avoid having to drag everything out or toppling everything over each time you remove a set.

Store the items you use most frequently, such as towels and bed linens, on shelves at or near eye level. Table linens can be assigned to a less accessible shelf—since they are used less frequently. And rotate usage—this keeps linens from sitting for too long and getting musty.

If you have antique linens, store them out of the flow of traffic. These should be in acid-free paper, if possible, to avoid discoloration and decay. Bulky items, such as comforters, quilts, and pillows that are for guests or that are rotated seasonally, can be stored in vacuum-sealed storage bags called Space Bags. They compress all the air out of the items, taking up less space and keeping them moisture- and bug-free.

> ● **Notable Note** ●
>
> **HOW TO FOLD TOWELS**
>
> Fold towels in half lengthwise, then fold in half (matching the ends to each other), then fold in thirds; this way, they'll stack perfectly and fit most shelves.

In my closet, I have each shelf labeled with the different sizes of linens: queen, king, twin. This is especially useful for guests looking for linens, who otherwise wouldn't easily be able to distinguish sizes without unfolding them. I use simple metal label holders to identify each shelf. You could just as easily use a label maker, adhesive tabs, or decorative tacks—anything that suits your taste and is easily legible.

Some folks like to store each set of linens in one of the pillowcases. I prefer seeing the individual pieces neatly stacked, but it's certainly another option. Seasonal sheets, like winter flannels, should live with other seasonal linens or stacked behind the everyday sheets.

Towels live on their own shelf, each in a neat stack. Beach towels should be kept on a separate shelf with other seasonal items, or behind your bath towels.

I store extra blankets and guest pillows on the top shelf of my linen closet. They're not often used, but they still belong with their brothers and sisters. I find that they stack nicely up top and are in a logical place when someone goes searching for an extra pillow or comforter. I keep them in the clear pliable zippered plastic "bag" that they came in, from either the store or the cleaners. If you don't have any of these, bags (or clear plastic tubs) are easily purchased at any number of stores.

As I mentioned above, this project doesn't necessarily call for any new purchases—so resist the urge to run off to a container store for new gadgets or toys to "help" you get organized. Once you know what you'll be storing, you can put together an accurate shopping list and pick up what you need.

When all the linens are reloaded in the closet, assess the remaining space, if any. Then begin reloading the other items removed, the sewing kit, surplus paper products, cosmetics, a first-aid kit (prominently stored and easily reached), etc.

Once those are in place, if there is still room available, consider storing luggage or totes and other bags or baskets here, either on the floor or on the top shelf, below the pillows and comforters. If there's no room here for these items, the entry or coat closet is an excellent alternative.

If you don't have a safe in your home, you may consider installing a kick-shelf underneath the bottom shelf. This is really more like a very thin recessed drawer, trimmed to match the base molding so as to remain undetectable. To gain access, you simply push the edge of it with your foot and the shelf releases and rolls out on wheels or glides. It's an excellent place to hide important items or documents, provided you aren't worried about them burning. Those kinds of items, if not in a fireproof safe, belong in a fireproof file box or off-site in a safe-deposit box at the bank.

Many folks consider the backs of doors to be valuable closet real estate. I typically disagree. While towel bars could be used to store table linens or other oversized items, or a mirror or display board could be mounted to the inside as a pleasant accent when the door is open, things that slap and bounce around every time the door is opened (ironing boards, brooms and mops, even clear shoe holders filled with items) are distractions that make opening the door noisy and a potential hazard. Wouldn't it be nicer, if possible, to just let a door be a door?

Cardboard boxes, paper bags, and some plastics can damage certain fabrics. Avoid them as storage containers. So can cedar chests, which are often only semisuccessful at killing moths or deterring carpet beetles. Paradichlorobenzene moth crystals may prove more reliable at controlling pests.

GUEST-ROOM CLOSETS

If your guest room is also your home office, or your living or family room, the closet in that room is most likely doing double duty. Anything from board games to office supplies could be sharing quarters with linens and extra bedding for your next guest. Keep it simple and containerize everything a guest would need in one clear plastic container. That way, any time company comes, they can find exactly what they need and you won't have to scramble around trying to assemble everything for them at the last moment.

Underutilized closet space in guest rooms is another place where overflow and infrequently used items can find adequate and reliable homes. Bulky appliances, such as bread machines, chafing dishes, and heated serving trays could all live neatly stacked on out-of-the-way shelves, ready for the few times each year they are needed.

UTILITY CLOSETS

A utility closet is where everything you use to run and maintain your home lives. Things stored here include cleaning products, lightbulbs, tools, surplus cables, paint and painting supplies, caulk, adhesives, brooms and mops, dustpans, rags, trash bags, and hardware. Flashlights, batteries, and emergency kits live here. If there's room in this closet, recycling and trash could also live here.

Take advantage of every square inch of this closet. Hang brooms, mops, and dustpans up and off the floor—business side up. Using Like with Like as a guideline, group cleaning supplies together or paint supplies together, so that when repairing or replacing something, everything you need to complete the job is within reach.

What you don't want living here are random items that serve no purpose. It's fine to have one container of mismatched fasteners, but don't turn this room into a way station for things that should have been tossed or recycled when you were finished with them. When you've completed assembling knockdown furniture and you're certain that everything is attached and functioning, and you find you have leftover hardware, toss it. Those unidentified extra pieces aren't going to come in handy someday—they're just leftovers. Paint dries out and hardens—keep small jars of each color for touchups, create a paint schedule (a master list of rooms, colors, and finishes), and toss the old paint. Color varies from batch to batch, so by the time you're ready to paint again, even if you're using the same color, you'll need enough fresh paint to completely cover the walls, anyway.

Cleaning supplies lose their strength—if you've gone organic, properly dispose of old toxic cleaners; don't just shove them to the back of the closet for "later." Make sure that what is in here is current to your house and current for your life. This closet in particular demands a simple and accessible layout—you should be able to find whatever you're looking for within thirty seconds of opening the door.

COAT/ENTRY CLOSETS AND MUDROOMS

These closets and areas are located near entryways to store outerwear and foul-weather gear. Ideally, all coats and jackets will find their way here to live. In addition, they're great places to store current seasonal sporting equipment, along with an ample supply of rain gear for the unfortunate guest caught out of the house when the weather changes. Baskets on the top shelf corral winter scarves, hats, and gloves, and another basket contains work and gardening gloves. A shoe rack and a floor mat catch snow and rain from snow boots and galoshes. Hooks hold pet leads and umbrellas.

In the case of mudrooms, ample cubbies and hooks for each member of the household provide plenty of places for book bags and knapsacks, lunch pails, and athletic gear. Any entryway benefits from a chair or bench where you can put on or take off shoes or boots or inline skates.

High shelves in closets and out-of-the-way cabinets also offer great resting places for seldom-used overflow storage from other rooms. Coffee urns, punch bowls, seasonal serving dishes—all of these can be stored based on the frequency they are used. I keep the leaves of the dining-room table in my entry closet, along with pressed table linens. When it's time to expand the table and set it for large gatherings, everything I need is in one location.

Our tech-heavy lifestyles point toward integrating an electronic charging station into these spaces as well. Everyone can have an outlet or station to plug in their phones, earpieces, and portable music players to charge overnight, and these items are then living near the entrance of the house to ensure that they are easily collected on the way out the door.

The limit of your imagination is the only limit on how these spaces can be structured so everyone comes and goes each day with all their stuff!

Dirty Laundry

Something I miss in my current home is a laundry chute. As a child growing up, I loved the convenience of dropping dirty laundry through a flap in the wall and coming home from school to find clean clothes folded and waiting for me on my bed. Today I understand that part of the magic of that memory involved my mother doing laundry while I was at school, but I also realize that the task of gathering dirty laundry from various rooms is a chore that a laundry chute simplifies.

If you, too, find the absence of a laundry chute in your home vexing, we must give careful consideration where best to place a hamper or two. When thinking of where to place baskets for laundry, dry cleaning, and alterations/mending, and whether there is sufficient space for all three or if one must do triple duty, take a logical approach.

Where are you most frequently without clothes? Either in the bathroom, a dressing room/walk-in closet, or your bedroom—these are the most likely places. Conveniently located and also out of sight seems to be the perfect marriage. So my first choice would be in a closet of some kind. My second choice would be in the bathroom, with a third choice being someplace visible in the bedroom. Certainly between all of them, you'll find the right choice for you. The key is to place the hamper somewhere convenient enough that you will actually use it. Too often they end up as another surface covered with lamps or clean clothes, or anything that prevents the lid from being opened. Please avoid this in your own home.

Maintaining the System

Like the mail and keys, the way to keep your closets from reverting back to a jumbled mess is not to exert some Herculean effort in desperate frantic spurts but rather to maintain the system on a daily basis. What you've accomplished in completing this chapter should never have to be done in this same way again, if you pay attention to the space daily.

You wouldn't think to not brush your teeth for several weeks and then suddenly scrub them silly in the hopes of erasing weeks of neglect. Likewise for these areas of your home. If you have a crazy day when you find yourself trying on thirteen outfits before running out the door, when you return home, hang up the twelve outfits you didn't end up wearing. Don't walk over them for another four days before restoring order. And drop the lucky thirteenth into the hamper when you take it off.

When adding something new to your wardrobe, consider if it's a replacement or an augmentation. As discussed, if and when you reach a level of equilibrium in your wardrobe, it would seem that more often than not, you're replacing and *not* augmenting. You should have enough clothes to wear to the variety of places and functions you're routinely called on to attend, from work to social events. There will, of course, always be an opportunity to pick up a new _____, when you need to attend an event and either it points to a gap in your clothing options or you just can't bring yourself to wear "that" dress one more time. And that is the appropriate time to augment.

If, instead, you're replacing a pair of jeans, it's okay to actually replace them; that was the plan when you bought the new pair. If resistance to letting the old ones go is based on some sense of "abundance," of feeling "rich" or somehow protected from once again finding yourself with "nothing to wear," think that feeling all the way through. Any comfort this lopsided sense of abundance may bring from now having one more pair of jeans needs to be seen for what it is—false. More of anything that doesn't serve you isn't more of anything you need.

Surrounding yourself with that kind of "more" will not adequately protect you from an imaginary crisis, whether that crisis is "nothing to wear," or suddenly finding yourself homeless and hungry. While that may seem like quite a leap from the comfort of where you're reading this now, I've witnessed irrational fear create outcomes at least that exaggerated within an instant. And once that happens, clinging to a pair of obsolete jeans starts to seem a reasonable way to prevent this imaginary disaster from striking fast and hard.

So let's inject some sanity back into the equation. Clothes are not groceries. You won't survive a blackout, hurricane, or blizzard by eating that extra pair of jeans. Seeking comfort from things and in places where comfort can't be secured sets you up for a frustrating merry-go-round of feelings that is like a junkie's worst nightmare. Desperate clinging is rapidly followed by forced deprivation, and round and round you spin between these two polar extremes—*I need more, I don't have enough, more is better, more feels safe, don't take that from me, I need more, I don't have enough*—again and again and again.

And all over a pair of jeans. Imagine what's possible with a few cashmere sweaters!

Buy another can of tuna or vegetarian chili, and give the jeans to the thrift store. You'll prevent going hungry, and you'll finally break the cycle of addiction to "more." That's the surest way to keep your closets (and yourself) in tip-top shape—satisfied and surrounded with everything you need and absolutely nothing you don't.

6 Auxiliary Spaces: Basements • Attics • Garages

> No person who can read is ever successful at cleaning out an attic.
>
> **ANN LANDERS**

> Only in America do we leave cars worth thousands of dollars in the driveway and put our useless junk in the garage.
>
> **AUTHOR UNKNOWN**

Did you ever think it possible that you would open the door to a closet in your home and see not a tangle of random items but some clear order? And that you would easily be able to put your hands on exactly what you were looking for quickly, without disturbing everything around it? Congratulations.

We're about to explore the many ways you can maximize these bonus spaces while avoiding new messes and jumbles in the process, keeping in mind that just because you *could* store something somewhere (such as the garage or attic or basement) doesn't mean you *should*. Resist the urge to get drunk on space and think that random chaos and disorder are more manageable because these spaces are less seldom seen. Clutter is clutter, whether it's constantly underfoot or encountered just twice a day, on your way to and from the car (or laundry or storeroom).

Almost like closets on steroids, these auxiliary spaces offer tremendous potential—both for storage and for clutter. And given their dimensions, they often require jumbo-sized efforts in getting and keeping them organized. That means wielding One Home for Everything and Like with Like with precision and consistency, especially when confronting historic neglect and chaos. We'll use the one-two punch of these two rules to clear out and reassemble these spaces, ensuring that whether we're looking for a half-inch washer or a wheelbarrow, we'll still have to look in only one place to put our hands on it quickly and easily. And whether what we're dealing with is a crawl space or a four-car garage, the result will be exactly the same—a neat and tidy space where anything can be found within thirty seconds. That may sound crazy now, but when we're finished, you'll see it's not an exaggeration.

What We're Going to Cover in This Chapter

- ☐ Auxiliary Spaces: What They Are and What They Aren't
- ☐ General Suggestions
- ☐ Space Limitations and Structural Elements
- ☐ The Particular Challenges Presented by the Garage
- ☐ Feelings and Stuff and Space, Oh My!
- ☐ Teamwork
- ☐ Scheduling the Time
- ☐ Creating Efficient Storage in Any Space
- ☐ Storage Systems and Shelving: An Overview
- ☐ Sorting and You
- ☐ Cleanliness Is Next to Garageliness (or Atticliness or Basementliness)
- ☐ The Kinds of Things You Store in Your Auxiliary Space(s)
- ☐ Containerizing the Categories
- ☐ The Importance of Labels—How, Why, and Where
- ☐ Organizing the Storage
- ☐ When Laundry Is Done in Auxiliary Spaces

- ☐ Managing Messy Projects Inside and Out
- ☐ Finishing Second-Tier Spaces for Living vs. Storage (and How That Impacts Where You Store Your Things)
- ☐ Trash or Treasure? Delusions of *National Geographic,* eBay, and Early Retirement
- ☐ The Thrift-Store Box Is Not a Grab Bag
- ☐ Maintaining the System

Auxiliary Spaces: What They Are and What They Aren't

Basement (noun):
The lowermost portion of a structure, partly or wholly below ground level; often used for storage.

Attic (noun):
A floor consisting of open space at the top of a house just below the roof; often used for storage.

Garage (noun):
An outbuilding (or part of a building) for housing automobiles; a building or indoor space in which to park or keep a motor vehicle.

Two of these three spaces are basically dedicated to general storage, with the third designated specifically for automobiles. Not that other things can't also be stored there, but first and foremost, we want to be able to get a car (or two) in there.

From a storage point of view, if you're lucky enough to have any one of these spaces in your home, you're pretty fortunate. If you're lucky enough to have more than one of them, you're probably either swimming in so much stuff that you can barely breathe, or you're fantasizing about an early retirement from all the money you'll make when you finally sell who knows what treasures you've been storing. Or maybe some combination of both scenarios.

To be clear, none of these spaces are museums to previous marriages, divorces, relationships, or hobbies. They are not altars to past design choices, future second homes, receding youth (yours or your offspring's), or historical educational activities. They are not final resting places for lost and misfit things cluttering your life. They are valuable real estate and the core of practical, functional, and efficient storage within your home and, by extension, your life. These spaces are where you store tools, building supplies, seasonal items, oversize items, and anything else that needs a home and can't seem to find one in any other room in your house.

Do you have a sad, scary corner somewhere? Like a bad date that never ends, you continue to pile just one more thing into that corner, vowing that "someday" you'll tackle the ever-expanding mound of stuff. Well, apparently, today is that day. Check, please.

General Suggestions

In any of these spaces, these tips and suggestions are useful.

- A working flashlight at or near the entrance to each space is a must. In case of power outages and burned-out bulbs, you need light to find your way in and out.

- Adequate and proper lighting: you can't have too much artificial lighting in spaces that have limited access to natural light.

- Water infiltration in basements is a huge problem for many home-owners. An easy and significant tool in the combat of wet basements is ensuring that roof gutters and downspouts direct water away from your foundation. Likewise, make sure that the grade of any soil around your house is sloped to channel rainwater away from the foundation.

- Review your homeowner's insurance policy to see what the limits of coverage are for sewer or drain backups or flooding. With limited coverage, think carefully before storing valuables (either monetary or sentimental) in your basement.

- Dryers should either be vented to the outside or ventless if your laundry center is located indoors.

- If you have an unfinished space, never store anything in direct contact with bare soil. This is an open invitation to termites and other pests, as well as mold, mildew, and decay.

- Do not store anything within three feet of the furnace, boiler, water heater, or other major appliances. Objects too close present service obstacles and potential hazards.

- Do not store any flammable and/or heat-sensitive items near gas-powered appliances or anything that has a lit pilot light.

- Make sure you've installed a smoke detector and carbon-monoxide alarm. Likewise, a fire extinguisher should be easily accessed in case of fire.

- Do not run a frost-free freezer in your basement if you have moisture problems.
- Do store wine in your basement (think wine cellars)—just not in the same room with hot appliances, such as the dryer, the boiler, or hot water heater.

Space Limitations and Structural Elements

Some of these spaces come with built-in limitations. Working with, rather than against, those limitations will maximize your storage capabilities. Few things besides hand tools don't mind fluctuations in temperature and humidity. For everything else, it's recommended to keep the temperature between 60 and 75 degrees Fahrenheit and the humidity between 35 and 40 percent. That may not always be possible, but it's useful as a benchmark when deciding what to store where.

Attic ceilings are sometimes low, limiting mobility. Part of the basement may be the laundry center or a workshop that limits additional available floor space. Maybe the basement is just a small room with an attached crawl space where the mechanicals of the house (furnace, boiler, water heater) are located. And perhaps structural columns or walls create very real obstructions or barriers to accessible space. Unless you're prepared to do major reconstruction to eliminate or compensate for some of these limitations, your best alternative is creative thinking.

If you have structural challenges that aren't going away—load-bearing partitions or low ceilings—spend enough time in the space studying those challenges to discover the best long-term solutions. "Right now" solutions may be fine in the short term, but in thinking them through, we want to make sure they have staying power. If spatial relations are not your thing or you find yourself particularly stuck, consult a contractor, structural engineer, or architect for a few hours—they may help you see a solution you've been missing.

DAMPNESS IN BASEMENTS

Below or above grade, dampness is always an issue when it comes to storage. Even if your space is sealed and finished and climate-controlled like the rest of the house, I still recommend waterproof storage anywhere dampness has been present or could still appear. I've seen many cardboard and other paper-based containers ruin more treasures from being stored in fluctuating humidity than from floods or direct contact with water. So just in case you had another cardboard box filled with your high-school yearbooks heading to the basement, I wanted to catch you first.

Run a dehumidifier in these spaces, and empty its tank regularly. The exception being a space where there is the absence of either a vapor barrier below the slab or sealed concrete, in which case you may actually draw moisture in from the outside with a dehumidifier.

Mildew loves dark, damp places. Be careful with books, papers, photographs, artwork, or important documents where there is no direct sunlight. Packets of silica gel desiccant in the containers will absorb some moisture, but is not a panacea. And in all cases, everything should be stored off the floor, on either pallets or shelves of some kind.

FLOOD ZONES (SEWERS AND DRAIN BACKUP)

Whether or not your basement is finished, the possibility of flooding still exists. Even if you've never experienced a flood, one could still happen, particularly if you have a source of water in the basement.

- Store all valuable items on shelves or tables above flood level (the calculated elevation of any expected flood, based on site-specific conditions).
- Install a sump pump to fight floods. Make sure it has an alarm attached to it.
- Consider installing an additional battery-operated sump pump for

backup during power failures or, alternatively, a generator that would power your sump pump (and other appliances) in case of power outages.

- Maintain critical equipment on a regular basis. Set up a maintenance schedule and post it visibly nearby.
- Keep the basement-floor drain clean and clear of debris.
- Do not risk turning your basement into a toxic soup by storing chemicals (gardening, cleaning, etc.) where rising floodwaters could reach them.

HEAT AND HUMIDITY IN ATTICS AND GARAGES

Unless your garage or attic has been converted into living space and sealed for air filtration or well insulated, or you live in a desert or extremely arid place, the temperature and humidity fluctuations that occur in these spaces prohibit storing valuable papers and other sensitive materials in them as well. The only paper I've found that can consistently and safely live here is surplus toilet paper or paper towels, still vacuum-sealed from the store. Likewise, luggage. You don't want to grab a suitcase at the last minute to find it teeming with mildew just as you're about to go on a trip. It's best to consider these as outdoor spaces, albeit with roofs and walls. So while nothing may actually be rained or snowed on, the effects of precipitation may still be felt by everything stored here.

Cold in the winter and swelteringly hot in the summer, these spaces should house only items that can withstand dramatic temperature swings. The effects of moisture coupled with heat are never good for much beyond your complexion. Many things, particularly anything cellulose-based—meaning made of wood or paper—could become a willing host for both mold and mildew under these conditions.

And at the risk of sounding like a broken record, precious items should never be stored in any place where the climate is not strictly regulated. Countless photo albums, baby books, and notebooks have been tucked away in unregulated spaces only to be consumed with black spotty mold and rendered completely unsalvageable. Save yourself a heap of grief and find another home for these irreplaceable items.

GO NORTH, YOUNG WOMAN OR MAN— CEILING HEIGHT AND STORAGE

Ceilings are a tremendous resource for storage space. Whether the space is finished or unfinished, a few well-placed hangers, hooks, or brackets will hold bicycles, ladders, lawn chairs, camping gear, and any other items used infrequently or seasonally. There are even nifty pulley systems designed specifically to aid in the raising and lowering of bikes up into the rafters. When hanging things overhead, always secure the fasteners (hooks, chains, etc.) from structural elements, such as ceiling joists.

If room allows, consider a loft platform to provide a bounty of space for everything from screens and storm windows to storm doors and spare lumber. The only limits on what you can store are the dimensions of the platform and its structural integrity. That said, rather than viewing any additional storage space as an invitation to shop to capacity, build it to suit the current volume of things you already own and use.

When going north, keep in mind the varying heights of people in your home. If everyone is 5'6" or shorter, things dangling overhead may not present a collision challenge. If you or someone else is taller, be sure to hang things out of the regular paths of traffic and, if necessary, hang a brightly colored cloth off either end to alert folks, like flags on oversized loads on the expressway.

Finally, never hang anything heavier than an empty clothes hanger from an exposed overhead plumbing pipe—too much weight will stress its joints and eventually cause damage. Hang your own dedicated storage rails alongside instead.

The Particular Challenges Presented by the Garage

Can you fit a car into your garage? If you have a multiple-car garage and multiple cars, is the number of spaces (or bays) in the garage actually available for the same number of vehicles? This is our starting point.

Imagine the garage as a giant cupboard. This cupboard should house your cars; any tools used to maintain said cars, as well as to maintain the physical structure of your home and your grounds; seasonal "quality of life" items, such as grills, inflatable swimming pools, and lawn chairs; and, if there's any room left over after all these things are assigned their proper homes, anything else you can easily fit inside without crowding out any of the above.

Too often the scale of a garage deceives you into thinking that order is less important because there's so much room, or that random or approximate piles of things are "good enough," since you're in here so infrequently. You still want to be able to find whatever it is you're looking for quickly and efficiently—even more so in such a large space.

If you cannot fit one or more cars into your garage, we need to know why. Do you have a pool table or ping-pong table set up here, or a home gym, or is someone practicing hockey in the empty bays? Maybe you're running a home business out of the garage and you've set up your office or workspace here? Or is it a less noble and more random reason, just an immovable pile of stuff that has accumulated over time, with no discernable beginning or end?

If cars do fit and there's just a bunch of clutter lining the perimeter of the garage, you're ahead of the game. Your garage is fulfilling its basic function. If the garage is currently so overrun with things that it's impossible to put a car inside, we're going to dismantle those snarls of stuff and disperse the myriad parts into Like with Like zones within the garage (or somewhere else inside your home). If they no longer serve you, we'll send them off to friends' and neighbors' and strangers' homes via gifts, garage sales, donations, and, when appropriate, placement at the curb (with signage clearly marked "Free!").

That goes for attics and basements as well. Too often, these spaces become repositories for the misplaced and forgotten, until useless clutter overtakes whatever remaining free space there had been.

If these piles of things have seemed overwhelming and impossible to untangle, time and willingness (and maybe a few trash bags) are all that now stand between you and order. Together we can clean up any and all of this stuff. But preventing this from happening again requires a shift in how you think about space, possessions, and their accumulation. More on that in a bit. Right now, grab your camera and this book, and head to the auxiliary space that has you most troubled. I'll meet you there.

Feelings and Stuff and Space, Oh My!

THE AUXILIARY SPACE AS REPOSITORY FOR YOUR SELF-ESTEEM

Excellent. Now snap a few pictures. Be sure to get some good wide-angle shots of the entire space. These will be your "before" shots. When you're finished taking pictures, just look around you, without starting to criticize or judge yourself. See what you're surrounded by. It might be kind of marvelous and horrifying at the same time, the sheer volume of it.

For everything that's lying around in a jumble pretty much useless, since you can't easily access it to use it, ask yourself if its practical absence from your life has negatively impacted you. Is there anything in these heaps that you haven't already replaced when you needed it—because you either couldn't remember that you already owned it or simply couldn't find it? Are there duplicates and triplicates of things that are piled up here, for similar reasons? How about things someone has outgrown or discarded here?

Take it all in. Pay attention to any conversations that may be starting up in your head. Perhaps you're hearing a voice describe yourself as "lazy" or "stupid" or "wasteful"? If you're getting overwhelmed and wanting to head back to the safety of a nice clean room, take a deep breath instead. You're fine. It's just stuff. And it really doesn't matter who's speaking, as long as you recognize that it isn't *you*. You would never speak that way to a friend in need, you'd roll up your sleeves, put your arm around their shoulders, pop a big grin, and say, "Is this what's making you crazy? It's no big deal. Let's dig in!"

So sidestepping any name-calling, fear, or shame at where we find ourselves right now, let's focus instead on how all this stuff got here in the first place.

DEPARTED RELATIVES AND FRIENDS, FROM HOUSTON TO HEAVEN, PART I: THE QUICK AND THE LIVING

It's quite possible that what you have in your auxiliary spaces belongs or belonged to someone else, not currently in residence with you. If that is the case, these are your choices in dealing with these things.

1. Continue to store the item, but organize it in the snuggest way possible to least inconvenience yourself.
2. Contact the owner and request that he or she collect the item by such and such date or you will move it to some off-site storage, where he or she can collect it within a larger deadline.
3. Contact the owner and inform him or her that you are disposing of the item by such and such date if you do not hear otherwise.
4. Don't contact the owner at all, and simply dispose of the item.

I'm not crazy about number four, but it is an option. Certainly if the items belong to someone you're not on good terms with, it can be uncomfortable to suddenly get in touch with them, particularly to discuss possessions. Even so, it's a courtesy that you may wish, were the shoe on the other foot, to have extended to you. Consider that before gleefully calling your local charity to come and collect everything or announcing a free-for-all at your curb. You've waited this long to get rid of it—if doing the respectful and courteous thing *would* be contacting them and giving them a clear timeline for the removal, another few weeks for a lifetime's worth of clear conscience seems a small price to pay.

Clients of mine, Patti and Nina, have lamented their own lack of space when faced with a version of one of the above scenarios, particularly when Patti began to telecommute for work. Patti was suddenly spending most of her work week at home, where she discovered a surprising lack of space, partly due to a piano and some furniture that were no longer in use, that Patti's father had loaned them some time ago. The piano occupied prime real estate in a small room off the dining room—an ideal location for a new home office. The furniture was not necessarily underfoot but still in the way.

At first Patti couldn't conceive of even raising the subject with her dad.

Patti: I just know he'll think me selfish and ungrateful.

VirgoMan: Why is that?

Patti: Because that's how I feel. I mean, I borrowed these things years ago; we had no furniture in the living room, and the piano was a great addition to our home.

VM: Okay. But do you really believe those things about yourself? Are you selfish and ungrateful?

Patti: No, of course not. And more important, we really need the space. We've had this stuff here forever. No one plays the piano, and we bought replacements for his furniture as we could afford to. Besides, I've got to get off the floor and out of the family room. I'm on the phone and computer all day, and if Nina comes in with the dogs, it becomes way too crazy and disruptive.

VM: Okay. Is money an issue for him?

Patti: No. He can afford to pay to move and store it. I just feel bad asking.

VM: Can you let go of those feelings about asking?

Patti: I can try.

VM: Great. Here's what I suggest. When you make the call, thank him for the use of everything. But rather than asking if it's okay with him for these things to be returned, ask him when and how you should arrange for this stuff to leave. Offer to contact a mover for him (ideally, with him reimbursing you) if that would be easier for him. Give him specific deadlines for things to leave. Again, be friendly and gracious about it. Just because you're finally asserting yourself doesn't mean you have to become defensive or confrontational. It's not his fault that you've had this stuff here as long as you have; you are as responsible as he is for the duration. There's also nothing to feel guilty about; it's simply a fact that you now need these things to be removed.

The phone call went off without a hitch. Her father easily arranged for a family friend to come by and collect the furniture, and by week's end a desk, an Internet connection, and a printer had replaced the piano and wicker furniture.

You, too, can encourage the still-living and fully functioning to once again become the stewards of their own possessions, whether that's your best friend or a grown child happily settled into his or her own home. If storing these things is no longer convenient or prevents you from properly storing your own things or fully utilizing your home, then I encourage you to make a phone call and kindly and firmly suggest that they make arrangements to reclaim their belongings.

DEPARTED RELATIVES AND FRIENDS, FROM HOUSTON TO HEAVEN, PART II: THE LATE, THE GREAT, AND THE BROKEN PLATE

If the items you're storing belonged to a deceased relative or friend, they typically fall into one of two categories—either they are deeply sentimental and things you treasure or they are things that ended up with you by default.

In either case, you have the following choices.

1. You can go through everything and find whatever you'd like to keep for yourself and then offer the balance to other family members who may have been close to the deceased. If there are no other family mem-

bers, after you've selected things, you could give the rest away to charity or attempt to sell anything with significant value.

2. You can offer it directly to another family member or friend, or to someone who is setting up house and needs things, without reviewing it.

3. You can donate everything directly to charity without reviewing it.

Certainly for anything you feel no attachment to, its absence should cause you no pain or inconvenience. If, on the other hand, these things *are* charged with emotional tugs and memories, it's important to allow enough time to adequately go through them, whether it's one box or an entire houseful's worth of items. It also may be useful to have either an impartial and disciplined friend or a professional on hand to guide or accompany you through the process.

For a client and friend of mine, my purchase of a house in Harlem came at the perfect time. While we were still renovating the mostly empty house, Valerie brought storage from four different facilities there to go through it all at one time in one place. An unfortunate series of losses came rapidly on top of one another for Valerie—first her grandparents died, then her remaining parent, and then she sold the home outside of Providence where she had lived and raised her children. Unable to deal with the sequential losses and overwhelmed with moving, storage seemed her best solution at the time. Even so, the cost to her was more than $1,200 a month, and she didn't even know all of what she was storing!

We made arrangements with each moving company to deliver the contents of her storage units to the house, and then with my help, she was able to examine everything and make critical decisions about what to keep and what to let go of. Timing also allowed her three children to come to New York and go through the house with her so they could each select anything they wanted. Valerie and I then arranged for the items to be shipped to their homes. Anything left over after she and her kids went through the stuff was given to friends and donated to local charities.

I realize not every situation works out this conveniently and smoothly. Still, the idea is there—get help if you need it, don't keep things in storage indefinitely, and do not allow the burden of other people's belongings to prevent you from ultimately moving forward.

In all cases, nothing is to be kept that doesn't mean something to you. It may be uncomfortable to hear, but you are not responsible for archiving the family's history. Unless you choose to. There's nothing requiring you to live with the accumulated possessions of deceased relatives—it does not make you ungrateful or selfish to let those things go. You inherited these things because someone thought you might have use of them or because you were the only surviving person left. Either way, nothing freely given is ever meant to be a burden. That is a certainty.

If you're feeling resistant right now, if a different conversation is starting in your head that I just don't understand your unique position or the responsibilities you shoulder, or any conversation that holds you apart and isolates you in its insistence that you must do something you do not want to do, or keep something that you don't want to keep, then know that I *do* understand. The fear, guilt, and other feelings that rise up are powerful when these kinds of self-notions are challenged. Remember, this process is about nothing less than liberation. Of course you will feel the shackles tighten most just before they are unlocked and falling away.

If you have any taste of your own independence or happiness, call that forward now. Draw strength from any experience you've had when you've asserted yourself successfully, when you clearly defined the end of someone else and the beginning of you. That's where this work takes place. Feelings can be overwhelming and frightening and confusing, but feelings cannot kill you. Breathe deeply and deliberately.

And my favorite part of all this is that as soon as you actually take the action, as soon as you move a muscle, your feelings will change. Try it right now and you will experience that for yourself.

MADISON AVENUE AND YOUR WALLET

If these things arrived in your home as part of a commercial transaction, there's a different responsibility you must shoulder in acknowledging how they got here, how they'll leave, and how you'll prevent a similar occurrence from happening again.

First let's look at what happens every moment of every day you interact with media, inside or outside the home. Throughout the day, we are summoned to purchase something, anything—mouthwash, snack foods, a new car, clothing, soda pop—the list is endless. We are hooked with promises of a better life, although that promise often remains surprisingly vague. Better how? Smarter, more stylish, more loved, better-smelling, always happy? But, of course, only after our purchase. Until then, I suppose we're just dull, stupid, stinky, lonely, unhappy people. Thank you, Madison Avenue, for rescuing us from our wretched state. None of the preceding is an excuse for irresponsible behavior, but it is an explanation for the pervasive grip so many of us feel caught in, consciously or otherwise.

With a constant feed of encouraged, almost mandated, consumption leveled at us, how are we to break free from our role in this often self-destructive pattern? Because after our purchase, we may be no smarter, stylish, loved, or happy than before, but we're certainly now the ones who are surrounded by the clutter of our attempts.

I'd like to say, "Just stop shopping," but that's unlikely and probably unreasonable. Most of us need to shop for some stuff—unless we're truly self-sufficient and living off the grid. So what I will say is, "Stop shopping indiscriminately." That seems defendable. Pay attention and move a little slower. Separate your happiness from consumption. Do not confuse the temporary rush of a new purchase with deep, soulful contentment—they are not the same, regardless of how many times you see that contradicted on TV and in print.

In a moment of desperation, you may buy something thinking, "I'm better safe than sorry." But looking around now, you may actually be a little more sorry than safe.

A PRACTICAL EXERCISE

Pick three items you can easily see from where you are that you purchased but don't use, have never used, or have used only once. Think about how they got here. Try to remember if you went to the store specifically for the item or if you just picked it up while you were shopping for something else. Write them down here.

1. **Item:** _____
   Were you shopping for this when you bought it? Y / N

2. **Item:** _____
   Were you shopping for this when you bought it? Y / N

3. **Item:** _____
   Were you shopping for this when you bought it? Y / N

Great. Now I'm going to suggest that these things find their way into a "leaving" area as soon as you can fish them out of wherever they're currently living. And at this point you may return to the safety of a comfortable chair, unless you're comfortable hanging out right here.

NASTY TALK—AND NOT THE GOOD KIND

Since both Hamlet and the Buddha seem to agree that "there is nothing either good or bad but thinking makes it so," let's turn our attention to those conversations we sometimes have with ourselves.

For myself, when I feel I'm wrong or I've made some error in judgment, it's very challenging to have some compassion for my mistake. I can easily jump right on that bandwagon, calling myself names and putting myself down for being all too human. It's difficult to see an opportunity for change and growth in those mistakes instead of feeling as though my whole world is falling in on itself. That rather than having made a mistake I actually *am* the mistake, and that how I feel in those moments is the way I'm going to feel forever.

This can happen regardless of scale—whether I've disappointed a friend or just left the mail at home on my way to the post office. Again.

It's touching and a bit amusing when we see someone else whaling on themselves for being human. From the outside, it's easy to see that what *feels* like a big deal really isn't, in the scheme of things. It's having that perspective when we're having those feelings ourselves that is sometimes challenging. So it's useful to remember that sense of the silly and tender when we feel ourselves narrowing down into tunnel vision, when our hearts start racing and panic or shame or something equally intense starts to present itself.

If a simple mistake can be either good or bad depending on our point of view, the sooner we can shift that point of view is the sooner we can get back on track and forgive ourselves. And I've found, when I remember it, that a belly laugh or singing out loud or a phone call to a good friend has a great ability to facilitate that shift quickly and easily.

NEW TOOLS, NEW CHOICES

These three things will help keep new stuff from showing up at home unexpectedly:

1. Shifting your thinking from viewing shopping as pleasure, diversion, or escape to a practical necessity.
2. Shifting your thinking from seeing mistakes as failures to opportunities for learning something new.
3. Staying present when running errands and not daydreaming or getting lost in your feelings.

We don't want to spend valuable time clearing out clutter only to find new things mindlessly filling up all that available space. Not to mention those debilitating conversations with ourselves—let's be done with those, too.

With these concepts in place slowing, if not eliminating, the inflow of unwanted new things, we can now get down to the business of unstuffing these spaces. Another deep breath or two, a look around, and we should be seeing through the clutter to what we know now are actually opportunities for change, piled high in some very interesting configurations!

Teamwork

When approaching these historically cluttered spaces, it's best to have help. And if you have a family, this is an excellent project for everyone to work on together. Chances are these spaces are filled with the result of more than a few people dropping and running, so you should not feel compelled to take this on by yourself. That's a surefire way to develop a huge resentment and strap on your martyr suit. And we know how that pinches and binds—never very flattering.

If you have the fortitude to survive the inevitable groans from these family members and their hyperbolic whining that they'd rather have a hot poker stuck in their eyes than sort through their stuff on such a lovely/rainy/busy/lazy day, you should be able to gently and firmly convince them that if they don't want to return home and find their precious treasures on the curb, joining you for a fun day in one (or more) of these spaces is in their best interest. Once they dig in, provided you have ample beverages and snacks, they will come to see the benefits of participating, not only on the micro level of reclaiming valuable space for proper storage but also on the macro level of laying claim to new ways of thinking about stuff and how you all share your home.

Working together to reclaim these spaces strengthens self-esteem—there is power in the "we made it together, we'll correct it together" spirit of team building and committing to common goals. It also presents ample opportunities to model healthy behavior. No amount of words or talking can compete with actually doing something—we've all survived some version of "Do as I say, not as I do." So picking up a piece of trash and putting it in the garbage speaks volumes, particularly when done not as a burden but as a step toward liberation. As a family, you are now engaged in building the life you desire, one moldy shoe or broken hockey stick at a time.

Perhaps more important is putting into place the very thing that will prevent this from ever occurring again. And that is a fundamental shift in how you all view space and stuff. As you sort through everything, it's imperative to discuss two things:

1. The scale of appropriate consumption, and what things coming in and out of the house should look like going forward.

2. How easily this space was turned into a chaotic mess, and how effortlessly it could return to this condition again—if any one of the family backslides on number one.

This is not a threat or blame conversation but a call to action for future prevention. Communal living demands rigorous participation and vigilance. Otherwise, you risk this project becoming a Band-Aid for a wound requiring surgery. Anyone can clean out a space—you and your kin may even have done this before. But making that core adjustment as a family, as a working unit, of how you manage your space and objects is what is necessary. Seeing stuff in different ways has to become a part of your daily lives to ensure that in a year's time we won't be back here again with a different set of objects but the same exact problem.

And, of course, if you live alone or it's clear that everything in these spaces belongs to or got there by you alone, it's going to be just you and me!

Scheduling the Time

Whether working alone or with others, the work we're about to embark on—installing or modifying storage systems and sorting the contents of your garage—will likely take two weekends or four days, at least two days of which should be consecutive. Those days are the sorting and reloading days. If you are working with others, you'll likely shave a day off the process—since building and installing the storage systems will go faster with more hands.

If you live alone, consider enlisting a friend or two to help you. Depending on your level of friendship, you all can determine exactly how involved they'd like to be. Particularly if the scale of your project is extensive and assistance is vital, consider a time swap, where you would agree to help them with a major project on their list in exchange for their assistance here. To protect against future resentments, consider this a contract—you don't need to memorialize it on paper, but you should schedule both parties' work sessions at the same time. That way, you avoid future scheduling conflicts and any hard feelings, and everyone remains enthusiastic while working.

Use the next sections to develop a plan of attack so you can direct the project from start to finish. Make a list of the tasks to be done and divide those up among your helpers to keep everyone on task without your needing to appear bossy or controlling.

Creating Efficient Storage in Any Space

While there are seemingly infinite flavors of storage components, the basic structures are pretty simple and finite. You're either storing things on something (shelves, either wall-mounted or freestanding; hooks; and hangers) or in something (cabinets; hanging baskets or bins). Your budget and aesthetic sense will determine what these things look like—the materials and finishes. Your space and skill will determine whether your belongings end up on things or inside them.

You may already have some of these elements in place. If what currently exists seems adequate and stable and well located, that's great. You just need to eliminate everything superfluous and reload. If some parts are there but a cohesive design is lacking, build around what's already installed. On the other hand, if all you've got are wobbly shelves and a few recycled kitchen cabinets threatening to fall off the wall, now would be the time to replace them with an overall new system. Always seek the balance between practical and efficient, keeping utility and conservation in mind.

GARAGE SPACE BONANZA

Most garages have two feet of depth on each wall before breaking the plane of the bays. In the average garage, those three twenty-four-foot-long walls equal seventy-two linear feet of potential storage from floor to ceiling—impressive. And that's without a single thing taking up any floor space at all. And speaking of which, the less stored on the ground, the better. Concrete is porous and constantly wicking moisture up through it. Tools can rust and paper bags disintegrate when left on unfinished floors over time. It's also safer and more convenient to minimize the need to bend over as one matures.

Storage Systems and Shelving: An Overview

As mentioned, shelves and storage systems come in a variety of materials, styles, and price points. Your budget, an understanding of what you're storing (both volume and kind of object), and the flexibility to modify the design as your needs change will be the guiding factors in determining what and which types of storage you'll choose. Different shelving types will obviously be better for storing certain kinds of items.

While many prefabricated systems offer tremendous diversity among their individual components, they are also the most expensive. If you're comfortable with several styles or designs living alongside one another and not afraid of potentially clashing looks, you can choose the best that each of these systems has to offer and custom-design your own system. That way, you can get exactly what you need and still keep your eye on the bottom line.

Stand-alone shelving units, whether plastic, wood, or steel, provide flexible storage while keeping things up and off the floor. Some shelving units can be fitted with casters or wheels, allowing even more flexibility in placement and access. Either roll them out of your way to gain access to more remote areas, or roll them closer for immediate access to their contents.

GUIDELINES FOR SIZING AND POSITIONING SHELVES AND OTHER STORAGE SYSTEMS

- Choose shelf heights that allow enough space between the shelves for items of assorted heights. The lowest shelf should be between 18" and 24" from the ground. The distance between the lowest shelf and the next shelf above it should also be between 18" and 24". After that, as you continue up, the minimum distance between finished surfaces is typically between 12" and 16".

- Make sure to leave enough space between the ceiling and the top shelf for any tall (and infrequently used) items you plan to store there. Think camping equipment and tall coolers.

- Make sure that all shelves, brackets, and hooks have clearance and will not interfere with interior doors, service doors, garage doors, and garage-door tracks.

- When hanging things directly from the walls, be sure to anchor hooks, nails, and screws into studs for secure support.

- Make sure that in all foot-traffic areas—near laundry, car doors, and doorways—you keep brackets and braces above head level so you won't bump into them.

- In the garage, do not cover every inch of wall space with shelving. Allow several areas, especially near the garage door, for hanging storage for gardening tools, such as rakes and hoses and wheelbarrows, and winter tools, such as snow shovels and buckets of snow melt.

- In the garage, allow additional space for SUV or pickup truck doors to open fully, ensuring that any shelving doesn't restrict them.

- Ensure a free-and-easy path from indoors to your trash and recycling areas, and from these bins to the curb. You don't want to run a gauntlet each time you bring something to the bins or on your weekly trip taking the bins to the street.

- Consider stackable recycling bins and the addition of a handcart. That allows you to wheel the entire tower of bins—metal, glass, and plastic—right to the curb.

- Ensure an unobstructed path for any motorized service vehicles. You don't want to move cars (or bikes or the grill) every time you want to get the riding mower or snow plow out. Design a space that makes using these machines easy and accessible.

SHELVING, STORAGE SYSTEM, AND HANGER OPTIONS

The following are listed roughly in descending order of cost by component, although costs may vary. A small amount of research up front will save both time and money, so you'll end up with exactly what you want at a price that seems reasonable. Remember when calculating costs to consider the measurements of the area(s) to be covered along with the cost for the materials themselves.

Customized Wall Systems

There are many whole-room conversion systems that are on the market now. They all offer similar features and install directly onto your walls. These systems provide a series of panels or tracks that various cabinets, shelves, and hooks lock into. They are the most flexible, should you want to modify your design down the road.

SLOTTED WALL PANELS

These are solid panels with rows of horizontal slots. Brackets and clips fit into the slots and suspend baskets, bins, cabinets, hooks, and shelves. Everything about these systems is uniform and proprietary, so once you commit to a certain manufacturer, you'll have to use only their components to complete your system. One potential advantage with this type of system is that you can also use this to finish off unfinished walls. Simply cover the wall with panels from floor to ceiling.

WALL TRACKS

These are metal rails that attach horizontally across studs. Some offer a decorative plastic cover that disguises the rail. They come in standard lengths and can be installed at any height. Again, with proprietary brackets or clips you can attach a wide variety of baskets, bins, cabinets, hooks, and other holders. With some systems (typically seen in residential closets), they also offer vertical standards that attach to the top rail. You can then attach brackets and support horizontal shelving across the brackets. This gives you the flexibility to break up shelving with other components from the rail's manufacturer.

Wall Storage Cabinets

Like kitchen cabinets, these come in a variety of materials, including wood, metal, and plastic, and are available in many different sizes, styles, and finishes. Some are freestanding (on legs or wheels), and some are wall-mounted. While these can be relocated once they're installed, you should consider these semi-permanent. Just like laying out a kitchen's cabinetry, you'll want to be fairly certain of your design before you begin installation.

Utility Storage Cabinets

These are made from multiple materials in multiple finishes and are free-standing but cumbersome to move once placed. You'll certainly have to empty them before you can relocate them. In addition, unlike shelving units, you'll need to allow clearance for door swings on these cabinets when figuring out placement.

Freestanding Shelving Units

These come in a variety of materials and combinations of materials, from steel to wood to plastic. They come in standard dimensions, and because each unit is independent, they offer great flexibility, as they can be moved from place to place. Units with wheels allow for even easier relocation.

Metal Standards and Brackets

These offer a low-cost, flexible alternative to both wall panels and wall tracks. Standards come in several lengths and attach vertically onto the studs, either over sheetrock or directly (in unfinished spaces). Interlocking brackets come in various depths and allow for incremental adjustment up and down. The only limits to height are the length of the standards themselves. For tall spaces, you can install standards on top of one another from floor to ceiling. Steel or wood or wire mesh shelves can be used, as long as they fit and are stable on top of the brackets. The thicker and more rigid the shelving material is, the less likely that it will buckle or warp under weight or humid conditions. One advantage to wire mesh is its breathability. Fabrics and other materials that need air circulation will benefit from mesh shelves.

Wire Grids

These grid panels are made of metal, are sometimes coated, are available in various sizes, and can be used to cover entire walls. They come with clips and spacers to secure them to studs. Baskets, bins, hooks, racks, and shelves can all be attached to the grids to customize storage.

Peg-Board (Perforated Hardboard)

This is the original grid panel. This ready-made surface is dotted with holes that accept a wide variety of clips, hooks, racks, and shelves. There are now also great accessories that let you store even heavy or bulky items without fear of things falling off or ripping free. Peg-Board is fastened directly to exposed studs or with spacers over drywall. The spacers hold the panels far enough away from the wall to allow hooks, etc., to be inserted or removed. There are different thicknesses of Peg-Board, so be sure to buy the correct corresponding hardware.

Tool Hangers and Hooks

Many hardware companies now sell individual and highly specialized hooks and tool hangers. These are designed for everything from garden tools, such as rakes and shovels and wheelbarrows, to ladders and bicycles and hockey equipment. These attach to studs and are perfect for all those narrow or corner spaces, to get things up off the ground and keep them easily seen and reached.

Before you install any of these systems, measure carefully and consider access to them from both the front and the sides. You don't want to have a great-looking system that you can't easily get to.

WHY YOU DON'T WANT TO
DO THIS OUT OF ORDER

Since these spaces are being "built to suit," if you cannot easily access every wall you plan to use for storage *prior* to sorting, I suggest studying your options and doing some research but waiting to install a system until after everything's been cleared away and sorted. When designing your layout and installing storage components, you need to be able to get to every part of the space, so your layout will have integrity and accessibility from inception to execution. A half-baked cake may taste sweet, but it's a mess to deal with.

Likewise, do not start to load any storage before everything has been sorted and categorized. It may be tempting to cut a corner here and there, thinking, "Well, I can certainly put X right here. I know where that wants to live." You may think that you can isolate certain items and store them while sorting, but you'll discover that as you sort, the volume of items in each category and the preferred location for these categories will continue to shift until everything has been touched and decided on. Until you have a completely empty space without any obstacles or space commitments, you can't actually see where the most efficient place to put anything will be.

Having to move things twice is not the end of the world, but a lot of loading and unloading is a waste of time during an already large project. Patience and a willingness to be methodical about this will pay huge dividends as you work through this process. Trust me.

Sorting and You

BRINGING THE SUPPLIES TO THE SORTING

If you've assembled and installed whatever storage systems you're going to be using, or are clear that it's preferable to wait until after the space is cleared, it's now time to start sorting. So get your supplies and bring them to the work area.

Those are:

- Camera
- Trash cans and bags
- Broom
- Dustpan
- Mop
- Wet-dry industrial vacuum
- Tubs/containers/baskets/tarps (to isolate, corral, and contain like things)
- Old carryout or food storage containers (clear plastic with sealing lids—for smaller storage items)
- A sizable magnet (for picking up nails, screws, or random pieces of metal)

Find a spot for your trash cans. A spot that you can easily get to with the bags of trash you'll soon be filling. And make sure there's enough room around them for the extra bags you'll end up with when the cans reach capacity. It'd be better not to have to move the trash twice before setting it at the curb. If you can arrange this process to fall close enough to trash-collection day, take it all to the curb immediately.

CLEVER ATTEMPTS TO DELAY OR AVOID SORTING

Having already taken your "before" pictures, at this point some people may choose to sidestep examining their possessions and prefer a quick trip to the store for containers—hoping that just corralling it all will be enough. This is only another variation of "out of sight, out of mind." By tossing everything into containers, you may be thinking you'll do the actual sorting "later" or "someday," when you win the time lottery and have an influx of unstructured time with no plans. At least everything's up off the floor and into bins, so that's progress, right? Wrong. Randomly stuffing things into bins and boxes brings you no closer to knowing where everything is or eliminating the things that you don't need, want, or care about but are still surrounded by. This hasty "fix" just delays the inevitable.

Alternatively, you may be thinking that heading off to the store and stocking up on all different sizes of tubs and bins will help you in your sorting process and is the best way to proceed. This, too, would be a mistake. No amount of shopping will cure this mess. Until you know the exact volume and content of the items to be stored, you can't possibly buy the right types or sizes of containers. And the last things you need are odd-sized and surplus containers creating more clutter and wasting money!

SORTING IN TWO EASY STEPS

Armed with our sorting categories and Stay-or-Go questions listed below, we're ready to begin sorting. This is where the rubber meets the road. Once you've sorted through everything, we'll evaluate whether there's more to store than room in which to store it. For now we'll focus on examining each individual item that makes up each category.

Step One: Eliminate Trash

The first thing to do is find everything that can clearly be identified as trash and discard it. At its simplest interpretation, trash is:

An unwanted or undesired material or substance; broken, discarded, or worthless things. It is also referred to as rubbish, waste, garbage, or junk, depending on the type of material and the regional terminology.

So now find the items that are unequivocally unwanted, broken, or worthless and throw them out. That includes anything missing key components that can't or won't be replaced; anything actually broken, including toys; and anything that no longer works, even when plugged in or after the batteries are swapped for fresh ones. Electronics and other things that contain heavy or toxic metals, chemicals, or rechargeable batteries should be isolated into a recycling pile—many places now offer recycling programs where you can drop these things off, either for a small fee or for free. Likewise, paint cans and other toxic liquids—isolate them for proper disposal (see the Resources section at the back of the book).

Step Two: Like with Like

With the trash gone, that leaves you with everything else to be sorted into families of like objects.

If there are still random items in a tangle, pry everything loose from its neighbors. Cords and cables have a way of strangling anything they come in contact with. No need to get frustrated or angry. Of course, any additional trash you come across should immediately get tossed.

If you're in the garage, relocate any motorized vehicles that are staying, whether they're cars, ATVs, riding mowers, motorcycles, or scooters and clear them out of the way. Likewise, any single large items, such as grills, bicycles, ladders, and wheelbarrows. These also need to be moved out of the way to create enough sorting and organizing space. Once you've established categories for sorting, some of these items can be brought back in and arranged with other items that share the same category.

Whichever space you're in, create areas into which like items can be sorted. Spread out tarps or bins to define areas, or take old cardboard or damaged sheets of foam core and a large marker and create signs, staking out specific regions and areas around the space. This way, camping gear doesn't spill over into seasonal gardening supplies.

When spreading things out and sorting, keep things to one level as much as possible, so you can easily recognize category contents and minimize handling times. Books and other flat and uniform items can be stacked, and clothes and other soft goods may end up in piles—just remember that ultimately you'll have to dismantle these piles as you make further decisions.

There are some global categories of things that don't require further specification. Those are the following.

Trash
Recycle (as in "green" recycling)
Return to Others (soon!)
Give Away (soon!)
 Thrift store/shelter
 Specific people or organizations
 Online classified sites (Freecycle/Craigslist) or out at the curb with
  a sign
Sell (only things that have significant value and easy-to-identify
 markets)
Sentimentaland
The Fence

For those items that you're keeping that will be containerized and stored, here are a few categories to get you started. Review this list, review your belongings, and identify any additional categories that you'll need for the proper labeling and storage of your stuff.

Artwork: intact or damaged, two- and three-dimensional
Automobile: all things to do with your cars, motor oil, windshield
 wiper fluid, tires
**Bicycles, tricycles, unicycles, inline skates, skateboards,
pogo sticks, stilts**
Books: in or out of boxes, current or historical or schoolbooks, etc.;
 ultimately, only books that you're keeping

Camping gear

Cleaning supplies: opened cleaning products, buckets, mops, brooms, dustpans

Clothing, children's outgrown

Clothing, "fat"

Clothing, seasonal: separated by season as well as by owner and wearer

Clothing, "skinny"

Collections: from Polly Pocket to Barbie to Hummels to stamps

Electronics, computer: surplus computer parts, printers, monitors

Electronics, other: surplus electronics—Walkmans, stereo components, TVs, adding machines, calculators

Fasteners: should always be stored near tools; includes nuts, bolts, screws, nails

Financial documents: Supporting documentation for tax returns, bank and credit card statements, receipts

Furniture: current and no longer used, intact and broken, missing parts, torn

Games and toys: board games, jigsaw puzzles, children's toys

Hobby supplies: scrapbooking; knitting and crocheting; model cars, planes, or trains

Holiday decorations: separated by individual holiday

Inherited things: in or out of any containers they arrived in

Laundry: as in dirty laundry, if you do laundry in this space

Lawn and landscaping: summer yard tools, such as hoses, rakes, shovels, leaf blowers, chain saws

Media: LPs, cassette tapes, 8-track tapes, 78s, 45s, VHS tapes, DVDs, CDs, floppy disks

Newspapers: current or old (e.g., documenting the day Kennedy was assassinated, your child's birth, the first moon landing)

Office supplies

Original cartons for equipment: just in case we have to return them!

Paint and painting supplies: including drop cloths, rollers, brushes

Pantry items: foods, dry goods, paper products

Periodicals: current or old magazines, catalogs

Photographs: in boxes, in albums, or loose

Seasonal lifestyle: grills, lawn chairs, cushions

Seasonal pastime supplies: pool equipment and toys, croquet equipment

Sports equipment: all seasons, from Frisbees to ice skates, further separated by sport

Surplus china and dishes: including crystal, stemware

Surplus goods: bulk cleaning supplies (unopened), lightbulbs, batteries

Surplus kitchen equipment: appliances, pots and pans, dishes, silverware

Surplus planting supplies: for houseplants rather than gardening, including planters and vases

Tools, all-season: ladders, saws, drills, hammers

Tools, cold-weather: snow shovels, scrapers, ice-melt products

---

Notable Note

Financial documents listed above should be stored in plastic, clearly labeled, water-resistant containers. These documents are typically discarded after seven years, or upon advice from an accountant or tax professional. Unlike supporting financial documents, permanent financial documents (tax returns) and financial instruments (stock certificates) should be stored with other documents that cannot be replaced or would be necessary in an emergency (insurance policies, wills, deeds, vehicle titles). These should all be stored in either a safe-deposit box at a bank (make sure there are multiple keys, with clearly noted and identified locations) or a fireproof, waterproof safe or file cabinet on the main level of the house.

STAY-OR-GO QUESTIONS

Now you'll handle each object and ask the following questions, and if the object makes the cut, it will then be placed with other similar items that are also staying.

- Do I really need this?
- How many do I need? (Once you pick a number, stick to it. Don't amend the number when you come across another one; swap the newest object you'd like to keep for one of the objects you've previously sorted.)
- Am I keeping it because of sentimental attachment? Would a photo of it suffice?
- Do I already have a better one?
- Is this better than the one I have?
- Am I keeping it for "someday"?
- Will I actually do the work required to restore or repair this? When?
- Am I keeping it because it was expensive and it's "still good"?
- Will my life change for the worse if I let this go? (Actually, really, not just in your imagination.)
- Am I keeping it because it's part of a set? Do I use the whole set or just one piece? Is it useless without the entire set, or could someone else benefit from the pieces I'm not using?

When in doubt, toss it out or let it go.

Other than snacking and bathroom breaks, this should be a continuous activity, and you should not stop until everything has been separated into some smaller pile or grouping organized by category or discarded. At that point, if it's getting dark or you're exhausted, you could be finished for the day. Of course, if you've taken things outdoors, you'll want to either cover everything up outside or relocate any big-ticket items back under lock and key for safekeeping overnight.

MORE PESKY CONVERSATIONS, FEELINGS AND IRIS

Sorting and purging may bring up other questions or thoughts or feelings. This is natural and not to be feared or judged as a sign of anything other than your humanness. The mind is a thought machine and the heart a feeling machine. Generating thoughts and feelings is what they do.

If these kinds of thoughts or feelings have stopped you in the past or prevented you from even beginning, you're not alone. And while they may be demanding and intrusive and annoying, they are nothing more than a product of your fertile imagination and vulnerable constitution—not always a great combination when sorting through random things, but certainly not deadly.

I recently spent three weeks in Chicago with a client, Iris, who had decided that she wanted to put her house on the market and move on. This was the house she had raised her two children in, and after twenty years, it was jam-packed from the attic to the basement with everything from fine art to toy drums. As we sorted through the basement, we came across lots of her kids' old clothes and toys. She never broke down and cried, but she told me the story of each thing we touched. Iris would hold each item and tenderly relate how her son had worn this little baseball cap or her daughter had performed in her ballet recital in these slippers. We kept three tubs and some trash bags nearby—one tub for each child, one tub for her, and trash bags for the local thrift store. As we sorted through box after box and pile after pile, some things were set aside for each child, a few for her—I could always tell which thing she wouldn't be able to part with by the way her smile lit up as she first handled it. She'd start to laugh, and I'd know this tiny jumpsuit was going straight into *her* tub. Anything that didn't make the cut was bagged and earmarked for charity. We continued this process through storerooms packed with books and sporting equipment and old bolts of fabric. Other than a few more sentimental objects, everything else was gathered up to be taken away.

There were times each day when Iris was clearly overcome with feelings as she sifted through years of accumulated belongings, each one representing a particular event or time in her life. When I sensed she had reached a threshold of emotion or exhaustion, or she just seemed to lose focus, I'd check in with her. Was she okay? Was she tired; did she want to take a break, get a snack or a cup of tea; did she want a hug? Most of the time she'd laugh and say she was fine, let's keep going, but there were times when we did pause, head downstairs, and put the water on for tea or grab a slice of cheese.

If you're working alone, you'll have to do that for yourself. Check in with yourself and pace yourself. I've laid out a rigorous plan of action in these pages, but you should consider the human component in this process as well. You don't want to get too hungry or tired when doing this work. Likewise, if strong emotions come up, shift gears; if you're overwhelmed going though your kids' childhood clothing, or an old dissertation that's not quite finished, or love letters from any number of exes, start shredding or go sort towels or do something equally unemotional. Get a snack. Take a walk around the block. No one's keeping track of the time. The goal is to complete the task or tasks described, from beginning to end. If that takes three hours or three days, that's fine. As long as you keep coming back to it, you can walk away for some fresh air as often as you need to. Just be mindful not to allow strong feelings, exhaustion, or hunger to derail you and prevent you from finishing altogether.

When we got to the attic, Iris and I found an old bedroom set that had belonged to her daughter. We cleaned it off and brought it down to the main floor to set up in one of the bedrooms. Unfortunately, most of what else was up there had been overrun by mice or moths. Surrendering to the situation, we filled bag after bag with trash and hauled it down to the curb. I think it was that much easier for Iris to empty the attic without looking back, having already sorted through the basement and selected her precious totems of two childhoods' worth of memories.

We can take away several lessons from Iris's experience. A few selective items can distill and capture the feelings behind whole swathes of time. And more practically, if you have the sense that time and unwelcome pests have destroyed the contents of some area of your home, sort through another area first and cull your treasures there. It will make the inevitable tolerable as you assess the damage and finally let it go.

OUR FEELINGS ABOUT TRASH

Undoubtedly, as you sort you will discover additional things that meet the definition of trash. Send them directly into a trash bag. There's no need to fret or talk yourself out of tossing something that is beyond repair or worthless. For those items that are still worth something, if not to you but to someone else, they can be gathered in another area (labeled "Give Away") and taken to your local resale shop or a shelter, or to some other place that accepts donations of still-functional things.

It can be sad to throw things away for a variety of reasons—most of them emotional and spurred on by stories we tell ourselves about either the monetary or the sentimental value of an item, or sometimes the monetary *and* the sentimental value. A popular story often told involves frugality and prudence, and the repairing of an item, restoring it to full functionality "someday" or even "someday soon." The sadder truth is that if you have not attempted to repair this item in the last nine months, it is almost certain that you never will. You may argue with me in your head, but I have been a party to this conversation countless times, and in each case not a single item needing repair was ever successfully repaired without my intervention.

And, of course, beyond money and feelings there are also the environmental consequences of throwing things away. Most of us are mindful of the growing mountains of trash just outside our cities or floating unwanted on barges on our waterways, and we want to keep as much as possible in circulation and away from these (mostly) dead ends. There are programs that convert some trash back into energy, and every day there are more options for recycling things that just last month were considered exclusively trash. I urge us all to pursue every avenue for the proper dismantling and recycling of any and every thing we discard. There will be times, however, when something is still destined for landfill. And in those cases, no one wants your trash any more than you do. If something is missing crucial parts or is destroyed beyond use or broken, be responsible and dispose of it properly. Do not pass along garbage to a local nonprofit, assuming they'll do the sorting for you. You may

> **Notable Note**
>
> When considering the toxic nature of something you're about to discard, a good rule of thumb is: if you wouldn't put it in your mouth, then it most likely has a correct way to be dismantled and recycled, and should not just be tossed into the trash to leach into water tables or food supplies.
>
> I realize this places a particular burden on some people who have limited mobility or live in more remote locations—even so, this just brings mindfulness further into focus. Before bringing home something potentially toxic and thereby tacitly agreeing to be responsible for its eventual disposal, consider your alternatives. Is there a "green" or nontoxic yet equally effective version of the item out there? There may not always be. In those cases, I encourage you to assume full responsibility for seeing your product/item through the complete arc of its life cycle— from arrival at your door to its departure for eventual dismantling and comprehensive recycling. See the Resources section at the back of the book for links to sites that offer more guidance and instruction on this.

believe that the remaining shoe of a pair might still find some use in the world, but you are mistaken. Throw it away. The exception being athletic shoes— these are collected and recycled!

The surest way to keep things out of a landfill is to use less and be more mindful about what you invite into your life. If you don't want to be responsible for something at the end of its life cycle, perhaps you should leave it where you found it in the first place. If we really do live in a supply-and-demand society, the sooner we stop demanding, the sooner they'll stop supplying. And while we wouldn't want that to include nutritious food, I don't know how many people would mind if that did include Chia Pets and the BeDazzler.

Cleanliness Is Next to Garageliness (or Atticliness or Basementliness)

Once everything is off its previous surface and now lying with its siblings in a clearly marked "like" zone, sweep or vacuum and mop the floor. If you are in the garage and have any oil or other fluid stains on the floor, now would be a good time to try to get them up. A quick Internet search should turn up solutions for any stain situation you might have on your hands. Wipe down every surface, paying special attention to cobwebs and other dust collectors. If you have cabinets or shelves that remain as part of your new storage system, wipe them down as well.

The Kinds of Things You Store in Your Auxiliary Space(s)

As you look around at the various Like with Like zones, get out your notebook. Create a new page in your notebook and title it "The Kinds of Things I Store in My _____" (whichever space you're currently working in), and then begin to record the categories you've identified and sorted things into. Remember to think in terms of groupings and categories rather than specifics—not "my heavy wool navy slack suit" but Winter Wardrobe. For fine-tuning, refer back to the list on pages 192 through 194 for guidance and suggestions as needed.

We'll do this exercise for each auxiliary space. Then with all the lists, we'll do a few things.

First, we'll look for duplications. If so, does one space house the bulk of a particular category, with just a few stragglers in another space, or are the items fairly evenly divided among spaces? This will inform your marrying together of categories spread across spaces, so that when you finish, all of any one category will be found only in one location. Like with Like comes to our aid once again.

Second, we'll review the lists with our understanding of any spatial limitations in mind, so you can evaluate whether what you've been storing is best suited to remain there, or if it should be relocated to one of the other spaces. Obviously, if you only have one or two of these kinds of spaces, that will alter your process and the outcome. In all cases, this exercise should help focus your efforts and clarify the kinds of things you're storing and how best to continue storing them for their protection and your easy access.

Depending on the size of your spaces, consider adjusting the scale of your belongings to match your available space. For example, if you often shop in bulk and it's also important to have generous open space around you when you're doing laundry, consider how much bulk shopping you *need* to do, rather than cramming forty-eight rolls of toilet paper and five hundred paper plates into your laundry-folding area and feeling unnecessarily crowded.

There is no absolute right or wrong way to organize your home—the guidelines are simple.

- Do you have adequate room for everything you own?
- If there is adequate room, is everything easy to locate and use?
- If there is not adequate room, you either need more room or less stuff.

And of course in these cases, I always vote for less stuff.

Containerizing the Categories

When everything has been sorted, it's time to put things away in containers. Measure or carefully guesstimate the volume of each category. Anything that is part of a set or is not a stand-alone item—for example, a shovel—should be containerized with its siblings—exceptions being lawn furniture (too bulky) and bulk supplies (these just need to all live together in one area) and collections of small things, such as fasteners. It's enough having each kind of fastener together in their own container; we don't need a container of containers of fasteners. All fasteners should live together near the tools and other hardware, however. When loading larger containers, make sure they don't become so heavy that moving them becomes awkward or requires more than one person.

Notable Note

FASTENERS

As you come across collections and assortments of fasteners, loose or in crumbling cardboard boxes, put each specific flavor of fastener in one of the resealable food containers. To be clear, if you have both ¾" and 1½" Sheetrock screws, *do not* combine them into one container of Sheetrock screws. Fasteners are utilized by size exclusively—as a rule, they are not interchangeable. So keep each specific size, shape, and kind of fastener separate but near its brothers and sisters. An alternative to the individual containers is a drawer cabinet system, a standalone cabinet with multiple drawers for small items. Each type and size of fastener could be isolated into its own drawer. You could then glue an example of each drawer's contents to the face of its drawer.

If your camping gear comprises a tent, two sleeping bags, a mess kit, a portable stove, two propane canisters, a tarp, and some stakes, find the container or containers that are large enough to house all these items in the fewest number of containers that will still fit someplace in your garage.

Now would be the time to go shopping for containers, if needed, since you have an accurate measurement of each category's size requirements. I'm not a big fan of plastic in everyday living, but I am a huge fan of clear plastic tubs and bins for storage. You may choose lovely decorator containers for all your storage needs *if* these containers are specifically labeled and those labels corrected anytime something is added or removed, *or* if you don't mind wasting time hunting through several look-alike containers searching for some item, because you don't remember *which* lovely container you stored that item in.

If repeatedly opening and closing a container to determine its contents seems like too much trouble (and it certainly does to me), the alternative is a container you can easily see through. This way, regardless of how often you change the contents, there's never any confusion about what it contains. Under no circumstances should you hold on to "decorative" containers if they don't serve you, regardless of their cost. Donate them or give them away and someone else will benefit from them.

Assuming you now have the right sizes and amounts of tubs, begin to fill them. Continue to put everything into a container until only stand-alone items remain. To guide you, we'll use Christmas decorations as an example. Within the category of Christmas decorations, there are several smaller categories. Because not everything is equally sturdy or has the same storage needs, it's important to further break things down as required. Note that when dealing with categories like books or seasonal clothing, several stackable tubs would be sufficient to house all the items without further subdivision. Most likely, no book will crush or damage another book when they are stacked on top of and against one another inside their own container. The same might not be true were you to combine your punch bowl, grandmother's china, and model airplanes into one tub.

CHRISTMAS DECORATIONS (AN EXAMPLE)

Lights, Indoor, and Lights, Outdoor

Here's a subcategory of a subcategory. Put all the lights together, but separated into each subcategory—indoors and out. Also include all extension cords, power strips, and spare parts/lightbulbs. It makes sense to have all the electrical wires and extra lights parts living with the lights—not the electrical parts for the model trains or power cords for various computers or appliances, just parts for the lights.

Ideally, each string or strand of indoor lights is individually wound around a paper towel roll or the core of an old roll of gift wrap or a very fat and short dowel. Lights should have their own container *unless* you have only one or two strings of lights, in which case you could store them in a smaller container within another larger decoration category and container. Three or more strands should be considered worthy of their own container.

Ornaments

Put all the tree ornaments in as many tubs as required. Only the tree orna-ments. These are fragile, and you don't want heavy items bumping into them on their way on or off the shelves. If you have the original boxes they came in, you can store them in their boxes inside the tubs. If not, recycle tissue paper from gift boxes and use that either to wrap the ornaments individually or to create layers, almost like a lasagna of ornaments and paper. Do not overpack these or crush them, and use as many tubs as needed for the amount of orna-ments you have. Included in one tub should be any packages of ornament hooks/hangers. If the hooks/hangers are loose and no packaging exists, a zip-lock plastic bag will do nicely to corral them.

Artificial Trees, Wreaths, Garlands, Swags, and Other Evergreen Trim/Decor

The tree, wreaths, and any other artificial evergreen decorations should all live together. While sturdier than glass ornaments, these are still subject to crushing and other damage. Take the tree apart into its smaller pieces. Lay the pieces in the tubs, allowing their own weight to determine volume. Never apply weight or pressure attempting to fit one more piece in a tub. If you have cardboard available, you could also place a section of cardboard between layers of greens, repeating the lasagna technique mentioned above. Do not overcrowd the tubs, or next year you'll discover flattened and unappealing components.

Natural wreaths and other decor will need to be discarded, ideally com-posted or chipped into mulch.

Flocking, Stockings, Other Soft Fabric Goods, Holiday Card Holders

These should all be kept together, laid flat and layered. Included in this tub should be stocking holders and any holiday-card holders.

Nativity Scenes, Small Figures, Snow Globes, Tabletop Decorations

Wrap each fragile item in tissue paper or Bubble Wrap, and lay them all neatly into the tubs. Everything else can be either wrapped or gently loaded into the tubs.

Large Figures, Indoors
Large Figures, Outdoors, Including Lawn Ornaments

All large figures should be stored in an open tub or in some sort of corral if possible (think repurposed playpen). If any are too large, store them together and next to or very near the tub of the others, preferably on a top shelf or shelves, depending on how many there are. An alternative site, if you have a garage, is to make or use a loft area to store these oversized items. If the garage is *not* climate-controlled, make sure to wrap the indoor items in some sort of protective material.

Christmas Collectibles

Like the Nativity figures above, any fragile items should be individually wrapped. Plush items or items that will not break, chip, or damage one

> ### Notable Note
>
> This chapter mentions storing things that burn as an example of a category of Christmas items. Here's where discernment and critical thinking come into play. While Sterno *is* something that burns and that you might use during the holidays, it *is not* a seasonal item and so should be stored with other fuels and chafing dishes someplace where it could be searched for year round (you might use it for a bridal shower or a Fourth of July party, for example) as opposed to only once a year during the winter holiday season. This kind of reasoning should be used whenever there are things that could be stored in two places. If everything has only *one* home, we need to really think through which is the broadest choice when determining *where* that home is.

another if they come in contact with another object may be laid into the tubs carefully.

Candles, Things That Burn

If you never burn these candles, they may be stored with other tabletop decorations. If you do burn them, keep them all together. *Do not* store matches in the tub with anything flammable. Also consider the climate and temperature when storing candles and other items that may melt or combust when exposed to prolonged heat.

Trains and Other Animated Decor

For trains, group all tracks, track-related fasteners, power adapters, etc., together. Keep the cars separate, and wrap delicate or fragile or antique cars individually. All signs, signals, lights, buildings, and other decor for the tracks and scenes should be stored separately as well. Things with moving or removable parts should be dismantled, and all specialized parts stored together in a ziplock bag. Do not mix similar-looking pieces without labeling them if there is any chance that you won't be able to tell them apart in a year.

The Importance of Labels —How, Why, and Where

Once everything is in a container of some kind, the containers should be labeled. Labels don't need to be fancy; they do need to be legible. Write in large block letters—avoid cursive and lowercase letters, since they are difficult to read from a distance. I prefer labels to writing directly on the container, because you may wish to put something different in the container in the future. That way you'll avoid a series of crossed-out names with each revision of its contents.

HOW TO LABEL SOMETHING PROPERLY

- Label all boxes/containers/tubs so you can tell at a glance what's in them.
- When you label your containers, label them with large enough and clear enough letters that you can see and read them from a distance of at least five feet.
- If printing labels or inventories from a computer, print an additional one and drop it in the container or tape it to the underside of the lid, in case the labels fall off the outside.
- There's no need to label the top of a container if you are stacking them—you'll never see it.
- Label both sides and either the front or the back of a container so you don't have to face it a certain direction when you put the container back in its place.
- Be mindful of label materials and where things are being stored. In hot climates, masking tape often dries and cracks off, or the glue melts. Likewise, when removed, some duct tapes leave a gummy mess behind.
- If you are using any drawer cabinet systems, a clever alternative to a label for the individual drawers is to glue one example of each drawer's occupant to the face of the drawer for an easy to see guide.

- Be specific with your labels. Don't just label something "Christmas Decorations." Especially if you have multiple boxes of Christmas decorations. Referring back to our work above, label them "Christmas: Lights, Indoor," or "Christmas: Artificial Tree," or "Christmas: Wreaths." That way you'll only have to open one container.

Organizing the Storage

With everything successfully containerized and labeled, it's time to organize the containers on shelves or pallets and put them away until you next need the contents. Two things will largely determine where you will store everything: frequency of use and volume of stuff. Use Like with Like for guidance in identifying where to store which items. Try to keep similar items on one shelf or on adjacent shelves.

Begin to load each cabinet and shelf with your sorted and containerized things. Do not be discouraged if your best guess of a category's volume does not match up with the actual capacity of a shelf or cabinet. When this happens, you have two choices—either reduce the volume of things in that category or find nearby storage that is adequate in size. If you feel strongly that everything that remains is necessary, I won't argue with you. If you feel that you have padded your category a bit with some questionable items, now is the time to fess up and let them go.

Keep in mind the weight of things, and always load heavier and bulkier items lower, with lighter things up high. For hazardous materials, such as chemicals, pesticides, and sharp tools, use storage cabinets with doors that can be closed and possibly even locked, well out of the reach of children and pets.

Once everything is up off the ground and on a pallet or shelf, in a cabinet, or hanging from a hook, take some pictures. These are your "afters." This is the way your space should look, and with a minimum of effort, consistently applied, this is the way your space will continue to look.

FREQUENCY OF USE: STORING HOLIDAY ITEMS, SEASONAL ITEMS, AND BULK ITEMS

For things used only once a year, such as holiday decorations, you'll want easy enough access, but these things don't need to be at your fingertips. Seasonal items that are rotated out for use each year might get higher priority, depending on where you live and whether you'd also take some of them on trips to other locales. Bulk staple items that you're often revisiting to replenish supplies should be the most accessible. Sentimental or nostalgic items or memorabilia (wedding gowns, yearbooks, etc.) should go in one section, usually the least accessible, as these items aren't taken out very often.

When Laundry Is Done in Auxiliary Spaces

If your laundry center is in one of these spaces, you want to make sure that you allow ample room for sorting clothes, hanging up any damp clothes to dry, and ideally a clean, uncluttered surface reserved for folding. You should also have a shelf or cabinet overhead or nearby that can house laundry soap, spot removers, and other products. Lazy Susans are useful to keep liquids on—they collect any spills and condense the space required for these necessities. If space is tight where you do the wash, you could also hang damp clothes to dry in a nearby shower and set up the ironing board in a temporary location as needed.

When evaluating your space and looking for ways to improve efficiency and minimize the footprint, think about how *you* like to do laundry by asking yourself the following questions..

- Can you finish the laundry in the same room or area that you wash it in?
- Is there room for a table or countertop to fold laundry on?
- What about an ironing board? Do you or does someone in your family press clothes?

- What about damp clothes that either shouldn't be dried at all or should be pulled out while still damp to avoid shrinkage or wrinkling?
- How often do you do laundry?
- Do you usually, or only, go to this space to do the wash?

All of these considerations will inform how you lay out your space and where you'll end up placing shelving and other storage solutions to organize everything that's being stored nearby.

Managing Messy Projects Inside and Out

Consider whether there are activities occurring indoors that generate dirt, dust, or other particulate matter that could possibly get into the things being stored. How about proper ventilation for hobbies, crafts, or repairs that involve toxic substances? Certainly you'll want to locate any sort of shop as far away from the laundry or stored food as possible. Beyond that, keeping any sort of woodworking, grinding, drilling, or chemical use isolated is your best bet at keeping your storage area clean, dust-free, and unaltered. That's one more argument for airtight containers with resealable lids.

If you do have a workshop indoors *and* also have a climate-controlled or all-season garage, consider relocating your shop to the garage. That's a sure way to prevent generating dust indoors.

When the garage doubles as a work area, stay mindful of mixed-use spaces and maintaining your workspace enough to keep projects and their components from migrating into common areas. And just because there is greater air circulation in this somewhat outdoor space, you'll still want to prevent sawdust and other particulate matter from infiltrating any items that are stored nearby. Regular sweeping, vacuuming, and air filtering will keep your debris from ending up anywhere besides the trash.

During this sorting-and-purging process you may have come across some things that needed repair or a project that has been incomplete for more than a year. Let me suggest a realistic assessment of what you actually have the time and interest to complete. If you are someone who is often building or assembling furniture, I wouldn't want to discourage you from continuing to do so. If, on the other hand, you've had a chair on your workbench for two years waiting to be reupholstered, consider taking it to an upholsterer or passing it along to someone who has a better history of completing these kinds of projects. You don't need to feel bad about it. Just be clear about where your interests and free time line up and intersect with one another. Even if I were retired, if I weren't going with my father, I'd never choose to go fishing. I might be missing a great time sitting on the dock with my pole in my hand, but I'd rather lie in a hammock, read a book, and take a nap. Different choice, just as relaxing.

Finishing Second-Tier Spaces for Living vs. Storage (and How That Impacts Where You Store Your Things)

If you've been planning to or are in the process of renovating an attic, basement, or garage to gain needed living space, consider carefully what that means for the things that are currently being stored there. I am adamantly opposed to using off-site storage facilities unless what you'd be placing there is any of the following.

- Fine art
- Serious antiques (with serious provenance, not a funky French hospital bed you picked up down the street)
- Other priceless artifacts

With any of the above, if you really have no intention of ever using these items again, and if you're not saving them for family members (or if you are saving them for family members but they don't want them), contemplate your de-acquisition timeline. At some point the market for any of these things will be as good as it's going to get, and it will be time to sell or donate them.

Just as you schedule other maintenance events, so too should you have a schedule for the liquidation of these kinds of assets. Otherwise they will linger in storage, possibly costing more to store than they are actually worth, particularly if interest in them is limited to you and a small group of other collectors, curators, or dealers.

If nothing you're considering storing falls into the above categories, find it a new home. Storing old bedding, marginal appliances, old magazines (those *National Geographics*), lawn furniture, etc., for hundreds of dollars each month makes no sense. The average length of rental for off-site storage is currently fifteen months. At an average cost of $150 for a 5'x8'x8' space—do the math. To store 320 cubic feet worth of stuff (and that would mean utilizing every cubic inch), it would cost you $2,250 over those fifteen months. If your goods aren't worth that much going in, I feel confident they certainly won't be worth that much coming out. If money is not a concern, the psychic burden of lingering stuff may be enough to motivate you to make different choices. And if money *is* a concern, the math speaks for itself.

Off-site storage is a short-term temporary solution at best. Like gym memberships, it's a monthly drain that's easily forgotten until the charge hits and you're reminded that "I really have to take care of this *this month*." Then something distracts you and it drifts away until next month's charge rolls around again.

Even avoiding off-site storage and successfully downsizing in preparation for a second-tier space conversion, make sure that you design sufficient storage into your new spaces for everything that renovation will displace but that still remains. If that's not possible, work smartly and cleverly to maximize storage wherever you can. A bank of closets or even a storage room in your new layout will pay off handsomely, not only for your usage but also in resale value when you eventually put your house on the market. As they say, you can never be too thin, too rich, or have too much storage!

Trash or Treasure? Delusions of *National Geographic,* eBay, and Early Retirement

Have you been threatening to have a yard sale as soon as the weather clears up or warms up or cools off? Or as soon as you get some time off? Perhaps you now have some newly organized additions to your "saleable" items that you've culled from your reorganization process.

Even so, the notion that you're sitting on a gold mine is probably exaggerated. No doubt with good used merchandise you can certainly make a weekend sale worth your time. It's unlikely, however, that you'll become wealthy. People don't often go to garage sales looking to spend hundreds of dollars, and any single item worth serious bucks is probably better off sold through an online or private auction, or a bulletin-board-posting site, such as Craigslist. And while there are people who collect anything—witness Beanie Babies, celebrity trash, and lawn gnomes—it again seems unlikely that the *National Geographics* you're stockpiling in the basement are going to put anyone through college, even a community college.

So while garage/yard/tag sales can be a lot of fun and a great way to interact with your neighbors as well as strangers, they can also be a lot of work. If you're really serious about having the sale, you must commit to a date or a series of dates and put them on the calendar. Once that's done, there are several websites that will walk you through the entire process of organizing a garage sale, so I won't detail that here. Suffice it to say, I hope we don't find the same pile of stuff still lying around six months from now.

If you can't get it together to have a yard or garage sale, it's unlikely you'll get it together to sell things on eBay or other online auction houses. If a tag sale seems labor-intensive and unappealing, online auctions will feel like climbing Mount Everest. Fortunately, there are more and more drop-off places springing up where someone else will do the selling for you. These folks keep a percentage (typically 50 percent) of what they bring in, plus you pay the cost of the listing. Even so, you'll be ahead of where you would be with everything still lying around your basement. Don't be penny-wise and pound-foolish about this one.

I've done plenty of online auctions, and it's time-consuming answering e-mails, packing things, and running to UPS or the post office. Be realistic about how much something is worth and how much time you want to spend trying to turn it into cash. It may well be worth dropping a carload of stuff off and opening the mailbox in a month or two to find a check. Rather than lamenting the exorbitant charges, be grateful for your newfound cash and the empty space where a load of stuff had been for years.

The Thrift-Store Box Is Not a Grab Bag

Regardless of whether you are planning a yard sale or not, you should establish a box or tub that becomes the thrift-store box. And this container should be easy to get to and clearly marked for everyone in the house to find. I suggest that anytime you come across something you're finished with, whether it's an article of clothing that doesn't fit or upgraded technology (as long as the older item still works properly) or a book you don't feel compelled to keep, these things should find their way into the thrift-store box.

I would also suggest that, as the title suggests, we do not view this as an ongoing grab bag of surprises and treats. With the exception of small children, who may mistakenly deposit something you would not want donated to charity, at least not yet, once something has made it into the tub, it should remain there until it is transported to the appropriate charity. We should be able to trust our housemates to determine for themselves when and how they are finished with their possessions. And rather than becoming bitter that they chose to give their old iPod away rather than offer it to you, celebrate their sense of generosity and thoughtfulness for those who are less fortunate. Of course, if you find that they've mistakenly tossed *your* iPod into the box, by all means rescue it!

Maintaining the System

The best and most reliable way to maintain these spaces in their current orderly state is twofold. Now that everything clearly has a home, make sure whenever you take something out of its home, you return it to its home when you're finished. And second, create an organizing schedule. If everyone participates in using and returning individual items to where they came from, you should never have to undertake a project on the scale of the one you just did. But no one or no system is perfect. So put a quarterly or biannual garage-, attic-, and/or basement-tweaking day on your calendar—because we also know that if it doesn't actually make it onto your calendar, it's unlikely to happen. If you live with other people, make sure it ends up on their calendars as well. Schedule the day to coincide with a change in the season, and you can combine swapping out seasonal items with cleaning the spaces as well. That way, it will seem less unpleasant and you'll have the added bonus of getting two necessary chores out of the way at the same time.

7 Car

If all the cars in the United States were placed end to end, it would probably be Labor Day weekend.

DOUG LARSON

If GM had kept up with technology like the computer industry has, we'd all be driving $25 cars that got 1,000 MPG.

BILL GATES

n the last chapter we talked about the car's home, the garage. Now we're turning our attention to the car itself.

Urban and suburban sprawl, shuttling the kids around, getting to mega-malls on the outskirts of town—these are but a few of the reasons we spend so much time in our cars. We commute for work, for play, to visit family and friends—if you do not live in a small town or within a large centralized urban area like New York where walking, biking, or public transportation are viable options, chances are you are spending time, considerable time, in a private vehicle.

For those people who drive to work in the United States, the nationwide average commuting time is now 48.6 minutes each day. That means that the average American now spends more than 210 hours a year commuting to work, according to the U.S. Census Bureau. Think about it—that's more than five full workweeks a year, just getting to work. I'm already exhausted typing it, let alone living it.

Wherever you live, if getting to and from work means driving a car, you're in that car for a while. Add into the mix that even the biggest vehicle (a Hummer, 87 cubic feet) is probably still smaller than most people's homes (3,200 cubic feet). So managing this limited space is even more challenging in some ways than tackling clutter in the home.

In such a small space, it would certainly make driving easier and more pleasant not to be wrestling with empty beverage containers, crumpled cigarette packs, old newspapers, and other effluvia as you're listening to a self-help tape, CD, or podcast, singing along with your favorite radio station, or trying to manage any number of children strapped into car seats, with or without tears, shouting, or flying food.

What We're Going to Cover in This Chapter

- What a Car Is and Isn't
- One Home for Everything and Like with Like (on Wheels!)
- What Belongs in a Car and What Doesn't
- Organizing the Car
- Categories and Locations in the Car
- Maintaining Order on Four Wheels
- Dead or Mortally Wounded Autos . . . and Their Final Destination (Which Isn't Your Front Lawn)
- Procrastinated Repairs, or Driving on Borrowed Time
- License and Registration, Please
- Road Trips
- Checklist Before a Trip

What a Car Is and Isn't

Automobile (noun):
A self-propelled passenger vehicle that usually has four wheels and an internal combustion engine, used for land transport

So that's what your car is.

Your car is not a rolling file cabinet, portable closet, phone booth, library, hobby center, "chick" or "dude" magnet, snack shop, head shop, or vanity or cosmetics counter in a department store—it's a vehicle used for land transport. Driving is a privilege and comes with rights and responsibilities. We'll get deeper into what should *not* be happening in your car a little further on.

If you consider your car to be an extension of yourself, meaning its purpose beyond transportation is to signify to others something about your personality, status, or rank, does that carry over to the car's contents?

- Do you consider your car to be an extension of your handbag, knapsack, or briefcase? Or your office?
- Are there schoolbooks or library books lying on the floor or seats?
- Do you carry work documents, brochures, etc., on the seats and/or in the trunk—not just when you're on your way to a particular meeting, but always, "just in case"?
- Do you have cosmetics stuffed into the glove compartment or between the seat cushions?
- Have you ever not offered a ride to someone because of the clutter in your car?
- Have you ever parked farther away from your destination than necessary to avoid having people see you exiting your car? Do you have blackout windows?

If you do not have blackout windows, any person passing your car on the street or in a parking lot can see into your car and assess its current state. Your secret, therefore, is not so secret. The solution is not to race out and *get* blackout film applied to your car windows. The solution is to clean out your car once and for all, and to neatly reassemble any necessary contents in a systematic way that allows you to find exactly what you are looking for in thirty seconds or less.

I approach organizing cars in two ways, which are *not* mutually exclusive. The car is a machine, and as such needs to be cared for and maintained in the ways that all machines need care and maintenance. I also think of cars as mini-rooms on wheels with specific areas of focus and function—this helps to keep the car organized and tidy.

One Home for Everything and Like with Like (on Wheels!)

As I mentioned above, particularly with limited space, applying these two principles will ensure your success when getting and keeping your car organized. Look for and gather together like items and assign each of these groupings a home. Use frequency of use and ease of access to guide you in selecting each home.

What Belongs in a Car and What Doesn't

The following are a series of checklists of things you may find in your car. Use these lists to identify what you currently have in your car. At the end of each list there are blank spaces for you to add additional items you also currently carry in your car.

APPROPRIATE CONTENTS

Emergency Needs

- ☐ Blanket (or two)
- ☐ Bottle of water (or two)
- ☐ Can of Fix-A-Flat or other aerosol tire inflation preparation
- ☐ Cigarette lighter
- ☐ Disposable camera
- ☐ Emergency cash (ideally enough for a tank of gas, a hotel room for a night, a meal, and towing)

- ☐ Fire extinguisher
- ☐ First-aid kit (a premade or homemade kit, including: Band-Aids, gauze, a tension bandage with clips and safety pins, rubbing alcohol, sunscreen, bug spray, and antiseptic cleanser)
- ☐ Flashlight
- ☐ Flares
- ☐ Fluorescent safety vest
- ☐ Hammer escape tool
- ☐ Help sign
- ☐ Jack
- ☐ Jumper cables
- ☐ Motor oil
- ☐ Reflective signs/triangles/tape
- ☐ Rubber mallet
- ☐ Spare tire (properly inflated)
- ☐ Tire iron
- ☐ _____
- ☐ _____
- ☐ _____

Maintenance

- ☐ Clear plastic folder or envelope containing copies of maintenance and warranty receipts and the cheat sheet you'll find at the end of the chapter.
- ☐ Duct tape
- ☐ Owner's manual
- ☐ Rope
- ☐ Spare fuses
- ☐ Tire pressure gauge
- ☐ Toolbox
- ☐ WD-40 or other mechanical lubricant
- ☐ Work gloves

☐ _____

☐ _____

☐ _____

Travel and Comfort Aids

☐ Adhesive Velcro strips

☐ Atlas (current, since roads are constantly being repaired, updated, or closed)

☐ Bluetooth or other hands-free device and charger

☐ Bottle of water (or two)

☐ Bungee cords

☐ Camping gear (if you camp frequently)

☐ CDs, DVDs, cassette tapes

☐ Cooler or other insulated container for groceries requiring refrigeration

- ☐ Coupons (inside a pocket, pouch, or envelope, for places you *only* drive to)
- ☐ Cradle for mobile phone and/or iPod
- ☐ EZ Pass or other toll-road transponder
- ☐ Garage door opener
- ☐ GPS device and power source
- ☐ iPod converter
- ☐ Maps (current, and all stored inside a pouch, clear plastic envelope, or folder)
- ☐ Medium-sized tote or shopping bag (or two)
- ☐ Mobile phone and charger
- ☐ Napkins/tissues
- ☐ Old towel (or two)
- ☐ Over-the-seat pocket organizers
- ☐ Pad of paper
- ☐ Parking permits, as needed
- ☐ Pen or pencil
- ☐ Sporting gear (if you are in a league or play weekly)

Notable Note

Anytime you have repairs done that carry a guarantee, make sure that you keep the receipt and any printed warranty papers you receive. These should be stored in a clear envelope inside your glove compartment.

You may also keep a copy of these receipts and warranties in your home filing system, and if you are prone to misplace things, backup copies at home are a good idea. The key, however, is to have a copy with you should your car break down while on the road—this ensures that any work covered by the warranty will be honored with few questions or fuss. While dealing with the inconvenience of an interrupted trip, you don't also want to deal with less-than-helpful staff trying to find proof or documentation of your claim to warranted coverage.

- ☐ Trash bags
- ☐ Tubs, bins, plastic crates, or laundry basket
- ☐ Umbrella
- ☐ Wet naps/baby wipes
- ☐ Ziplock bags (gallon, quart, and sandwich sizes)

WINTER

- ☐ Bottle of water (or several)
- ☐ Candles
- ☐ Cat litter (for traction on icy or wet roads)
- ☐ Collapsible or small garden shovel
- ☐ Energy bars or candy bars
- ☐ Gloves, winter weather (one pair per typical number of passengers)
- ☐ Graphite/lock de-icer
- ☐ Hand/feet warmers
- ☐ Hats, winter weather (one per typical number of passengers)
- ☐ Ice scraper
- ☐ Waterproof matches
- ☐ Wool or sport socks

KIDS

- ☐ Books or magazines
- ☐ Diapers, etc. (if needed)
- ☐ Games/puzzles/distractions
- ☐ More water
- ☐ MP3, cassette, or CD player; headphones; batteries; and DVDs, CDs, or tapes of movies, music, and stories
- ☐ Napkins or wet naps
- ☐ Snacks that don't spoil

Work Product

These are any brochures or other printed material, samples, and displays that you regularly use for your current work. What this isn't is the box of stuff you emptied from your desk at your last job that's never left your trunk.

☐ _____

☐ _____

☐ _____

INAPPROPRIATE CONTENTS

- Alcohol opened and being consumed while driving
- Broken machinery
- Broken tools
- Dry cleaning or laundry, unless you are on your way to drop it off or have just picked it up
- Illegal drugs of any kind
- Old beverage containers, with or without beverages still inside
- Old food containers, with or without food inside
- Overdue library books, unless you are currently driving to return them
- Returnable items, destined for their original home "someday" but not today
- Thrift-store items to be dropped off, unless you are on your way to drop them off
- Trash of any kind

A FEW WORDS ABOUT TRASH

If you have purchased food from a convenience store or fast-food restaurant, you were probably handed that food in a bag of some kind. A simple way to corral food trash in the car is simply to put the food wrappers, napkins, etc., back *into* the bag they came in when you are finished eating. Feel free to also add any other trash you find lying around the car. The next time you exit the car, take the bag with you and deposit it in the first trash receptacle you see. No more trash in the car.

Trash is never thrown out of a car window onto the side of the road. If one lives in a home where trash is lying about, you may view the world outside your home as an extension of your home, and therefore feel comfortable littering. You would be mistaken.

We all share the world outside our homes, and as such it is common courtesy to transport any food or gum wrappers, popsicle sticks, cigarette butts, empty packages, or bottles or cans to the nearest receptacle and deposit trash there instead. Remember, you or your friends are not lost and leaving a trail of trash behind you to help you find your way home (like Hansel and Gretel). If you're littering, you're merely unconscious and need to wake up. Please do so.

Organizing the Car

If you are doing this alone, then an area near your home (driveway, parking lot, or at the curb) is the best place to do this. If you have someone with you who can watch your stuff for you, a car wash is another excellent place to empty your car and get it organized. That way, you can run it through the wash while the other person keeps an eye on your belongings. A mild sunny day that is not too windy is your best choice for this activity—you don't want the weather to interrupt your process once you begin.

STEP ONE: EMPTY THE CAR OF ITS CONTENTS

Things you'll need for this task:

- Bins/tubs (8)
- Bucket of soapy water or other cleanser, rags, sponges, or cloth
- Camera
- Clear 9"x12" envelopes or pocket folders
- Rags

- Tarp
- Trash bag (or several)
- Vacuum cleaner
- Ziplock bags

By now, this should be familiar, if not easy. You'll want to have all the items listed above on hand before you begin this process. If you don't have them assembled, put down the book and go get them—we don't want to interrupt the flow because of a missing component.

Great. Now open the tarp and spread it out. Open a trash bag and set it aside.

Before you remove anything, take a few photos to document the current state of your car. Open the trunk as well, if there's chaos in there.

Now begin removing everything that isn't actually a part of the car and lay it all out on the tarp to examine. Avoid placing things in piles or clumps or stacks for now. When we begin sorting and arranging, that's when grouping Like with Like will be used. Throw away any trash as you remove it from the car—trash is the one thing we don't need to sort through. If you need a refresher on what exactly trash is, see the definition below.

An unwanted or undesired material or substance; broken, discarded, or worthless things. It is also referred to as rubbish, waste, garbage, or junk, depending on the type of material and regional terminology.

Any items that you find that originated in your home (coffee mugs, Thermoses, reusable food storage containers) should be set inside a bin or tub to return to your home.

Be sure to empty out:

- Any roof compartments
- Ashtrays
- Behind the visors
- Cubbies

- Cup holders
- Door pockets
- Glove compartment
- Rear cargo areas
- Rear-of-seat pockets
- Trunk
- Under the seats

Now would be an excellent time to wash and vacuum the interior and possibly the exterior of your car. Clean all the interior surfaces—vacuum between all the seats and their backs, between cushions, and under every seat. Remove, shake out, and vacuum all floor mats. Fold down any foldable seats to get deeper into seldom-reached areas. Wipe down the dashboard and inside any cubbies and compartments; wipe down all the doors and clean the windows. When that is done, we'll begin the sorting.

STEP TWO: SORT

These are the categories you're going to sort everything into:

Emergency Needs
Maintenance
Travel and Comfort Aids
   Winter
   Kids
Work Product
Going Away—Keep
Going Away—Away

Refer to the lists above in the section What Belongs in a Car and What Doesn't for examples of which items and their siblings belong in which category. Remember Like with Like, so that all DVDs and CDs end up together, all tools together, all service and repair receipts together, all maps together, etc.

The Going Away category has two parts: Keep is for anything that still has a purpose but doesn't belong in your car. And Away is for things that still have a purpose but no longer belong in your life. Items in Keep will end up someplace in your home or your garage, and Away things will end up at a thrift store or shelter, ready to become a part of someone else's life.

Notable Note

Maps need to be checked for date and accuracy. If you are holding on to maps from a road trip several years ago "just in case" you happen to return there, think about how often the roads where you live change. If any map is more that two years old, chances are that enough changes have taken place to render that map obsolete. Recycle it.

The same holds true for atlases and GPS systems. While I'm sure that a certain amount of motivation to print new atlases or update software each year is based on profit, a certain amount of motivation is also based on providing people with accurate information. Check out the latest editions of atlases annually to see if they indicate the amount of new information they contain. Likewise, visit the online site for your GPS system to check for crucial updates there as well.

Just like with trash before, anything that can easily be culled from the former contents of your car at this time should be. If you see that you have four flashlights, it may be simple to test them all, find whichever ones work, choose the best one, and set the other three aside. For anything that you need to think about, it's fine right now to just group Like with Like and wait for the next section to begin whittling down the number of things. It will become apparent soon enough that you have things you can let go of if you have seventy-five CDs in your car and a half-dozen Welcome Center maps of Maryland.

STEP THREE: PURGE

As you did for your kitchen, think about how you use your car.

- Do you work from it—are you a salesperson, regional rep, or real-estate agent?
- Do you shuttle kids all day in it?
- Do you volunteer for Meals on Wheels or use it for other kinds of deliveries?
- What are you regularly reaching for and not being able to put your hands on—mobile phone, CDs, pen and paper?

Touch everything. This physical contact is important, as it shifts your relationship from hypothetical to actual. This is not a step to sidestep. If you make yourself touch each item as you're going through them, you will be clearer as you determine what is necessary to have with you in your car versus what you think may be fun or useful to "someday" have in your car.

Things that are obsolete or outdated can leave. If you have work product in the car, realistically assess if you have enough for the next few weeks or the next few years. How often do you hand out brochures? How many lawn signs do you need to have with you right now? If you're not even working today, perhaps those lawn signs can live in the garage until you *actually* need them?

Recognize the faulty logic in thinking that the more things that surround you, the better prepared you are for anything, should a situation suddenly come up. Unless you literally live in your car, you can't be in need of that much stuff for a day's outing. When taking a serious road trip, you would, of course, be packing things specifically for that trip. For day trips around town, you don't need a wilderness survival kit at your fingertips.

Pay attention to multiples of the same item—a bottle of water is a welcome addition to your car. Random half-empty bottles, less so. Likewise, multiple bungee cords, screwdrivers, etc.—if they aren't unique in size or shape, consider how many are necessary. And if you struggle with how to answer that question, I'll give you the answer: one. These items already are "spares"—you don't need spares of spares.

Anything that could still work but doesn't, such as flashlights missing batteries or a DVD player without a power adapter, can be set aside to either cure what needs curing or just let go of.

When purging, if you find yourself getting stuck or having conversations with yourself about how useful something might be "someday," then what you're struggling with does not belong in your car. This kind of debate is easily solved by using the junior version of "If your house was on fire, what would you grab?" Ask yourself, "When was the last time I used this?" If the answer is either more than six months ago or never, it doesn't go back into the car—the welcome exceptions to this are, of course, emergency supplies and the first-aid kit. I hope you'll never need either, but you should always have both.

Whenever you have to spend time either debating or convincing yourself of something's ultimate usefulness, pay attention. Whether it's another abs exerciser or a third pair of spare sunglasses, if you have to really search for the answer to the above question, you already have your answer. It may not be the answer you want to hear, but it's there, and it's speaking as loudly and as clearly as it can. And what it's saying is "Let me go."

Once you've set aside everything that doesn't need to be in your car, do not revisit those items. Don't second-guess yourself. Let them be, and turn your attention to organizing the remaining items so you'll be able to find them whenever you need or want them.

STEP FOUR: ORGANIZE EVERYTHING THAT REMAINS

Now that we have our piles of Like with Like items, it's time to corral them. Enter the bins, tubs, or crates. If you find all the containers you've brought are too large, load things into them anyway. This will give you the best understanding of what size container to replace it with. Then you can either find that container inside your home or head to a store to purchase the right size containers for what you'll be carrying around in your car.

Unfortunately, this works the opposite way as well. If, overly optimistically, you have brought a series of shoe boxes to this party and everything requires a laundry basket, you simply have too much stuff. Return to step three above and take another pass through your things.

Categories and Locations in the Car

Emergency Needs—trunk (exception: first-aid kit—under front passenger seat)

Maintenance—trunk (exception: owner's manual; envelope with warranties, receipts, cheat sheet—glove compartment)

Travel and Comfort Aids Inside the Car

Atlas (current)

Bluetooth or other hands-free device and charger

Bottle of water (or two)

CDs/DVDs/cassette tapes

Coupons (inside a pocket, pouch, or envelope, for places you *only* drive to)

Cradle for mobile phone and/or iPod

EZ Pass or other toll-road transponder—on the windshield, behind the rearview mirror

Garage door openers—on the driver's visor or in a ceiling compartment designed specifically for them

GPS device and power source

iPod converter

Maps (current, all stored inside a pouch, clear plastic envelope, or folder)—inside side pocket of passenger's door

Mobile phone and charger

Napkins/tissues

Over-the-seat pocket organizers

Pad of paper

Parking permits, as needed

Pen or pencil

Permanent marker

Trash bags

Umbrella

Wet naps/baby wipes

Travel and Comfort Aids Inside the Trunk

Bungee cords

Camping gear (if you camp frequently)

Cooler or other insulated container for groceries requiring refrigeration

Medium-sized tote or shopping bag (or two)

Old towel (or two)

Resealable zip bags (gallon, quart, and sandwich sizes)

Sporting gear (if you are in a league or play weekly)

Tubs, bins, plastic crates, or laundry basket

Winter—trunk (for the duration of the cold-weather season where you live)

Kids—inside car, easily accessible—either in a pocket organizer that fits over the back of your front seat or in a bin on the floor in front of the child—somewhere the child could get to quickly and without assistance.

Work Product—inside trunk, unless you are en route to a business meeting

Maintaining Order on Four Wheels

Now that the car is clean and organized, how will you keep it that way? The best principle for this is "bring something in, take something out." If you bring a new CD (or three) into the car, look through the discs already in the car and find others to swap them for. Keep a trash bag or small container handy, and use it rather than tossing trash on the floor or on the seat next to you.

All people who use or ride in the car are also to be responsible for removing what they bring into the car. If they fail to do so, they should know that items left behind will be considered abandoned and discarded. These kinds of rules take a bit of time to establish, so once the rule is put in place, allow two weeks for learning and complying. After two weeks, no one can act surprised when they find you've kept your word. Make it a habit to empty the car immediately when returning home from a sporting event or other activity involving gear, and after the grumbling dies down, it will soon become second nature.

Don't allow items to pile up. Make a daily or weekly sweep through the car, searching for items out of their bins or needing to be returned to the house. Empty the trash bag or can frequently. When stopping for gas, gather the trash and toss it. Almost any store or mall you'll drive to also has trash receptacles outside—use them. Likewise, the trash can in or near your house: get into the habit of removing the trash when exiting the car at the end of the day. It's that much nicer to get into the car the next morning not faced with yesterday's or last week's garbage.

Plan a regular washing schedule. Kids still like the opportunity to get wet and play with hoses, so make it a family affair. You could add the incentive of paying them a bonus equivalent to the cost of a drive-through car wash if enthusiasm seems lacking. If the idea of washing your car yourself is unappealing for any reason, take the car to the local car wash—just make sure you've organized your things first, as the workers at mine seldom seem interested in moving anything out of their way to vacuum beneath or around any obstacles.

Dead or Mortally Wounded Autos . . .
and Their Final Destination
(Which Isn't Your Front Lawn)

There are any number of local charities that seem ready and willing to take dead or dying cars off people's hands. There are also junkyards and auto-parts places that may be willing to buy or haul your car away for parts. In either case, if a car is no longer roadworthy or is beyond repair, don't clutter your yard or your neighborhood with dead vehicles. Pick up the phone and have it removed.

Procrastinated Repairs, or
Driving on Borrowed Time

Besides keeping your car clean and neat, you'll also want to keep it running smoothly and efficiently, and therefore safely. In your day planner or on your electronic calendar, enter the date of the most recent services performed to your car. While many service providers now place a little plastic reminder in the far-upper-left corner of the windshield as a reminder for your next oil change, other services can easily be overlooked until it's too late.

The time to respond to warning lights is when they first go on, not weeks later.

When I was seventeen, I was driving a Plymouth Duster I got from my mom. It was a little top-heavy, as Dusters were, but it was a neat and clean car in excellent working condition. The oil light went on one afternoon on my way home from school. Between my ignorance and disinterest, I saw that light every time I started the car and drove somewhere. I figured I had plenty of time and would eventually "get around to it." I was a high-school student, quite busy with whatever I was doing—too busy certainly to pick up a quart of oil. Fast forward to an early evening several months later. Still that lit-up oil light . . .

I'm driving my friend Ann Ritchie and myself down to Cobo Hall to see Rod Stewart in concert. We were very excited, WRIF was playing back-to-back-to-back Rod Stewart songs, even old Faces songs, and we were having a great time anticipating the show. About seven miles from the exit of the expressway, there was a sudden loud bang and the car shut down. I managed to pull us over to the side of the expressway out of the way of traffic and open the hood. Lots of black smoke. Bewildering. What could possibly be the problem?

The state police pulled up soon, and after explaining what had happened and where we were heading, in a stroke of luck they decided to drive us down to Cobo Hall so we could make the show. And it was amazing. Rod Stewart was in rare form and good voice . . . for Rod Stewart. We had a great time. Of course, my father had to come down there at eleven p.m. to collect us. That was less of a good time.

The next day the car was towed to a mechanic friend of my dad's, who examined the car and determined that a piston rod had been blown through the engine block of the car. Cause: insufficient oil. The car was totaled. The cost of replacing the engine was more than I could afford or my father was interested in spending. As the saying goes, "for the want of a nail," or in my case, for the want of a quart of oil. A painful and costly lesson learned.

License and Registration, Please

As mentioned earlier, always have the registration and insurance card with you when driving your car. And just like noting due dates for service on your calendar, it's a good idea to also add reminders to your calendar for the renewal dates for your vehicle's inspection and registration. I like to place these reminders four to six weeks prior to the actual expiration date, allowing ample time for me to take the car in and receive the new materials back in the mail.

In some states, the registration and inspection run concurrently, according to month—however, a vehicle's registration is renewed for multiples of years, whereas the inspection is due each year. Check with your local DMV or Secretary of State's office to avoid a ticket for lapsed inspection because you assumed that everything renews at the same time.

Road Trips

Pack the night before any road trips, and stack everything by the door you'll exit your home through. That way, you'll never walk out of the house without everything you planned to take with you.

Check traffic and weather reports before you depart, and print any maps or directions you'll need and keep them handy. Review your emergency kit and make sure everything is fully stocked and up-to-date. Make any important phone calls *before* you get in your car to avoid unnecessary phone calls while driving.

Checklist Before a Trip

A week before your trip, use this checklist to make sure everything is in good working order and get any necessary repairs done at that time. You don't want a needed repair to delay your departure.

- ☐ Check wiper blades.
- ☐ Check the windshield-washing reservoir—fill as needed.
- ☐ Check all lights—headlights, bright lights, and fog lights.
- ☐ Check all signal indicators—turn signal, and brake and emergency flashers.
- ☐ Check the radiator for any visible leaks.
- ☐ Check the oil—is the reservoir full, and is the oil clean? Check the oil when the car is off and cold.
- ☐ Check the level of antifreeze, and make sure the radiator cap's seal is in good shape and not worn.

☐ Check all belts and hoses for proper tension and wear.

☐ Check your brakes. If they have been making noises or have been spongy and not responsive, have these looked at *prior* to leaving on a trip.

☐ Check tires for proper pressure. Always check tire pressure when the tires are cold.

☐ Do not overfill the car so much that you can no longer see out the rear window.

Have a safe trip!

AUTOMOBILE FACTS AND FIGURES (CHEAT SHEET)

Make, year, and model of auto: _____

VIN number: _____

Tire size: _____   Tire inflation: _____

Engine size: _____

Oil weight and type (e.g. 10W30, synthetic):_____

_____

Emergency contact numbers:

Name: _____   Home number: _____

Relationship: _____

Work number: _____   Mobile number: _____

Name: _____   Home number: _____

Relationship: _____

Work number: _____   Mobile number: _____

Doctor (primary care or family physician):

Name: _____   Home number: _____

Work number: _____   Mobile number: _____

Insurance company and policy number:

_____

Insurance claims: _____

Roadside assistance: _____

Registration expires on: _____/_____/_____

Annual inspection due by: _____/_____/_____

Oil changed on: _____/_____/_____, _____ miles

Air filter changed on: _____/_____/_____, _____ miles

Tires rotated on: _____/_____/_____, _____ miles

Battery replaced on: _____/_____/_____, _____ miles

Mementos • Sentimental Objects • Gifts • Collections

Souvenirs are perishable; fortunately, memories are not.

SUSAN SPANO

Sentimentality—that's what we call the sentiment we don't share.

GRAHAM GREENE

Most of those who make collections . . . are like men eating cherries or oysters: they choose out the best at first, and end by eating all.

NICOLAS CHAMFORT

I n this chapter we turn our attention to conceptual clutter as opposed to location-specific clutter. The subjects of this chapter—mementos, sentimental objects, gifts, and collections (and by extension, decor)—are the kinds of things you may find all over your home. When on display, they are a matter of taste. When lying in piles, unsorted, underfoot, or in the way, they become clutter. Learn to tell the difference and to honor one and safely store or discard the other.

What We're Going to Cover in This Chapter

☐ Mementos, Sentimental Objects, Gifts, and Collections: What They Are and What They Aren't

- ☐ One Home for Everything and Like with Like
- ☐ Sentimentaland
- ☐ If You Visit It, You Will Bring Me Home (Mementos of Travel), Part I
- ☐ Departed Relatives and Friends, from Houston to Heaven, Part III
- ☐ Good Gifts, Bad Gifts
- ☐ I Am My Own Museum
- ☐ Collections—Cool or Crazy?
- ☐ Will You Hate Me if I Get Rid Of . . . ?
- ☐ This Might Be Worth a Fortune—*Antiques Roadshow* or Thrift Store?
- ☐ Dry Storage vs. Wet Storage (Reminder)
- ☐ Approaching Sorting, and How to Sort
- ☐ Actually Sorting
- ☐ Containerizing the Objects
- ☐ The Importance of Labels—How, Why, and Where
- ☐ Organizing the Storage
- ☐ Maintaining the System

Things You Will Need for the Work in This Chapter

- Trash bags
- Timer or stopwatch
- Eight tarps or blankets for sorting items into categories
- Dust cloths
- Acid-free paper
- Noninvasive adhesives (tapes, glues, etc.)
- Tubs, containers, or baskets to corral and contain like things
- Label maker, or labels and a fine-point marker

Mementos, Sentimental Objects, Gifts, and Collections: What They Are and What They Aren't

MEMENTOS

Memento (noun):
An object or item that serves to remind one of a person, past event, etc.; keepsake; souvenir.

This could be just about anything, from a Roman Catholic relic to an old soda-pop cap, and everything in between. The idea here is to discriminate, in the best sense. In sorting through mementos, I suggest you find a quiet place where you will not be disturbed as you examine them. Set aside a comfortable length of time, between thirty minutes and three hours. People sometimes question the wide parameters of time allotted, and this is my reply: Less than thirty minutes is not enough time to settle down and dig in. And more than three hours and one loses focus. Beyond that, if one day you have two hours and feel you can sit still that long and look through things and make thorough and thoughtful decisions, then go for it. If on another day, forty-five minutes is all you can spare, that will work, too. The key is to remain sharp, undistracted, and productive for the entire allotted time.

So establish the amount of time that you will dedicate to sorting for your first session. Set your timer. Whatever you determine that to be, even if you find yourself on a roll, when the timer goes off, finish the last piece, clump, pile, or area you're working through and set the rest aside for the next time. It's better to be pleasantly surprised and looking forward to the sorting than cranky and exhausted and watching the clock.

We don't want to stray into reminiscing, which is dangerous territory when sorting. A certain amount of reverie is acceptable and expected when handling mementos. Still, the time to linger is on the other side of the sorting process.

Sitting still and reviewing these items, really imagine yourself going through this tub in another twenty years. What do you think you'll want to be handling at that time? Old chewing gum (really, food in any form) is inappropriate as a souvenir. Ditto for dirty clothing; while the smell of someone in or on a worn garment may seem evocative today, in twenty years their sweet aroma will turn sour—not to mention how body oils and perspiration accelerate the discoloration and deterioration of most fabrics.

SENTIMENTAL OBJECTS

Sentimental (adjective):
Having or showing tender, gentle, or delicate feelings, as in aesthetic expression; having or showing such feelings in an excessive, superficial, or maudlin way.

Here we have a definition illustrating the best sense of sentiment. We also have a cautionary tale of what sentiment can morph into when indulged in, in the worst ways. I encourage clients to retain sentimental objects and mementos in a focused and disciplined way—almost as if distilling the memory or experience and charging the item with clear intention. As in cooking, we work to reduce the experience, but here not with steady heat but with steady focus, so that the objects selected to hold the memory are saturated and rich with the experience and memory, rather than having the experience and memory thinly spread out over many random or unspecific objects.

At the same time, I think it is a mistake to fetishize any object, elevating it above the actual memory. Too often we charge the object with so much responsibility for containing complex and extended memories that the object's significance becomes distorted and our ability to actually remember events and people fades without the object present. As we will see, any object may fail or break apart or disappear at any time, and it would be a sadness for the memory or memories to depart along with said object.

I strongly suggest that any item that evokes maudlin feelings or hurtful memories be discarded. Promptly. There's no need to sustain that form of grief.

GIFTS

Gift (noun):
Something given voluntarily without payment in return, as to show favor toward someone, honor an occasion, or make a gesture of assistance.

I do not believe in obligatory gift giving—it contradicts the very definition of a gift. Likewise, I strongly believe that nothing freely given is ever meant to be a burden. If it is meant to be a saddle or an imposition in its offering, I suggest, whenever possible, that you decline the offer. If that seems not possible, for any number of reasons, which we'll discuss further on in the chapter, release the "gift" as soon as possible. It may be given to someone else who has no relationship with the intended imposition, or donated to a local charity, where the sale or use of the object will be free of any negative associations.

COLLECTIONS AND DECOR

Collection (noun):
Something that is collected; a group of objects or an amount of material accumulated in one location, especially for some purpose or as a result of some process: a stamp collection; a collection of books on Lewis and Clark.

Decor (noun):
Decoration consisting of the layout and furnishings of a livable interior.

They say that beauty is in the eye of the beholder. Nowhere is this more evident than in one's taste in decor. I am not a big fan of collections of objects as decor. I think they seldom reflect a strong curatorial vision and typically devolve into clutter . . . as a rule. I believe there are exceptions to all rules, this one included, and the best examples of standing exceptions to this rule include most museums and libraries, where collections are both actively curated and consistently revolving. We'll explore both of these concepts as they relate to collections later in the chapter.

One Home for Everything and Like with Like

These two principles are your foundation for all organizing, particularly with sentimental objects and mementos. I cannot stress this enough. These principles should be rigorously and consistently employed, not saved for special occasions. One Home for Everything and Like with Like ensure that when you need to find something, anything, you have to look in only one place, and there it will be.

Sentimentaland

In previous chapters, we've created the virtual place Sentimentaland, which exists in our imaginations as well as in a number of tubs and bins. Here, again, is the definition:

> Sentimentaland, as its name suggests, is a mythical land defined by clear plastic tubs containing objects of dubious monetary value but, as the commercial says, ultimately "priceless."

As we've worked through other areas, we've uncovered random things that we determined ultimately belonged in Sentimentaland. Now, with our focus directed specifically on mementos and sentimental objects, Sentimentaland is about to become far more populated. It's possible that you'll need more than one container for Sentimentaland before you're done with your entire house and this chapter. That's okay. The containers just all need to live together, and we need to ensure that their contents are consistent. Never mix general items seeking a home with meaningful touchstones of life's important moments. Like with Like!

The ultimate location of these containers that make up Sentimentaland is open to some negotiation. They may reside in a closet, the basement or attic, under the stairs . . . anywhere you have adequate room, provided that that place is someplace climate-controlled. Welcome to Sentimentaland—like everything in Goldilocks's world, we want to avoid anything too hot or too cold; we want the temperature to be "just right."

While Sentimentaland is a country without borders, it does have a few laws that are useful to obey. There are only two of them, so remaining law-abiding should not be too challenging.

SENTIMENTALAND LAWS

Like with Like. You see, it's everywhere! Here it means, for example, that all baby clothes and other childhood artifacts reside together. If you still retain your own baby clothes in addition to the clothes of your children, they should be further subdivided by child or generation. Chances are that your baby clothes are more fragile than your children's, due to sheer longevity. What I typically suggest is that each child's objects be given their own container, so that childhood art, report cards, crib blankets, stuffed animals, and the like can all remain together, and that each child's totems are not commingled, requiring later sorting. Why put off until tomorrow what you can do today? Think of these as time capsules carefully and lovingly curated by you for either yourself, your children, or both.

When everything is precious, nothing is precious. In curating these items, you must select what will ultimately be kept. It is at once highly personal and subjective, and at the same time, an easy reflection of your memory and history. You will certainly remember which outfits most amused you and tormented your child. Likewise, the artwork that heralded nascent genius versus the scribbling that expressed core rage at being cut off from the stash of juice boxes.

Upon your shoulders rests the responsibility for choosing what is significant and what is either not significant or perhaps even trash. Relax, though. It isn't that difficult. When actually sorting through things, you'll be amazed at how the important totems will assert themselves. If years later, you can still giggle at a memory simply by handling a tiny shirt or pair of shorts, you'll have your touchstone. You really only have to stay present and pay attention. Like most things, showing up is the most important piece of the work.

Remembering that *you cannot keep everything* will assist you in making strong and confident choices. This is mostly an exercise for you—your kids either have already rescued the things that are most important to them or will be pleasantly surprised at whatever you've kept from their childhood, since they were busy living it, and you were there to guide and witness it. Iris's story in chapter six has a few examples of this process.

Notable Note

I've talked a lot about childhood and childhood artifacts because for parents, this is often the most difficult category of objects to sift through and select from. The Sentimentaland "laws" in this chapter apply to all objects—yours as well as your children's. Old baseball cards, concert tickets and playbills, T-shirts, sports equipment, Christmas decorations, school textbooks and class notes, journals and diaries, games and toys . . . the list is seemingly infinite. Every grouping of sentimental objects could benefit from careful editing.

One of the benefits of creating these tubs is to corral and thereby preserve these items. If they remain in a jumbled heap, you would be less likely to find something if and when you wanted it, and its properly maintained condition at that time would not be assured.

If You Visit It, You Will Bring Me Home (Mementos of Travel), Part I

Document the event, not the approach or preparation. Simply put, the sandwich was special, not the waxed paper or wrapper that it came in. Free maps and brochures from tourist centers are still being printed every day, so what about your trip was unique to your experience? Find that—that's the souvenir to hold on to, not the map that got you there or the envelope from the gift store that used to hold postcards but is now torn and empty. If the gift store is a place you'd like to visit again, log the address into your address book, electronic or otherwise, and note the entry so when you return to the town or city of the store, you'll remember to visit there again—then recycle the envelope.

Use this as a guide for future travel and adventures as well. Avoid the mass-produced junk hyped as souvenirs that tourists are encouraged to consume, and find the local oddities that distill your experience into something specific and meaningful for you. Did you stumble on a funky dive somewhere and decide this was the perfect place to propose marriage? That's the site of

Notable Note

I'm all for photos from trips and travels, but I also find that many people spend so much time documenting their excursions that the first time they actually experience being someplace different is when they get home and look back at photos taken and souvenirs gathered. By then, the experience is over and all you're left with are artifacts from history, albeit recent history. Put down the camera and put away the traveler's checks and explore, experience, drink up the adventure *while* having the adventure—you'll surely have more interesting stories to share when you get home than simply arranging a slide show for friends and family and trying to remember what exactly you did while away.

something special—keep the matchbook or coaster from there. A disposable paper cup or T-shirt from Euro Disney is something anyone could have brought home and probably has.

Departed Relatives and Friends, from Houston to Heaven, Part III

Now to inherited things—including broken clocks, chipped dishes, and the like. For whatever reason, however it happened, these things are now in your possession. Things you love, things you use—these are not the issue. Things you love that don't work or are broken, things you love and don't use, and things you don't love and don't use—all of these *are* the issue.

Let's start with the last one first. **Things you don't love and don't use**— let them go.

The fact that a family member once owned an object is never a good enough reason to keep anything. You are not the family archivist—if your family is that significant in historic terms, find a historian or archivist who will be able to advise you about what belongs in a museum or someplace of note. If you are not from a storied or notable family, find the family member who actually wants the responsibility or role of preserving history, and if you find that no one does, *pay attention to that.* You needn't take it on by default. That's a useless story. You're not a bad child, parent, or sibling for not wanting things that you don't like or can't use. They are only objects, even if Grandma traveled from the old country with it strapped to her back. She chose to do so for her own reasons, not to saddle you with it one hundred years later.

If it has some actual value, consider selling it on eBay or Craigslist, or through an auction house. If not, a reselling charitable organization would welcome your contribution.

Things you love and don't use. Waiting for "someday"? As mentioned in chapter six, if these items are charged with emotional tugs and memories, it's important to allow enough time to adequately go through them, whether it's one box or an entire household. Consider enlisting an impartial and disciplined friend or professional for support and guidance.

Ask yourself, "Why am I keeping things that I don't or won't use?"

Are you afraid of damaging them, thereby diminishing their value? As an example, let's look at antique sterling silverware. You always run the risk of someone cleaning them with a scrub brush and scratching the finish or mistakenly dropping a utensil down the drain and accidentally turning on the garbage disposal with the fork or spoon still inside. Things happen. If the monetary value of the silver is the most important thing to you, then perhaps you should consider selling it and using the money to buy something you wouldn't be afraid to use. Or pass it along or trade it to another family member who has something you really cherish that you would be willing to use.

Given that financial markets are unpredictable—in this example, both the antiques and the silver markets—it seems imprudent to simply sit on the silverware, hoping that it will hold its value, possibly even appreciate, and in the meantime leave it unused in a closet somewhere. There are smarter ways to handle this part of your portfolio.

Or perhaps you don't use something because you're afraid that use will speed its decay. No doubt you're right. If you use antique linens, they will eventually fall apart after many, many uses and launderings, but probably not tomorrow. Linen in particular is a remarkably strong and resilient material. Unless it's dry-rotted, in which case it's already ruined, so there's no point in saving it anyway.

Gandhi told his followers to imagine a brand-new *anything* broken and at the end of its usefulness, as this was the natural progression of its life cycle. He felt that by doing this, the preciousness of anything was dispelled, and if you were in touch with the inevitable conclusion at the outset, when that conclusion occurred, it would be welcomed and not arrive as a surprise. I agree.

Lovely things are lovely. And doing one's best to keep them that way is noble and appropriate. But denying yourself the use of lovely things to preserve them for future, perhaps unknown, generations seems sad and pointless, whatever the Patek Philippe ads say to the contrary ("You never actually own a Patek Philippe. You merely look after it for the next generation").

So if you find yourself the steward of beautiful heirlooms, I encourage you to use them. Celebrate the foresight your forebears exercised in selecting something so durable and enduring. And we can hope that in passing down these things to you, their very intention was for you to use them as well, and create another generation's memories in the process.

Things you love that don't work or are broken. Meet Laurie. And her father's broken clock. From as far back as she could remember, Laurie's dad had a small mantel clock on his desk. It took pride of place at the center of the rear edge of his desk. So whenever she would visit him in his study, the clock was there—solid, reliable, warm, and steady. Just like her dad.

It's now many years later. Laurie's father has passed away. And the clock no longer keeps time. The hands are loose and don't progress, and the internal workings are frozen. She even took the clock to several watchmakers in the hopes of having the clock restored, but each horologist confirmed that the clock was beyond repair. Laurie was disappointed and surprisingly stuck.

Laurie is a highly efficient educator and trainer, and doesn't keep broken or unusable things around her. Things are either working, being repaired, or discarded. But this was her father's clock. She couldn't get rid of it—that would be like getting rid of her dad. Not really, but that's how it felt. So the broken Dad clock sat on the credenza behind *her* desk, an unsettling and nagging presence.

VirgoMan: So, Laurie, tell me about the clock.
Laurie: It was my dad's.

And then she told me about learning to tell time on the clock, and the pipe that used to sit in a stand next to the clock, and the great conversations she would have with her father in his study, underscored by the gentle rhythmic ticking of the clock.

VM: Wow. Lots of memories.

Laurie: Yeah. That clock was always there, keeping time.

VM: Yep. It sounds even more like your dad was always there, keeping time. Steady and reliable, and now he's not around, either. Does that sound accurate?

Laurie: But it's the last thing I have of his. I can't let it go. I mean, there's a part of me that totally wants to let it go, but it feels like too much of a betrayal.

VM: I know it feels that way, but I want you to know that letting the clock go isn't the same thing as letting your dad go. Your dad is not the clock, and of course the clock is not your father. You had great times with your dad, in and out of that study. Those memories are not, *will not be,* diminished by the absence of this clock. I'd like you to consider a few things.

One, it's possible that in holding on to the clock—which if it had not been your father's would have left a long time ago—that you're actually fetishizing the clock, charging it with the responsibility of holding all your memories of your dad, and so you become afraid to let it go because then all the memories leave with it. Perhaps you can first release the clock from carrying all that weight, and that will open up opportunities to remember your dad through a variety of objects. Maybe none of them even having belonged to your dad, but all of them capable of evoking a memory through association—as in a favorite book or meal or song.

And two, an ancillary of number one above. In shifting the focus off the broken clock, take some time and reconnect with the person that you're missing, in this case your dad, and what you miss about him, what you think about when you think about him, the conversations you may still be having with him. Move back into your powerful imagination and memory to spend time with your dad, all the great times you had with him. None of those memories or images are diminished or altered by whether the clock is here or not. In fact, take it a step further and choose not to reduce them down to a broken clock. Metaphorically, something that doesn't even work. That's definitely not your dad—he's so much more; let him be more than a broken clock.

Laurie: It just bums me out that it doesn't work, that I can't get it working.

VM: I know.

Laurie: And I would have let it go if it hadn't been his.

VM: I know.

Laurie: Uucchhh. *(Pause.)* He's not the clock, is he?

VM: Nope, that's for sure. He is not the clock.

Laurie: He's not the clock. I love him, and he's not the clock. He is not the clock. *(Pause.)* Okay. Let's let it go, I'm ready, I'm done. I'm done with the clock. The clock that doesn't work. My dad is not a broken clock.

VM: Excellent. Good work, my friend. Really good. Congratulations.

If you, like Laurie, find yourself caught between remorse and release regarding a treasured object, as a step in the letting go process, consider taking a picture of the object in question. As you journey toward releasing the actual object, the photo can be a tool in softening the transition for you. You can carry or reference the photo as a touchstone and active reminder of your process. And once you do decide to let the photographed object go, you could choose to retain the photo—that way, you can still "see" the object, but it takes up a fraction of the space occupied by the original item. Do make sure the photos are in focus and well lit. And if you are inclined toward art projects or scrapbooking, the photos might even find their way into any number of collages or image assemblies.

Things you love and use. Bravo! The only issues that might arise around these items are where they live and whether they are living with their sisters and brothers. It all comes down to One Home for Everything and Like with Like.

Good Gifts, Bad Gifts

Nothing freely given is ever meant to be a burden. Gifts are: an expression of someone's appreciation, recognition of a significant event or that event's anniversary, or a token of affection. They are not offered, and should not be offered, as a punishment or a pointed reminder of what you "should" be doing or "shouldn't" be doing. Like a framed photo of someone suffering from mouth cancer given to someone who smokes—this is not a gift; this is an assault.

When these kinds of "gifts" are from a relative, a colleague, or someone you see regularly, social custom requires you to accept the gift graciously, but you are under no obligation to retain the "gift" a moment longer than absolutely necessary. Get rid of it as soon as possible. Any object that upon sight causes you pain, grief, regret, embarrassment, disappointment, or any other form of debilitating sorrow has no place in your life. There is a clear distinction between torment and the bittersweet sadness we feel when remembering certain past tender moments. That sadness is colored by the absence of a particular time or a loved one and is not the sorrow I'm describing above. One feels as if something aggressive is being visited upon you and the other occurs as a natural result of intense feelings of loss or separation.

Short of veiled criticism or pointed communication arriving in the form of a gift, let's assume that most gifts are being offered in a spirit of kindness and thoughtfulness, a desire to enhance the quality of your life, not to burden you with an unnecessary object. If any gift doesn't seem either aesthetically pleasing or practical—a brightly colored sweater and you wear only earth tones; a car radio and you don't own a car—you may pass it along. There is nothing wrong with re-gifting; just avoid embarrassment to both parties by ensuring that the re-gifting takes place beyond the extended network of the original gift giver. If there's any opportunity for recognition of the re-gifted item, you're still too close to home.

These principles should inform our gift giving as well. No strings or it isn't a gift. And always consider the recipient.

I have a friend; we'll call her Louise. Steve, Louise's boyfriend of many years, had read a book that he loved. It was about relationships and communication between couples. Steve talked enthusiastically about this book with Louise several times while he was reading it. He even mentioned giving Louise a copy of the book as a gift.

Louise is a particularly self-possessed woman. She had, of her own accord, glanced through the book while Steve was reading it and found that the tone of the book and the message were not to her liking. She shared as much with Steve. Steve was hurt and disappointed—the book had been significant to him, and he felt that some of the information in the book would be useful for them as a couple, addressing challenges and areas of conflict within their relationship. Louise was adamant that she was not interested and that he should not consider the book an appropriate gift under any circumstance. I hope I have successfully conveyed how direct and clear Louise was in her communication.

Valentine's Day arrives. You guessed it. In spite of her direct plea to Steve, he presented her with the book, neatly gift-wrapped along with some gourmet chocolates. Louise was livid. A huge fight ensued, so huge they almost broke up, that's how upset Louise became. And Steve seemed genuinely confused. He could not grasp that in his willful desire for her to read the book he had explicitly ignored her wishes. For him it was a loving expression of something significant that he wanted to share. He could not recognize or comprehend that respecting her desires should have been the guiding principle in this instance. And, of course, for Louise that was what was so disturbing—not the book as gift, but that in his insistence, he completely dismissed her, disrespected her, and rendered her invisible. Not really an effective way of expressing affection on a special occasion.

The lesson is clear: the gift is for the intended, not for you. It ceases to be a gift when you give someone something that they don't want or won't use, simply because you think they should want it or should use it.

Endless opportunities exist for expanding our thinking around gift giving. There are many ways to express or demonstrate your affection for another. In some ways the easiest choice is to buy something. In considering the quality of the intended's life, in supporting his or her choices, what else might make a noticeable impact that doesn't necessarily involve the exchange of a purchased object? Perhaps a home-cooked meal or some day care? Maybe a scholarship to attend a workshop or class? A week's worth of carpooling for the recipient or her kids? Really imagine what you have to offer your loved ones besides a manufactured token—you'll no doubt come up with many great ideas that will mean so much more when given.

I Am My Own Museum

No, you're not. Pull back the drapes and let some light in. You can't live for posterity and for the moment at the same time. And shrines to fallen movie stars, ex-lovers, or the hot clerk at the local drugstore are all equally disturbing. Hold things gently in your hands, and if that isn't possible, it may be better to simply set them down or let them go.

If everything is precious, nothing is precious. Learn to distinguish between trash and treasure. A dime-store hairbrush is not the same as your last published article. No one is interested in your discarded toothbrush or Q-tips, except perhaps a stalker or an unstable ex-lover. The products of your effort are what have value—whether that's a quilt, a collection of short stories, a film, or a casserole.

In cases where one is engaged in creative activities, when an archive somewhere actually would be interested in your notes and research and working process, actively identify and pursue that archive and begin a relationship with them. Completed projects, particularly published work or work that is out in the world, stands alone as well as within the context of your creative process. Film-makers may sift through outtakes and unreleased footage for "DVD extras" and other curiosities, writers through old notes for inclusion in an anthology of works, photographers through old files and possibly even negatives for a new view of an older image. But in all of these cases and others, almost everything still has a finite time limit or expiration date of practicality.

At some point, even for artists, it's useful to acknowledge that an opportunity may have passed and that current and future projects are where your attention now lies, and that going backward to unearth a potential hidden or overlooked gem is unlikely. Again, if the work product is important enough to be retained, there will no doubt be places interested in preserving it that will do a much better job of inventorying and cataloging it than you might, stacked and jumbled together in your studio with old junk mail and other less specific "stuff."

Collections—Cool or Crazy?

Do you have a matchbook collection? A large jar full of coins you're using as a doorstop? Coasters from around the world? Sand from every beach you've ever swum at? A glass menagerie of woodland creatures? Do you see where I'm headed?

Do you use the matchbooks or just accumulate them? Has it become indiscriminate, just picking up a book of matches anywhere, from a corner bodega to a recent meal out? Likewise the coasters. What qualifies inclusion in the collection—a particularly memorable brew or just the last place you grabbed a beer? Will you eventually cash in the jar of coins and use them for a "rainy day"? Have you carefully labeled the sand, noting the beach's name and country of origin? Attached a photo of you in your swimsuit?

What makes a collection special? It is the care with which the collection is curated. Rather than going for sheer volume, there ought to be a reason for each piece to be included. Each piece should be capable of standing on its own, possessing a degree of excellence in its own right—this lends greater integrity to the entire collection when viewed as a whole.

Consider carefully when beginning a collection of anything—typically, within the collection there are the one or two pieces that gave birth to the collection in the first

> ● **Notable Note** ●
>
> Unless you're a nineteen-year-old college student, a collection of beer bottles or cans is neither a collection nor appropriate decor, not even in your wet-bar area.

place, and these are the strongest examples and favorite iterations. Too often they are then surrounded by "filler," creating ample bulk so as to qualify as a collection. Do you really need to collect anything? Perhaps it is best to simply keep the few *whatevers* that you cherish and let the rest go.

In addition to people who have embarked on collecting things themselves, I've also encountered many people inundated with objects from well-meaning folks who know that so-and-so likes rabbits or elephants or turtles. Most of these collections began innocently enough with one object—clients Carol and Becca successfully illustrate this point.

On a trip once, and not a safari, a single giraffe was purchased as a token from Becca to Carol. It was displayed on a glass curio shelf in the main hallway of their home, where all could see it. Suddenly, as if floodgates had opened, every time a friend or colleague was stumped for an appropriate gift idea, the lightbulb went on and bingo!—another giraffe found its way to their home. Likewise, mermaids.

When I arrived at Carol and Becca's home for the first time, their bathroom was lousy with mermaids. Cards depicting mermaids were taped to the walls, the nightlights featured frolicking mermaids, and the tub and shower area was swimming in them. All because they had one framed picture of a mermaid hanging in the bathroom—a not-uncommon image for a wet room, particularly in the home of playful and creative women who appreciate other women.

This one picture became an unspoken invitation for anyone and everyone to inundate Carol and Becca with mermaids in every form—from Disney figurines to stickers, apparel, even toothbrushes. What was once a note of whimsy became a stifling theme, and one not of their own design. They were either too embarrassed or too polite to offer any resistance to the onslaught of merchandise, so they resignedly decorated their bathroom with every piece of mermaidalia they received. My arrival finally gave them permission to dismantle the collection and "come out," as it were, about their "new" desire to simplify and cease collecting.

If you too are the reticent recipient of people's generous but misguided assumptions, you are empowered and encouraged to disperse any unnatural or forced collection of objects and to gently and consistently mention to folks that you're no longer "collecting" whatever it was that they had thought you were collecting.

Will You Hate Me if I Get Rid Of . . . ?

I love my mom. This is not news. Several years ago she gave me her wedding china. It's all intact, full service for twelve—sweet, Bavarian, lots of serving pieces. She hasn't been married to my father since the 1970s, so she was done with it. And she inherited her mother's china when my grandmother died. Double done with it. So she gave her china to me.

It's lovely but a little too scalloped and floral—daisies—for my taste. I'm a bit of a minimalist, not surprisingly, and would prefer something elegant but simple—no pattern, no design.

I also don't want to upset my mother or hurt her feelings. Clearly she was done with something, so it could be fair to conclude that if she was done with it, it would be okay for me to be done with it. But one never knows until one asks.

I called her the other day and broached the subject with her. I mentioned that I was thinking of getting some new dishes and that I wanted to know how she felt about that. I could hear her catch her breath a bit and pause. I think she may have uttered, "Oh?" And then she changed the subject. When she starts talking about the Tigers or the Pistons, it's clear she's uncomfortable with whatever we had just been speaking about.

I rushed in with "Forget it, it's fine. You know I love the fact that it was yours, and I certainly appreciate the thought; it's just not really my pattern. But it's fine. I won't do anything right now."

We talked for a few more minutes, and then it was time to go. The end of the call was typical, not strained, and we both said "I love you" and hung up.

A few minutes later, the phone rang. It was my mom.

Mom: It's fine. Do whatever you want with the china. I'm done with it, and if you're done with it, let it go.

VirgoMan: Really? Are you sure?

Mom: Absolutely. You know that stuff just takes me a little bit of time to get over. And then I'm over it. So I'm over it. I'm fine with whatever you decide.

VM: That's great, Mom. Thanks.

Mom: Now, you're not getting rid of it completely, are you? You just want to get new dishes in addition to the china?

VM: I can do that. Is that what you want me to do?

Mom: It's good china, right?

VM: Sure. It's great. It's in great shape.

Mom: Well . . . I don't know. I guess not. This stuff is hard! This is what you do with your clients every day?

VM: Pretty much.

Mom: That's amazing. You're amazing.

VM: And that's my mom talking. But thank you.

Mom: Do you know anyone you think would like the china?

VM: Not off the top of my head, but I can give it some thought.

Mom: Or you could just give it to a local charity. There's a couple by you that you like, right?

VM: That's more what I was thinking. I spoke with an online company that buys china and cutlery but they offer you a fraction of what they sell it for; you have to pack it up and ship it to them; if they don't want something, they ship it back. . . . It just sounds like a nightmare. I'm more inclined to give it to some charity and let them sell it. It's in perfect condition, all the pieces are there, they should be able to get some good money for it.

Mom: That sounds better. Do that.

VM: Thanks, Mom. I will. I love you.

Mom: I love you, too. And you are pretty amazing.

This Might Be Worth a Fortune—*Antiques Roadshow* or Thrift Store?

We discussed a version of this idea in chapter six, Auxiliary Spaces, when discussing garage sales.

If you think you have an actual treasure, take it to an appraiser or someone qualified yet disinterested (meaning they don't stand to benefit from either a high or low appraisal) to determine if you're right. We've all heard stories of the garage-sale Jackson Pollock or seventeenth-century silver bed warmer found in the corner of an attic that turned out to be one of only three that Paul Revere signed. If you have something similar in your possession, it would be good to know it.

If instead you have a quirky and interesting thing that has no deep value, the local thrift store will probably be happy to turn it into some operating capital.

Finding the best advisor for your possible treasure will require some footwork, so take the time to do it right once and the first time. Look online, ask friends and neighbors and colleagues for referrals, and check the appraiser's references. You don't want to turn a rare and beautiful thing over to a complete stranger until you're certain that she or he won't disappear with it and that she or he has demonstrated expertise with objects like yours. And this is what I mean: don't assume that after a five-minute phone conversation, because you "had a good feeling about" the appraiser, that you can tell whether he or she is reputable and reliable. Remember Bernie Madoff.

Once it's been appraised, even if you decide you're not going to sell it and it will remain on display in your home, it should then be properly documented and insured.

Dry Storage vs. Wet Storage (Reminder)

As discussed in previous chapters, precious things are not to be subjected to fluctuations in humidity or temperature. Mold, mildew, rot, and pests—you name it and moisture will foster and welcome it.

Once you've gathered everything and completed the sorting process discussed in the next sections, make sure that wherever you ultimately store your mementos, they are safe and dry and protected from the elements.

Approaching Sorting, and How to Sort

If you're apprehensive about sorting through things—in particular, sentimental objects and touchstones from your past—a calm and steady approach is best: breathe deeply, settling down emotionally and mentally. You're not about to run a gauntlet of swinging bloody spikes, so manic frenetic energy will not be useful here.

The goal and result of sorting is knowing exactly what it is you're holding on to and why you're holding on to it. And the most direct way to achieve that goal is to sort through everything, make reasonable and heartfelt decisions, discard that which you are done with, and lovingly and respectfully store or display what remains. So while this may not be like a day at an amusement park, it also kind of is. You'll be scared, you'll be thrilled, you'll be tuckered out, you'll laugh, and you may even surprise yourself and want to go back for more.

There are only three rules for sorting:

Establish an amount of time for each sorting session. We've already discussed that it should be no less than thirty minutes but not longer than three hours.

Find a quiet place where you will not be disturbed. If you're sorting in the space where everything is currently living, see if you can close off that space so other folks or pets are not randomly wandering through or constantly interrupting you. If having company (pet, friend, or family) will help you stay calm and focused, by all means have them with you. Just be sure they can be there while you maintain the equilibrium and the pace and not create or become a distraction.

Be true to yourself. No one is looking over your shoulder, and this is a private and personal task. So you are the final word on what you think is important and what you can let go of. You needn't have conversations with anyone who is not in the room with you about whether you "should" let something go or not. And you absolutely do not need to answer to anyone else for your choices (unless the things still belong to someone living and that person isn't you!).

This is by no means a grave or overly serious task; it just requires concentration and deliberateness. Which is why I'm being so explicit about how and where. You want to be comfortable and focused so that whatever "comes up," you're in the best place possible to address it without becoming overly disturbed.

If you haven't done so already, select a place in your home that can be dedicated to this next process of sorting until the process is complete. Even if the space is modest, it's best not to have to set up and tear down this whole operation every time you want to continue the work.

Once that space has been identified, collect all the mementos and sentimental objects you've accumulated and bring them to this place. If you've created Sentimentaland containers as you've worked through previous chapters, now would be the time to bring them here as well. Without tearing apart your home, I suggest that you be thorough in searching out every item of sentimental import and gather them all up until you've isolated them to this one area of your home. You can always address the random object you've overlooked and discovered later, but a comprehensive sorting saves time and minimizes emotional upheaval.

Actually Sorting

Great. You've found a quiet place to be. You're surrounded by things to sort. It's now time to gather the supplies listed on page 242. Once you've got your tools and supplies on hand, you're ready to begin.

Perhaps it's worth saying a little prayer or meditation at this time: "Let me be careful and conscious, respectful and thoughtful. Let me be deliberate and diligent and thorough. Let me be strong and patient and flexible and resilient. Let me be kind and generous and gracious and fearless. And let this be pleasant."

Define your workspace by spreading out a tarp or blanket. You'll use this to isolate areas where like items can be grouped together and still be seen. Remember not to stack things too high in piles when sorting; we want them to be mostly spread out on a single plane. This won't always be possible—space may be limited, and with books and other flat items stacks are probably inevitable. All piles and stacks will eventually be dismantled as you make further decisions. The following are the categories you should be thinking of when sorting.

Sorting Categories: Sentimental Objects
Keep
Return to Others
Give Away/Donate
    Specific people or organizations
    Thrift store/shelter
    Freecycle or at the curb with a sign
Sell
Trash
The Fence

Keep: These are items that you really love today, not items that you
    only loved many years ago, and items you feel confident you'll con-

tinue to love in many years to come. These will be wrapped in acid-free paper or other protective coverings (as needed) and placed in containers for safekeeping.

Return to Others: These are things that belong to other people that are currently in your possession. It doesn't matter how long you've had them; they need to go home, and they should get there sooner rather than later. Do not procrastinate any longer; swallow whatever feelings you may have about the amount of time you've had them, and get them gone. In these rare cases you may give the object to a thrift store *rather* than returning it to its rightful owner:

- The owner is deceased and you are unable (not unwilling) to contact next of kin.
- The return of the object would cause harm to the recipient or someone other than yourself.

Give Away/Donate: These are things you are clearly done with, for whatever reason, that you're now willing to give away. Regarding personal mementos, it's uncertain how many of these kinds of things have a life beyond you—for any that could, determine where they would best be further used and send or deliver them there. Do not allow these things to linger as you search for the "perfect" home for them.

Sell: These are things you are clearly done with that have adequate value to demand a sale. These things will be taken to a local consignment shop or sold online, either by yourself or through a drop-off service that manages online auctions for you.

Trash: These are the unfortunate things you've kept that have no value to anyone and are to now be discarded.

The Fence: As in "on the fence," or unable to make a decision. This category is to be used with hyper-vigilance, and only in cases of extreme confusion. It is never to be used as a mask for procrastination or regret, but only in cases of true confoundment. This is not a "get out of jail free" card—use it only as a last resort!

STEP ONE: LIKE WITH LIKE

Set and start your timer. Then begin simply by getting similar things into groupings. This means yearbooks together, journals together, baby clothes together, love letters together, etc. Throughout this initial sorting into groups, toss out all the trash you come across—there's no need to leave that for later. Likewise, now on the first pass, wipe down everything—we don't want to store anything that is dusty, mildewy, or grimy in any way.

It's possible that all you'll accomplish in the first session is sorting into like categories. That's fine, and not a small achievement, so don't be discouraged. Make sure you set up your next date with yourself so you don't lose momentum and don't have to look at the sorted piles for too long.

STEP TWO: STAY OR GO?

Once everything has been sorted into like categories and obvious trash has been discarded, it's time to make some decisions. Sitting quietly and handling each item, carefully consider what has real meaning for you. What seems lasting and enduring? What is mildly amusing? And what holds no meaning, because the memory is either not so compelling any longer or possibly even forgotten or unpleasant? Anything that doesn't seem lasting and enduring should be released. If any of these items have significant monetary value, or they perform a function, such as an appliance or an electronic device or even a T-shirt or wine key, then sell them or pass them along to a charity. If they are less functional, such as a menu or a wrapper or a bag, they are destined for recycling or trash.

Spend enough time with each object to make an informed decision but not so much time as to get lost in reminiscing or distracted by feelings, either fond sentimental feelings or any sort of shame or embarrassment, disappointment, or frustration. If or when you become aware that you're drifting and are no longer focused on the task at hand, stand up and move around. The surest way to shift feelings is to physically shift your body. Go get a glass of water, leave the room and walk around outside—anything to physically break the mood. If you choose to call someone, make it someone who is supportive of you and this process—do not call anyone who might offer you any criticism, constructive or otherwise. Likewise, do not call someone related to the items being sorted if there's any chance you'll be drawn into further reminiscing and get pulled off track. Once you've cleared your head and feel ready to resume, return to where you're working and dig back in.

This is really a "rinse and repeat" task. You'll keep sorting through these objects until they are all sorted, until each one has been touched and a decision has been made to keep it or let it go. As in other sorting projects, you may very occasionally set an object aside in a "wait and see" place called "the fence"—but this is only to be used when you really can't make a decision, not in cases where you just don't *want* to make a decision. Keep in mind, too, whether the things you've come across are things you'd like to have in your home on display or neatly stored away in Sentimentaland.

When everything has been sorted, it's now time to containerize it.

Containerizing the Objects

As I suggested earlier, if you have multiple people's mementos and objects, you should have a tub or series of tubs for each individual. All the containers should be see-through. Additionally, you may want to have slightly different sizes and/or colored lids that signify each person. For example, all of your tubs have purple lids and/or are ten gallons, your child's are blue and/or eight gallons, your partner's red and/or twelve gallons, etc. If this isn't practical, consider using different-colored electrical tape as an easy-to-read identifier. Of course, all the tubs will also be labeled as well.

At this time, if you haven't done so already, anything that is fragile or requires additional protection should be wrapped or enclosed to keep it safe from damage. Load heavier and bulkier items toward the bottom, with lighter things resting toward the top. Do not overload the containers so that moving them is awkward or requires more than one person to manage them.

If you have multiple containers for each person, consider segregating the contents by category as well (for example, one tub for printed materials, such as journals, yearbooks, or magazines; one tub for clothing; one tub for tchotchkes and other objects, etc.).

The Importance of Labels—
How, Why, and Where

In chapter six, I give a detailed description and explanation of labeling. Please review pages 207–209. Here I'll simply stress that labeling the containers is critical for anyone to successfully interact with their contents.

Organizing the Storage

Once each category has been successfully containerized and labeled, it's time to store them until you next need or want the contents. Find an area of your home that is large enough to house the full collection of Sentimentaland containers.

If this isn't possible, then divide up the containers by person and find a home for each person's Sentimentaland. Remember to store them somewhere climate-controlled and as accessible as these kinds of items need to be. If you frequently look through memorabilia, don't bury the containers behind old furniture and seldom-used paint. Common sense will inform how and where everything should be stored so it's out of the flow of traffic but still within easy reach.

Maintaining the System

Moving forward, whenever anything is destined for Sentimentaland, add the newish item to the appropriate container in a timely fashion. It's fine to set something aside for a few days until you can get back to Sentimentaland, but don't leave things lying around indefinitely. Find the container the item wants to be deposited into and place it inside. Obviously, if the item is fragile or requires additional packing, do that prior to your arrival at Sentimentaland. If you find that you possess enough energy to identify something as Sentimentaland-worthy but seem to lack the energy enough to then transport it there, talk yourself through the procrastination, and the potential damage to this item you claim to value, and you should find adequate motivation and impetus to pick up the object, travel to Sentimentaland, and make the deposit.

9 | Photos

All photos are accurate. None of them is the truth.

RICHARD AVEDON

A photograph is like the recipe—a memory of the finished dish.

CARRIE LATET

A picture is worth a thousand words—but not if you can't find it.

GOOD HOUSEKEEPING MAGAZINE

Are you overwhelmed by your photographs?

Do you have envelopes of photos shoved into various drawers around the house?

Do you have rolls of film lying around that have never been developed?

Have you ever bought a new memory card rather than downloading images from your digital camera?

Have you ever gone in search of a particular photo and given up in frustration?

Do you think that "someday" you're going to create a photo album of your trip to _____?

Have you ever created a photo album before?

Have you recently inherited old photos and don't even know who's in them?

Do you contemplate stopping taking pictures because you're so overwhelmed?

Are you now overwhelmed with your answers to these questions?

Take a deep breath and count to ten.

This entire chapter is dedicated to photographs—sorting them and storing them, accessing them and utilizing/enjoying them. After all, if we don't enjoy our photographs, what purpose do they serve? As a frozen window into events we have lived or events we have missed (that have somehow been described to us or left for us to imagine), they exist to conjure those scenes anew with each viewing, inviting us to relive and share past events in the present time.

Almost every home I visit—either a client's or friend's or family's—has at least one photo "challenge." We love to take pictures, and then we are quickly overwhelmed with keeping them organized or storing them. And as with so many other "advances" in technology, digital photographs can further complicate, rather than simplify, the situation. The very fact that the photos live somewhere on our hard drives encourages an "out of sight, out of mind" attitude, particularly if we have limited computing skills.

Together we'll tackle the challenges of sorting and organizing and storing photos, and by the time you're done with this chapter, your photos may not be in perfect order, but they will all be together, more manageable, and much easier to interact with.

What We're Going to Cover in This Chapter

- ☐ Photographs: What They Are and What They Aren't
- ☐ One Home for Everything and Like with Like
- ☐ Does This Photo Make My Butt Look Fat? Or, Good Pics, Bad Pics
- ☐ If You Visit It, You Will Bring Me Home (Mementos of Travel), Part II
- ☐ Who's That Strange Man Standing Next to Aunt Ida?
- ☐ Digital vs. Analog Images—Not an Either-Or Proposition

Things You Will Need for the Work in This Chapter

- Trash bags
- Timer or stopwatch
- Spray can of compressed air
- Tubs, containers, or baskets to corral and contain like things
- Photo boxes and/or albums and/or scrapbooks and/or frames
- Lint-free cloths
- Acid-free paper
- Cotton negative sleeves
- Clean white cotton gloves
- Acid-free and noninvasive adhesives (tapes, glues, etc.)
- Label maker (but stick-on labels should not touch photos or negatives)
- Acid-free labels

- Acid-free markers
- Scissors or paper cutter
- Sorting surface (3'x6' or larger, and ideally not a surface that needs to be cleared off before the sorting is complete)

Photographs: What They Are and What They Aren't

Photograph (noun):
A picture produced by photography.

Photography (noun):
The art or process of producing images of objects on photosensitive surfaces.

Notable Note

If you're intimidated or agitated by the threat of destroying your photographs because of your current mistreatment of them, let that go. What's done is done. There are recommended ways to store photographs, and they are detailed in this chapter. Sentences ending in exclamation marks are meant to excite you—if you read something on the Internet that warns of the irreparable damage you are doing to your photographs, remember that right after that exclamatory sentence is probably an offer to sell you just what you need to prevent or reverse years of neglect and potential damage. Learn what to avoid and what is safe, and then go about protecting your photos—it's no more demanding or scary than that.

Some people claim that photographs are your most precious possessions. People also say that "the camera never lies," and that "one picture is worth a thousand words." We charge photographs with the responsibility of documenting our lives, telling us the truth about events even if our memories contradict the image's represented narrative, and condensing conversations and relationships into a series of still images. I'm unconvinced.

No doubt they capture moments in time, but those moments are colored and shaped by so many variables—the photographer, the subject, the location, and the circumstances, to name just a few. I can look at a photograph of my father and me on a trip to Tahquamenon Falls in Michigan's Upper Peninsula, and see us embracing and smiling at the camera. The falls behind us are rushing deep copper and rust with tannin. The sunlight is fractured through the thick canopy of green leaves overhead. What the photo doesn't reveal is the horrible fight we had fifteen minutes before we asked a passing tourist to snap our picture in front of the falls. But I still remember it. In fact, the argument was so significant that I can't look at the photo and *not* remember it. It doesn't diminish the beauty of the setting, my fond remembering of the trip, or my affection for my father—it's just an added component of the memory that the image itself can't supply.

So photographs may be records, but even more they are interpretations of the events they purport to record. The photos we take, the pictures we gather and hold on to, are touchstones for real events and real encounters with real people; the photos are not the events or the encounters or the relationships. They are powerful tools, certainly, they are expressions of creativity and artistry, of surprise and wonder and circumstance and timing, but they are not, should not be confused with, intimacy and breath and scent and touch. Cherish them as windows into places you have been or dream of going, and protect them as documents of people you have known or people whom you've never met that may have made your life possible. But know that you will not, cannot, replace the actual experiences with a two-dimensional image of light reflected. Believing so would be a tragedy far greater than losing every photograph you've ever owned in a natural disaster or fire.

One Home for Everything
and Like with Like

Applying One Home for Everything and Like with Like to photographs means digging out those developed rolls of film and their corresponding images that may be shoved into various drawers, or tucked into corners or stacked up on shelves, and bringing them all together to sort through and organize. And then, once they've been sorted and organized, finding the one place in your home where they'll all live. Even the CDs of pictures that friends and family have given you or you've had "developed" and the historic family photos you may have inherited—if it's a photo, it's to be with its brothers and sisters in one place in your home or office. The *only* exception to this is, of course, the hard drive of your computer. When we get to organizing your computer in chapter ten, we'll address those photos as files on your computer; in this chapter we'll deal with getting them from the camera to your hard drive and into folders and identified. The same techniques we'll use to organize your physical photos will be applied to their digital counterparts as well, meaning you won't be learning two different ways to keep your pictures together—one way fits all.

Does This Photo Make My Butt Look Fat?
Or, Good Pics, Bad Pics

When we talk about sorting photos later in this chapter, we'll address the larger task of making sense out of accumulated photos. But from this moment forward, whenever you get pictures developed or receive them from someone else, immediately go through them and eliminate the "dogs," and by that I mean the following.

- Bad exposures
- Blurry or out-of-focus shots

- Off-center pics
- Bloopers
- Photos you'd rather not remember
- Photos that you're not proud to share
- Photos that don't evoke an immediate emotional response
- Photos with a foreign object obscuring part of the frame, be it a finger, a camera strap, or some other object

As we've discussed before, most likely you are not the subject of an anthropological study or documentary, so fortunately you don't need to keep any photos of you where the little tummy roll you've recently been sporting is pushing down the waistband of your slacks. Or the photo of you with food on your shirt or mascara running down your face or with your fly open. Unless they amuse you. If they don't, there's no reason to hold on to them for someone else's amusement, especially if that amusement would come at your expense. Just like buying pistachio nuts—you accept that not every one will be opened, that some are duds; you factor that into the price of the nuts. So, too, expect that a roll of thirty-six exposures will not automatically yield thirty-six "keepers." Ditto for digital cameras—the bonus there being the ability to immediately delete any image you don't wish to retain.

If You Visit It, You Will Bring Me Home (Mementos of Travel), Part II

Taking vacation pictures is fun, whether the trip involves trekking the Himalayas or visiting family in Des Moines. Living behind your camera as you descend into the Grand Canyon or teeter on a rope bridge suspended four hundred feet over a gorge in Bhutan is both dangerous and imprudent. Even insisting on taking excessive photos of your children's athletic competitions robs everyone involved of primary involvement—your kids don't get an enthusiastic cheerleader, and you will miss the most important moments of the event while attempting to capture the most important moments of the event.

Like so many things in life, balance is a key element for full and easy enjoyment and participation. Buddhists speak of "the middle way" as instruction that the path to enlightenment lies neither in exaggerated asceticism nor in self-indulgence, and we can benefit from applying this concept to the taking and keeping of photographs. Certainly you'll take more photos than you intend to keep, knowing that not every photo will merit holding on to. So, too, you probably won't want to never take another picture for fear of missing an experience. Take the photos, stay present, and then be prepared to cull the best and let go of the rest.

As we discussed in chapter eight (Mementos • Sentimental Objects • Gifts • Collections), we're looking for the exceptional in touchstones for memories. So aim to capture unique images when taking pictures. There are masterful shots of the falls at Niagara that professionals have waited days, perhaps months, to capture. Buy a postcard—you won't do better. But the image of your companion leaning over the rail and being drenched in her or his yellow slicker is a once-in-a-lifetime shot—don't miss that.

Find the moments that are never to be repeated without rehearsal, and those are the images you'll cherish, those are the images that will instantly remind you of the smell of fresh grilled panino in Venice or a thick-and-syrupy coffee in Turkey or your grandchild's first birthday cake. How many pictures do you need of your African accommodations, luxurious as they may be, when you can capture the moment a lion pounces on a gazelle on safari in Kenya? Why take a photo of a generic roadside mile marker when you could just as easily take a picture of the luridly vivid purple pickled eggs swimming in a jar on the counter at Stuckey's on your first road trip to Nashville, Tennessee? That first birthday cake may be interesting to document as an achievement of baking and decorating, but the bite that ends with frosting on the nose is far more evocative of the moment.

In capturing the shocking, the absurd, the ridiculous, the sublime, and the quietly mundane, you record the history of your travels and lay the emotional map you'll follow to remember each taste, each step, each sound, each smell. Be thoughtful and creative and you cannot lose. Just remember to remove your lens cap—and, of course, fully charge the battery and carry extra film, batteries, and memory cards.

Who's That Strange Man Standing Next to Aunt Ida?

Probably Uncle Albert, her first husband, who died tragically before your mother was born. But you might not have known that if some other relative had not written on the back of the photo, identifying all the people in it.

Not long before my father died, we went through everything he owned that was important to him. He knew his time was shortening, and it was a beautiful and simple exchange between the two of us. He let me know what was important to him that I keep and was also very clear about what no longer meant anything to him. His ease and matter-of-factness was refreshing and inspiring. Clearly, where he was going, these things weren't going with him and he was as content to toss something into the trash that he was finished with as he was to place it in my hand and tell me its story, encouraging me to care for it as he had.

We also went through a bunch of old family photos. As we looked through them, he identified many of the players for me, some of whom I knew or still know and others that I had never and would never meet. There were other folks in some pictures that he either couldn't remember or had no clue about. My dad was the youngest and the last surviving sibling of his generation—so if he didn't recognize someone, there was no other source to go to, and these people were now relegated to a vague and unknowable history. And while any old photograph holds some fascination for me—the clothes and cars, wondering about a stranger's life and what may have been going on when the picture was snapped—ultimately these people are lost. And as I am not my own museum and certainly not the family historian (and given that we can't identify some of these people, it's quite possible I'm not even related to them), there was no reason, good or bad, to hang on to those photos. So like old coupons and calendars he was no longer interested in, these he simply tossed into the trash as well.

As we sorted, we came across various early photos of family members who are still living, and my dad gave me specific instructions on whom to send what to. Which I did. And I found some great pictures of my grandparents and great-grandparents, cousins I'm fond of, and my dad and his sibs. These I kept for myself. The greater point I'm making is that just because a photograph comes into your possession at some time for whatever reason, you are not required to retain it. And this is amplified when you or anyone else either does not know or just doesn't care who is in the picture.

Digital vs. Analog Images—Not an Either-Or Proposition

There are advantages and disadvantages to both film and digital photography, and I think the merits of each advocate for the continued existence and use of both. So I'll leave it to you to do adequate research if what you're considering is selecting one over the other. Whether you use film or digital cameras, the question of what to do with the prints or images is the same. One Home for Everything and Like with Like should guide your organizational efforts in dealing with all photos, physical and virtual.

Photo Albums—Fun or Frustrating?

To answer the above question, take a few minutes, check in with yourself, and answer the questions below:

- Are you someone who is already organized and motivated to make positive changes in your life?
- Are you constantly "on the go" and moving from one project to the next?

- Are you, for whatever reason, still searching for something to unlock that well of potential inside?
- Are you curious and tenuous when you step outside of your comfort zone?
- Do you dream of doing projects but seldom actually get them started and then typically don't finish them?
- Do you complete some things but lose interest when you encounter an obstacle or resistance?
- Are you easily distracted?
- Are you relentless in the pursuit of your goals, sometimes to the exclusion of other priorities?

I don't want to rain on your parade, but if you are not already a project person, attempting to become one with photo albums may be a stretch. Mow the lawn first. Do the dishes or the laundry. Take on some projects that require less creativity, have more inherent structure, and yield tangible and immediate results. We want you to build on success, not provide you with another argument for why you never seem to get anything done. Of course, doing the laundry is not nearly as sexy as creating a travelogue picture book of your trip around the world. But being honest with yourself about how long ago that trip was and where exactly and which photos you would even include is sexier than starting the project in a flurry of activity and then burning out two hours into it, after you've torn apart several drawers and the dining-room table is littered with snapshots. Honesty = hot. A cluttered dining-room table = not so hot.

For those uninterested or intimidated by photo albums, a great alternative is "memory" or "keepsake" boxes—distinct from Sentimentaland but in the same hemisphere. These boxes allow you to corral photos (and even other related sentimental objects) into one container, creating a mini time capsule of a trip or an event. They come in many sizes and colors, and are a no-brainer when it comes to keeping things together—open the lid, fill the contents thoughtfully, and store them away.

Albums can be small enough to fit just one trip's worth of pictures, or large enough to hold multiple years of photos. What makes the most sense for you? Many people choose the easiest route and just insert photos as they get them, adding new pages or creating new albums as required. If this is you, make sure to label pages with dates to provide some structure, both for organizing and to offer some context for the viewer.

For those interested in creating photo albums, here are a few tips:

- Basic photo albums or blank-page scrapbooks can be bought at most drugstores and greeting card or stationery shops.
- Consider albums with a window or frame on the front cover—then insert a decorative card or evocative image to introduce the album's content.
- Label the binder's spine for easy reference.
- All pages and any adhesive should be acid-free and lignin-free, and should have passed the Photographic Activity Test (PAT) to avoid destruction to the photos. Any product that has passed the PAT test will state so on its packaging.
- Avoid magnetic and self-stick photo albums for that very reason—they damage your photos.
- Any plastic sleeves should be made from uncoated pure polyethylene or a similar material. Plastic containing PVC generates acid as well. Read the label carefully for composition.
- Select photo albums that are expandable. You may want to add pages in the future.
- Do not overstuff photo albums—this can cause the pages to buckle and damage the photographs.
- Select an organizing principle (for example, chronological order, by subject, etc.).

For chronology: Put a beginning date in each album, and a final date when the album is full.
For subject: These are some examples: baby album, travel album (either each trip in its own album or a large

album of all travels), holiday album (same idea, perhaps a year of holidays, or every Christmas for the past few years).

- Always plan the layout of each page before permanently affixing images.
- Clip phrases or names from magazines for captions, or type or print labels for all pictures, including setting and subjects. Any label should be attached to the page, avoiding contact with any photographs.
- Whenever possible, store albums vertically. Laying them on their side can warp the photos.
- If you're drawn toward scrapbooks, consider a big blank book. Then add keepsakes to the pages, such as ticket stubs or other paper-based memorabilia, even swatches of fabric or locks of hair. Use caution with glitter or sparkles to ensure that they will not decompose or come loose over time and damage your photos. Always use an acid-free adhesive. For the most protection, use duplicate prints whenever possible to minimize potential loss.

Amateur or Pro—the Disease of "I Made It-ism"

I have several friends and clients who are photographers, and many of them have the same particular ailment: "I made it–ism." Far on the other side of "I might need it someday," "I made it–ism" endows any and every thing created by the afflicted with an unwarranted significance, just because it came from his or her hand. It's possible that this illness was first contracted at a summer camp with the creation of a God's-eye made from yarn and Popsicle sticks or maybe a ceramic ashtray. In the adult photographer, it manifests itself in the need to keep every photograph and negative ever shot. The photo could be out of focus, it could be a partial exposure, it could be a duplicate of another shot— the simple fact that some effort of theirs produced the picture seems to them reason enough to hold on to it. Artists working in other mediums also sometimes suffer from this condition, but it seems particularly acute with photographers. What I find doubly remarkable is that while they won't let anything go, they are hyper-selective about what they will actually exhibit or display. So the bulk of these photographs, once printed, never see the light of day. They are stored in any number of flat file boxes and kept indefinitely. When I've asked several of them about this, this is how the conversation often plays out.

VirgoMan: So tell me about all the photos.

Photographer: I took them.

VM *(chuckling):* Okay. Got it. What are you intending to do with them?

Photographer: Nothing.

VM: Nothing now, or nothing ever, or . . . Can you be a bit more specific about "nothing"?

Photographer: I don't know. I mean, I took them; I'm not getting rid of them, if that's what you're thinking.

VM: Well, I don't think I was implying just tossing them out willy-nilly. I guess I was thinking that maybe you'd go through them and cull the images that you like, or that are useful, or that you might or would print again, or . . .

Photographer: Yeah. I'm not going to do that. I took them. They're my photographs.

VM: I understand that. No one's trying to do anything to you or take anything from you. What I'm trying to understand, and I'm trying to relate this to other art forms . . . When I write something, for instance, I'll go through several drafts until I arrive at a completed manuscript. And then I don't really have the need for all the previous drafts. I pull out phrases here and there that I might be able to use somewhere else, but then the rest of it is either redundant or just not needed, so I end up deleting it or tossing it in the trash.

Painters, too, that I know will sketch things out and then begin a canvas, and unless the sketch was significant in some way, once they start working on the canvas the sketch is set aside and eventually discarded.

Chefs pick out the choice parts of their ingredients and then use the remains for either a stock or compost.

Photographer: I don't know what to tell you. I took all these photographs. I don't want to get rid of any of them. I made them. They're little parts of me.

VM: Hmm, really? I think I'm going to disagree with you on that. And

---

Notable Note

There are numerous online photography resources—too many to list here. Whether you're looking to purchase supplies or have your film developed and the photos posted online, a quick search will yield a variety of options. Here's a few to get you started:

www.smilebox.com (online scrapbooking)
www.shutterfly.com
www.snapfish.com
www.exposuresonline.com
www.archivalmethods.com
www.archivalusa.com

If you'd like your pictures in albums but you don't want to spend a lot of time creating them, consider having a digital or online company create a custom photography book for you and your loved ones.

Remember that online storage does not negate storage on your hard drive and a backup copy on a disk or external drive as well. Do not rely on some external company's technology to protect and save your images for you. There are too many horror stories of servers crashing and other technical glitches that gives an electronic spin to the adage "Don't put all your eggs in one basket." Just like with investments, when it comes to backing up, *diversify*!

if you think about it, they're not really even extensions of you. They're certainly expressions of you, but they are not in any way actually little pieces of you. *(Pause.)* Okay, then. Let's move on.

Approaching Sorting, and How to Sort

When you're ready to sort through photos, I suggest you find a quiet place to examine them, where you will not be disturbed. Remember that this is a task—a not-unpleasant task but a task. Approach it as such, remembering that every task has a beginning and an end, and that the result of a task well done *is* the goal. A delightful by-product of a task well done is a pleasant experience. There's far too much emphasis these days placed on having fun at all times. I'm all for amusement and enjoyment. When they occur organically as part of this work, that's great. If they don't, I don't consider their absence to be a failure or a deficit in any way. The absence of amusement does not automatically equate to drudgery. Something can be challenging or interesting or demanding without being unpleasant. So do yourself a favor and don't torment yourself unnecessarily by heaping expectations on top of a process that may already be loaded with some procrastination and trepidation.

When ready to begin, set your timer for a comfortable length of time, between thirty minutes and an hour. It helps to have a time limit—that way, you'll stay focused on moving briskly and deliberately through the task at hand and are less likely to stray into reminiscing, which is dangerous territory when sorting photos. Do this every time you sit down to sort them. Do not try to be a hero or think yourself exceptional—that time limits are for mere mortals and you're feeling so motivated or clearheaded that you'll work for hours uninterrupted, impervious to fatigue or sentiment. You will fail. Trust me on this. No more than an hour at a time. Even if all you do during breaks is get up and stretch and walk around the house. It clears the head.

A certain amount of reverie is acceptable and expected when handling photos. Still, the time to linger will be on the other side of the sorting process.

Actually Sorting

If you haven't already done so, gather up all your photos now. Find them wherever they live—in boxes, in drawers, in piles. Bring them all together. You do not need to take apart or undo photo albums already created, just collect them together with all the random other photos so they can all be together.

Decide on how you will sort them. I recently reviewed the several boxes of photos that I live with. And they break down into the following basic categories defined here:

Old Family Photos: These are typically black-and-white and are pictures of people who are older and even possibly deceased. What I would call "ancestors."

Current Family Photos: These are typically in color and feature blood relatives. I don't sort further than that, meaning distinguishing between my nuclear family versus my extended family, and then further into various nuclear versions of the extended family, but you could. I don't have so many relatives that distinguishing between cousins is that important, at least photographically.

Friends: These are pictures of friends that transcend a particular event or were taken at no event at all, just because I or some other photographer wanted to capture something specific yet random.

Travel: These are sorted by trip, so all the India pictures are together, the camping in Canada pictures are together, the backpacking summer through Europe pictures are together. They are then arranged in either alphabetical or chronological order. I chose alphabetical.

Events: These, like travel, are grouped by specific event (for example, piano recitals, bar mitzvah, senior prom, high-school graduation, shows and gigs during college, college graduation, significant birthdays, weddings, work gatherings, etc.). Mine are in chronological order of events as well, so piano recitals (when I was nine or ten) are grouped before high-school graduation, and so on.

Theme: These are images whose relationship with other images is based on an external or abstract theme. I did a series once of single riders reading books on the NYC subway. I took another series of photos of roadside produce stands. So a theme or common subject ties them together, not my relationship with them.

Utility: These are not pictures of the gas meter. They are photos of valuables in my home that I've taken for insurance purposes, or photos I've taken of water lines run through newly constructed walls when those walls were still open. By "utility" we mean that the photo's only purpose is utilitarian or functional.

What are the categories of photos that you have? List them here.

_____

_____

_____

_____

_____

Once you've gotten all the photos in one place and are clear on your categories, set the timer and begin. With each photo, ask yourself the following questions. The answers will determine if it is a keeper or a leaver.

- Is the print under- or overexposed?
- Is the subject in focus?
- Is the subject completely in the frame?
- Is the subject obscured by anything (thumbs, straps, signs, etc.)? Is any part of the image obscured by anything?
- Is it flattering? If it's not flattering, is it amusingly or uncomfortably unflattering? Spinach in the teeth might be okay, runny makeup following a fight less so.

- Going further, is it a photo you would rather not remember?
- Would you be embarrassed for anyone else to see this image?
- Do you know everyone (or anyone) in the photo?
- Do you care about everyone (or anyone) in the photo? Really think about pictures of exes. I'm not a fan of cutting people out of a photograph to reflect the way you've cut people out of your life. Toss the whole thing instead. Several clients took great pleasure in shredding pictures of their exes—it was very liberating for them.
- Are you keeping the photo because you're afraid of . . . ? What? Say it out loud—name it, know it.
- Will you ever want reprints of this image? Would anyone else?
- If it's a close duplicate of other shots, is it superior or inferior?
- Do you have an immediate emotional response to the photo, or is it just a picture?

You need only one disqualifying answer to determine a photograph's fate, so after your first response that identifies the image as a clunker, you needn't proceed asking the rest of the questions—just discard the picture. A photo that fails any of the questions above should be discarded. Also consider letting go of duplicates or near-duplicates. If you have good double shots, distribute them to family members or to anybody else who might appreciate them.

Sift out any image that could be improved by cropping or other adjustment, and set them aside for a future project. But be realistic. If you end up with one hundred images that would benefit from some kind of altering, how feasible is it that you'll have the time *and* then choose to spend that time actually altering images? Or spend the money for someone else to do it? If you had to choose between gardening and altering photos, which would it be? How about visiting family? Really evaluate how important and valuable projects like this are to you, and then prioritize them. It's fine to identify the need for altering and to recognize that your eye is that sharp and your aesthetic sense so developed. And it's also possible to acknowledge that time and/or budget limitations may mean that altering won't be happening. If this is your case, and if you don't love the photo pre-altering, then let it go.

Once you've determined whether it stays or goes, label each image you're keeping with some key information so you don't have to go through them twice. Then sort the prints into the categories that you've identified above. If the final destinations for your photographs are photo boxes, create one for each category and sort the pictures directly into each box. That may be all the sorting you need or want to do.

If you're planning to store them in acid-free sleeves or pouches with their negatives nearby, once you've completed your categorical sorting, you can begin to assemble these sleeves or pouches. Likewise, albums or scrapbooks. After applying the categories, you'll have your raw material for your individual books.

There is no one perfect way to sort and organize photos, so there's no need to stress about this process. What you're doing is creating a system where there was previously chaos. All progress is good progress. And what we're aiming for is completion rather than perfection. No one is testing or judging you if you end up with a few pictures out of order. This doesn't give you permission to be sloppy—pay attention to what you're doing so you can get the results you desire. When this project is finished, you want to end up with a photo collection that is safely organized in a way that makes sense to you. Where you can find the photos you want easily and quickly. Be cautious of overreaching and creating a monster. You may build a meticulous, highly structured organizational system for your photos, but if it's so complicated that you'll never use it again, you've defeated its purpose.

Once all the photos have been culled, sorted, and labeled, and they are in either photo-safe boxes, sleeves for storage, or sleeves headed for scrapbooks or albums, it's time to put them away. Using One Home for Everything and Like with Like to guide you, find a place to store them all that is climate-controlled, easy to access, and large enough for them all to live alongside each other. So whether they're in photo boxes, albums, or sleeves, they'll be together, not scattered throughout the house or even the room. Keep them together and you'll always know where to find them, day or night.

Digital Photos

Digital photography has revolutionized the world of photography. Unfortunately, it hasn't revolutionized photo storage. We've traded in piles of prints for random images scattered across our hard drives, in and out of digital folders, labeled or not, almost impossible to locate without a razor-sharp memory, superior computer skills, and a heap of luck. Add to the mix the technical way in which your camera and computer "name" each picture or file as it's imported, and unless you specify or remember exactly which folder you downloaded an image into, you'll be lucky to see it again before your next birthday. Your only hope is recognizing the .jpg suffix at the end of a file's name and then manually opening each file until you find the image you're seeking.

Downloading from the Camera

When you get home from taking pictures or soon thereafter is the time to download them to your computer. Do not procrastinate. Because eventually you'll be rushing out the door, frantically grabbing the camera, racing to your grandkid's birthday party, and when you go to take that first picture, you'll discover that your memory card is full and you don't have a spare. And that will be a big fat disappointment.

I have a client who never downloads his images; he simply buys new memory cards. This is not an adequate solution for several reasons. The first is the most obvious—he's yet to enjoy a single image he's ever photographed. The other reason is more about convenience and delaying the inevitable—the more memory cards one ends up with, the longer the downloading process will be when one finally commits to it. It would seem, at some point, that one *does* want to see the photos, not just handle the memory cards!

When transferring photos from your camera to your computer, direct them into specific folders immediately. Do not dump them all randomly into any folder labeled "My Pictures" or "Pictures" or "Photos," thinking you'll get back to this "later" to clean up and organize. Create subfolders that accurately describe the photos you're about to deposit into them—like "August 21, 20XX, Billy's Birthday" or "Summer 20XX, Cape Cod." A short description is more likely to jog your memory than just a date, so be sure to include both. Every computer has a default location it prefers to download images into—you can either globally alter that under a "preferences" or "options" tab, or simply manually redirect the downloading each time your camera is hooked up to your computer.

For example, instead of just dumping the camera's contents randomly into "My Pictures," create a series of subfolders inside it as follows:

My Pictures
2010
November 2010
Nona's 90th Birthday

If you already have many photos dumped into your "My Pictures" folder, schedule a chunk of time (or several) to create these subfolders as described above, and slowly and deliberately sort your photos into the appropriate folder.

> ● **Notable Note** ●
>
> If you will be posting any of your photos to a website, make sure to save the original, higher-resolution image as well. The smaller, lower-resolution image desired for Web publishing will not make an adequate high-quality print if you want to print one out later.

Renaming or Tagging?

When digital cameras first became widely available and affordable, you'd take your pictures, then download those pictures to your computer. When you wanted to find them or name them or organize them in any way, you'd have to remember which folder you had downloaded them into. Sometimes the computer would put them into a default random folder, perhaps the last folder previously opened. Eventually, you'd find them and then manually rename them.

Even today, renaming photos can be a tedious process, and when you're finished, you're still limited in how you can view related images. If they all reside in the same folder, you can open that folder. But if you have photos of a particular subject or person stored within several folders, there's no way to view them all without manually creating a new folder and duplicating each image or creating shortcuts in the new folder as well. And then you'd have two versions of the same picture in two locations.

With the innovation of tagging, you can now use photo-organizing software to assign "tags" (i.e., labels) to each of your photos. Tags are really only keywords or categories used to describe a piece of digital data—in this case, a photograph. But rather than call them "keywords" or "categories," they're called "tags," a more friendly and less jargony way to refer to something that ultimately works behind the scenes, anyway. Anyone can visualize sticking a tag or a series of tags on an image—it's simple.

With some care and thought, you'll create a list of categories that reflect common subjects—these will become your tags. Use these to get you started: Mon, Dad, Grandma, Grandpa, skiing, boating, road trips, birthdays, etc. Too many and the list becomes unwieldy; too few and there's little distinction between images.

The power and ease of tags are apparent when you want to find a particular photo or photos. You no longer have to sort through various folders looking for them, trying to remember what you may have called the folder or opening each photo, especially if they're still bearing some digital number identifier as their only name. Instead, you just think of some aspect of the photo that you would have used in a tag, like "skiing" or "birthdays" or "Mom." Search on that tag and all the photos associated with that tag will come up. And unlike renaming each picture, you don't need to retype the same tag again and again. Once you create your tags, assigning them is a simple drag-and-drop activity.

Tags are especially useful when it comes to finding specific people in your photos as well. By tagging each picture with the names of each face in the picture, you'll be able to search and find every picture of a particular person instantly. You can further refine any search by including or excluding additional tags. For example, a search for "Gary" and "Ethel" will bring up all photos in your collection of Gary and Ethel. By excluding "wedding" from the same search string, you'll end up with all the photos of Gary and Ethel except for those also tagged "wedding."

Digital Frames

Digital frames continue to drop in price and increase in functionality and storage capacity. These devices are a great way to stream a slide show of favorite images, a photo album displayed within a frame where you need never turn a page. Some even have built-in speakers and allow you to stream a piece of music as your photos rotate through their cycle. They may not appeal to everyone, but for some these frames' flexibility and functionality may be an excellent and expedient alternative to creating photos albums the old-fashioned, time-intensive way.

Software Solutions

There are a variety of photo-organizing programs out now with great photo-tagging features. Some are free, and some you'll have to buy. Technology changes so fast, I'll refrain from specific recommendations and instead suggest that you search online for "photo-organizing software" and see what comes up. Do some research, talk to your tech-savvy friends, and see what looks user-friendly and within your budget.

All programs should allow you to assign tags to your photos and then search by any combination of tags to view any group of photos that contain those tags. And in many of them, you literally drag a representation of a tag to drop on your pictures. Very simple.

The one software I'll mention by name is iPhoto, which Apple wrote for Mac users. Taking tags one step further, iPhoto has a feature they call "Faces," which employs face-detection technology to identify faces of people in your photos, and face recognition to match faces that look like the same person. They have another feature called "Places," which allows you to search and sort photos by location (which can be tagged with GPS metadata).

Whatever program you choose, make sure it offers the ability for the tags to remain with the image, so that if you change software or give the image away, its tags stay with it. The language to look for is anything that describes "embedding the tag into the metadata of the photo."

File-Renaming Options

If tags seem too complicated or involved for you or you don't want to get new software, you should at least rename your photos from obscure camera-speak like DSC000014 to "20XX, Sally's Graduation."

With Microsoft Windows, you can rename your photos in groups. Open a subfolder, such as "20XX Christmas," select all the images in the folder, right-click and choose "Rename," then type "20XX Christmas" and press "Enter." The photos will all be given that name, along with a sequential number tacked onto the end.

If you're looking for software that speeds up renaming photo files, again look for a program that gives you access to the metadata associated with each file. That way the info, including any name, becomes embedded into the photo's data file.

Tagging and Folders: A Digital One-Two Punch

Tagging is great progress but not yet a revolution that eliminates the need for some order and organization. Since each tag is the same "weight" and no tag is more significant than any other, tagging can be a bit too democratic in how it returns results. You may also be so specific in your creation of tags that you soon have too many tags to control and keep track of—so that managing the tags becomes as involved as managing the photos used to be.

As a significant advance in the way digital data will be sorted, saved, and even shared, tagging is an excellent addition to our organizing arsenal. But we are not finished with hierarchical folders (folders within folders). Together with tags, they provide an excellent way to corral and maintain your digital images.

So instead of just dumping all your photos in one folder, thinking that tags will help you keep track of them as you search for and sort them, you can create subfolders to hold those particular tag searches.

One More Plug for Folders

Regardless of whether or not you use photo-organizing software, you still want to sort your photos into subfolders by year, category, and subject. There will always be times when you want to get to a specific photo directly, and having it labeled in a folder is one of the surest ways to do that.

I suggest that with tags and/or subfolders, you keep a simple list of them someplace, either as a digital text file on your hard drive in your "My Pictures" folder, printed for easy reference, or both. Whatever categories, tags, or folders you use are less important (they can be completely idiosyncratic to you, including pet phrases, etc.) than ensuring that you'll remember them and be consistent in using them.

Maintaining the System

Take the time to sort through all your old photos, either film-based or digital; put them in appropriately named folders or boxes; tag, label, and/or rename the images; and you'll be finished with the historic challenge, however large. This now becomes your base for future organizing.

Use the following steps to keep the system working. Remember that each task has a beginning and an end, so complete each step in order, and if you are diligent and consistent you will never not find a photo again. Ever.

For new film-based photos, follow these steps:

1. Develop film in a timely fashion.
2. Review prints and cull the best, discarding the rest.
3. Label each image with some sort of information: who, what, when, where.
4. Transfer the keepers from the developer's sleeve into an acid-free sleeve or the appropriate photo-safe box, accurately labeled.

For digital photos, follow these steps:

1. Download the images from the camera.
2. Sort the images into appropriate subfolders, creating new folders when necessary.
3. Rename the picture file from gobbledygook to a few actual words that make sense to you.
4. Label or tag all images.

Back Up Your Digital Photos Regularly

Anyone who's had the nightmare of having their computer crash knows the necessity of backing up their files and pictures on an external drive. As the saying goes, "Back up early; back up often." Most external drives now come bundled with backup software that simplifies the entire process. You select which folders you'd like to back up, select a schedule for the backing up, and leave it alone. As long as the drive and computer are powered up, at the appointed time the drive will scan the computer and back up all the folders indicated. Some even scan for additions, adding just those files to the folders already stored.

In addition to an external drive, make a CD backup—which you can store with your prints. A bonus of CD backups is that you can also insert the disk into a CD or DVD player to view on your TV.

This may seem like overkill to you while reading this book. It's not. More than a few clients and even I have suffered through failed hard drives and the anxiety of trying to harvest whatever data could still be salvaged after the technical failure. At that point, you'll be grateful for whatever morsels can be pulled together, and you'll be cursing yourself for procrastinating. Save yourself the future headache and back up now.

If you don't use digital cameras, choose the option to get a disk of your prints at the same time you get your rolls of film developed. It's simpler and safer than storing paper double prints—even if you lose hard copies and your hard drive, the disk of the pics will survive.

When backing up, some people limit the contents on each CD to a particular subject, such as "holidays" or "gardening." Label all disks clearly with the subject name. Then you'll never have to look through "holidays" to get to "gardening." At the risk of flinging more clichés around, "an ounce of prevention is worth a pound of cure," and when it comes to digital files, that pound of cure can be breathtakingly expensive. Spend a little time now to prevent having to spend a king's ransom later.

Notable Note

PHOTO SORTING AND ORGANIZING DO'S

Sorting

- ☐ Immediately toss any pics that are not keepers (see the list of questions on pages 288 to 289). A photo that fails any of those questions should be discarded.
- ☐ If your photos are going in boxes, sort them directly into those boxes. No need to touch them twice.
- ☐ If your photos are going in albums or scrapbooks, in addition to sorting them by category or event, sort them into groups destined for each album or book. Then create test layouts to play with design before the glue comes out and you're committed to a permanent arrangement.
- ☐ When sorting, record an identifying description on the back of each photo (for example, the date taken or the key subjects or people in the photo).
- ☐ When sorting, separate favorite pics to display as you come across them; likewise, segregate pics (duplicates, etc.) that are earmarked for friends or family.

Storage

- ☐ When purchasing photo boxes, buy several at a time. This keeps the look uniform and gives you room to grow.
- ☐ Store negatives separately from prints, as negatives can release acidic gases that will damage nearby photos.
- ☐ Store negatives with one another, clearly labeled, protected in the same way as photos.
- ☐ Store all photo and negative boxes away from light and heat.
- ☐ As soon as prints are developed, transfer them from photo-center packaging to protective acid-free envelopes.
- ☐ Immediately and clearly label each new envelope with dates and concise, specific descriptions. Do not save this task for "someday." An example of accurate and specific labeling would be: "September 2004, Marybeth's Wedding" or "June 2002, Alaskan Cruise."

- Each labeled envelope should then be stored with its brothers and sisters, grouped by their common category.
- When establishing categories, be specific enough so that you'll be able to find photos and general enough that each category contains more than one image.
- If using photo boxes, use acid-free tabbed dividers to further organize into subcategories (for example, "Family Gatherings" or "Trips" or "Friends").

Care and Maintenance

- Keep film negatives. Just because the developer *also* provided a disk of images, negatives of images you'd like to retain should not be tossed. The jury is out on whether to clip your negative strips or not. Some labs won't reprint individual frames; others require it. Everyone agrees they should be kept as flat as possible to avoid curling.
- Oils from skin can degrade photos and negatives, so handle pics by their edges only. Clean white cotton gloves offer added protection.
- These plastic products are currently considered safe for contact with photos: polypropylene, polyethylene, Mylar, Tyvek, and cellulose triacetate.
- When writing on photos, always use a light touch, and use only acid-free, photo-safe pencils or pens.
- Keep a box organized with all your photo supplies: acid-free glue sticks, labels, markers, and photo corners. Acid-free, acid-free, acid-free! Having them on hand means you're more likely to actually use them.
- Sort each roll as it is developed to avoid ever ending up with an unmanageable pile of photos again.
- Set aside any photos or negatives that you want to reprint or enlarge, and keep them together with negatives or disks in one location, to be dropped off on your next errand run.

PHOTO SORTING AND ORGANIZING DON'TS

Storage

☐ Never use manila envelopes, file folders, envelopes provided by the developer, plastic bags, corrugated boxes, or shoe boxes to store photos.

☐ Never use "magnetic" photo albums—the glues used are bonded onto the pages and will damage your photos after minimal contact.

☐ Acid, lignin, and polyvinyl chloride (PVC) will ruin photographs. Make sure that any storage option you choose (photo box, album, scrapbook) is labeled as acid-free, archival-safe, and lignin-free, and is not made of PVC.

☐ Do not store photos in any space where temperatures and humidity fluctuate.

Sorting

☐ Do not start a big sort on the dining-room table (or other multiuse surface) and then leave the photos cluttering that surface. If you don't have a space in your home that you can dedicate to a sizable project, then spread out only enough photos to sort through in one sitting. This may mean your sort will take a bit longer, but you won't become anxious or agitated when you want to use the dining-room table and find it otherwise occupied.

Care and Maintenance

☐ Nothing (adhesives of any kind, paper clips, rubber bands, etc.) should come in contact with photos, unless specifically designed and identified as safe for photos.

☐ Photos should not come into contact with wood or engineered wood products (plywood, chipboard, etc.), polyvinyl chloride (PVC), or porous marking pens.

☐ Never hang framed photos on a wall that gets direct sunlight—your photos will fade. Or use blinds, shades, or draperies to control the light.

10

E-mail • Organizing Computer Files • Social Networking Sites

Programming today is a race between software engineers striving to build bigger and better idiot-proof programs, and the Universe trying to produce bigger and better idiots. So far, the Universe is winning.

RICK COOK

Diamonds are forever. E-mail comes close.

JUNE KRONHOLZ

his chapter is not a how-to instruction manual on using the computer. A chapter would be insufficient, and other people have already written those books. What we're going to cover in this chapter is how to organize the contents of your computer, and by that I mean your files. Not your software, also called applications or programs. Your computer files can be considered the modern counterpart of paper documents that traditionally would be found in an office or file cabinet. Organizing your computer files assumes that you already possess basic computing skills. That means that you know what your hard drive is, that you know where to locate it on your computer, and that locating, navigating, and altering the hierarchy of your computer's subfolders are things you feel are within your grasp.

We're not going to modify software (programs or applications running on your computer) or remove viruses or worms, and we're not going to optimize your computer so it can run faster. We're going to optimize you, so that you can run more efficiently and actually find things when you're looking for them.

Like any other power tool, whether a drill or a chain saw or a dishwasher, your computer is a tool to leverage time and accelerate a process. What we want to avoid is any situation where the tool ceases to be useful and becomes a burden and an obstacle to efficiency and speed. Likewise, we want to establish or shift your habits around e-mail correspondence to align with your core values while at the same time creating realistic expectations and timelines—so that you are running your e-mail rather than your e-mail running you.

We're also going to address social networking sites and instant messaging (IM) as additional resources for communication and better time management. While many people use them in the most basic or personal ways to keep in touch with friends and family, they are also potentially powerful communication tools. Few people in your professional world may be interested in what you had for breakfast, but posting an update to a social networking group on the status of a project you need support with instantly updates key players with a clear directive and articulated goals.

In the way that so many innovations can either suck time out of a day or increase productivity, these electronic communication tools can be either potent or trivial, depending on your intention. Hanging out in cyberspace chatting and visiting all day can be fun, but quickly and succinctly reaching people with the information they desire using focused communication is also possible with the same tools. And if that is something that would serve you and you're not currently doing it, you could be after this chapter.

If you lack basic computer skills, I suggest you pick up an instructional book or take a class or both—computing is not theoretical, it's a series of actions and activities strung together. Learning your way around a computer requires practice—while computers may be used for rocket science, answering e-mails and surfing the Web is definitely not advanced computer use. You just need to spend enough time repeating certain actions until they no longer feel foreign. Think of chopping onions. There are efficient and effective ways to hold a knife and complete the task briskly, and there are similar techniques when it comes to your computer. And fortunately, using the computer is not guaranteed to make you cry.

Some basic training will do much to increase your confidence and get you comfortable in front of a computer. When you're feeling strong, return to this chapter and I'll be here waiting. At that point, reading this chapter will help you establish superior work habits before you have the chance to learn bad ones, ensuring that chaos and confusion won't overtake your hard drive and that using a computer won't devolve into a tedious chore.

What We're Going to Cover in This Chapter

☐ E-mail: What It Is and What It Isn't
☐ One Home for Everything and Like with Like
☐ Establishing a Personal E-mail Policy
☐ Managing Incoming E-mail
☐ E-mail Vampires
☐ Online Shopping—A Potential Personal Hell
☐ Organizing Your Bookmarks
☐ Managing Spam—Not the Potted Meat
☐ Organizing Your Computer
☐ Backing Up!
☐ Social Networking Sites—What's in It for Me?
☐ Instant Messaging? I'm Just Getting Used to Instant Pudding . . .
☐ In Conclusion

Things You Will Need for the Work in This Chapter

• A computer
• Internet access
• Timer or stopwatch
• A heaping dose of patience!

E-mail: What It Is and What It Isn't

Electronic mail, often abbreviated as e-mail (noun):
A method of exchanging digital messages, designed primarily for human use; a system for sending and receiving messages electronically over a computer network.

E-mail is not a siren call; it is not an emergency broadcast system; it is not the fire department banging on your front door. It's a string of symbols that have been electronically transmitted between computers for the benefit of humans (and in a few labs somewhere, probably chimps).

> ### Notable Note
>
> In the United States alone, more than $650 billion a year in productivity is lost because of unnecessary interruptions, predominantly mundane matters, according to Basex, a leading knowledge economy research and advisory firm. The firm states that a large part of that $650 billion is the result of time lost recovering from interruptions and trying to refocus on work. E-mail junkies, take note.

Unless you're a surgeon and the way that you are called to the operating room is via e-mail (unlikely) *or* you are on a clearly articulated deadline and you're awaiting key information in an e-mail message (possibly), you are not obligated to check e-mail or answer e-mail constantly. They call the BlackBerry "CrackBerry" for a reason. The illusion of speed is seductive and intoxicating. But be clear, e-mail's almost immediate arrival into your inbox does *not* automatically require an instantaneous response (the one exception being in a customer-focused business. In those cases, customers have come to expect quick responses, and you may want to adjust your response time for customer inquiries *only*). Just as you needn't bolt for the phone every time it rings, you can break the cycle of obsessively checking your e-mail, responding like one of Pavlov's dogs to notifications of new messages. Nor should you confuse the ability to receive e-mail with a signifier of one's importance—for matters of national security, the President is not relying on e-mails and text messages from the Joint Chiefs.

"Snail mail" still arrives once a day, six days a week, and that hasn't changed since the 1890s. While your creditors would now prefer to contact you electronically (under the guise of saving the planet by saving paper—when it's really about saving printing costs and postage for them), even they seldom demand an immediate response. So it's okay to slow down—you are not under attack and and arriving messages cannot hurt you. And regardless of what other people might opine, moving slower and more deliberately when composing e-mails does not mean that you don't care or that you're irresponsible or rude.

One Home for Everything and Like with Like

Perhaps with electronic files and e-mails, these two rules are even more important than they are in your home or office. One Home for Everything and Like with Like guide us in the organizing of our computer's files and in keeping track of e-mails arriving and being sent. You can't afford not to know where every document on your computer lives—unlike your desk, you'll never move a book or folder to discover a stray receipt lying there that you had been looking for just minutes ago. The chances of randomly stumbling across a misplaced digital file are stacked against you—which is why it is imperative that you always pay close attention when saving or moving files and folders around on your hard drive. This is a time when you do *not* want to be multitasking. I've tracked down files inadvertently grabbed by clients and dragged to the oddest of places, all because they were talking on the phone or not paying attention when moving something else, something completely unrelated, and the missing file had just gone along for the ride.

Establishing One Home for Everything and maintaining it will save you hours of frustration. If all Word documents live together, you'll always know where to search to find the one file you need when you've got to have it. And Like with Like ensures that, for example, all the Word documents pertaining to a particular subject or project are all in the same folder, easily identified and distinguished from their siblings.

Establishing a Personal E-mail Policy

To support employees in remaining productive and focused, most companies have implemented e-mail policies for their workers. We should follow their lead.

Originally created to define appropriate content and usage, more and more e-mail policies are expanding to include the how and when of replying and sending e-mail as well. In establishing your own e-mail policy, it's important to remember that you are in control of your e-mail. You may not always be able to control what ends up in your inbox, but you can control when and how often you check your e-mail, and when and how often you reply.

It's only within the last fifteen or so years that e-mail, officially created in 1971, has taken over as *the* means of communication. Techies and time-management folks have both begun advocating for alternatives to this de facto monopoly. Each with its own agenda around efficiency and expediency, these different groups of thinkers have begun pushing for the adoption of other methods of sharing information, encouraging broader use of blogs, Twitter, IM or chat, text messaging, wiki, and so on. But until this movement reaches a tipping point, e-mail is here to stay, and given that, here are my suggestions on how to better manage it. Feel free to use or modify this list as it serves you, with the exception of the first rule, which is not open to negotiation.

CHECK E-MAIL ONLY WHEN YOU HAVE TIME TO REVIEW IT AND REPLY TO IT

Similar to handling the physical mail—don't open it if you don't have time to process it (as discussed in chapter two)—here I'm suggesting that you not open an e-mail if you don't have time to answer it as well. If you open a message without enough time to respond to it, not only will you need to reread it when you *do* have time, but if the content is at all disturbing, it will become a distraction until you have time to adequately respond. I have ruined more than one night's sleep by opening an e-mail I was too tired to deal with but not too tired to be upset by.

When you do get around to checking e-mail, start and finish dealing with every new message when you first see it. You will waste much time reading e-mails and not responding at the same time. The one caveat is anything that is too emotionally charged for you—replies composed in the heat of the moment are always well-served by careful review and editing, after you're calmed down and had some time to think. Prudence of pen and tongue is an excellent guide when composing e-mails to intimates—you don't want to commit to something in writing that with some clarity and calm wouldn't accurately reflect your true feelings.

Excluding this exception, these three steps should guide your e-mail process.

- Read it.
- Reply to it.
- File it (or trash it).

CHECK E-MAIL ON DEMAND—DISABLE AUTOMATIC CHECKING

Either close your e-mail program completely or turn off automatic mail checking and turn off the program's announcement features, such as sounds or pop-up screens that herald the arrival of e-mail. Again, unless you're expecting something specific from someone specific, you don't need to see or know about each e-mail as it arrives.

DON'T READ AND ANSWER E-MAIL THROUGHOUT THE DAY

I easily receive between fifty and two hundred e-mails each day—some are informational, some need to be answered, but very few of them need to be answered immediately. And I tell everyone that in the case of an emergency, calling my mobile phone is the surest way to reach me. You can't be productive and constantly interrupted at the same time. Establish a particular time or times each day and an appropriate duration for the review and answering of e-mail. Set a timer, and when the time is up, you're finished. Obsessive slavishness to some perceived obligation to e-mail is counterproductive at best and dangerous at worst when you're more concerned with appearing rude than completing a major project in front of you.

I remember calling author Suzanne Pharr once and being struck by the directness of her outgoing answering machine message. It announced that if you had phoned between certain morning hours, she was writing and would not be answering the phone. It made an impression. While writing this book, I created my own auto-responder to all e-mails stating that until the book was finished, I would not be checking e-mails between the hours of nine a.m. and six p.m. It afforded me a manageable boundary so I could work with fewer interruptions. Thank you, Suzanne!

Once you've figured out how long you need to answer the volume of e-mails that actually require a response, budget that amount of time into your day. I find that twice a day, once mid-morning and once later in the day, works best for me. Whatever you decide, make it a part of your routine and stick to it.

DON'T ANSWER E-MAIL AT YOUR MOST PRODUCTIVE TIME OF DAY

I'm a morning person. I'm up early and at my most productive between seven a.m. and eleven a.m. So I prefer not to get lost in e-mail first thing in the morning. Answer the following question for yourself.

I'm most productive between _____ and _____.

Now that you've defined it, that time is sacrosanct. Not only should you not be answering e-mails, you really should not accept any commitments for that time if you can avoid it. Schedule less-demanding tasks, including managing e-mail, outside of your optimal work time to ensure making the most of your day. I find that when I'm losing steam and growing fatigued from extended focus on a particular project, the distraction of e-mail is sometimes a welcome shift from more rigorous brain activity.

INBOX MEANS INBOX

Your inbox should show only unread messages. It is not a task list, a shopping list, or a reminder area where lingering "to-do" items hang out until they're forgotten or deleted. I have one client who had more than thirty thousand e-mails in her inbox and would attempt to search through them to find recent correspondence about a particular project. The sheer volume of e-mails would slow her processor down to a crawl as it sorted through all those e-mails. We've spent several long hours trying to eliminate all duplicates and Listserv and subscription e-mails that are now obsolete or redundant, and have finally gotten her down to less than eight thousand, with more sorting still to do. Which leads us directly to the next point on the list.

LET YOUR E-MAIL PROGRAM
MANAGE YOUR E-MAIL

Successful e-mail management must include setting up and using filters. All e-mail programs offer the ability to configure e-mail "rules" or "filters" to direct e-mails to specific folders based on any number of criteria: the sender, subject, and/or content. If you're not using some external spam filter, you can have any spam directed immediately to the trash, so you don't have to waste time reviewing and deleting it.

I have many folders labeled for specific categories of e-mails. My e-mail program automatically filters all incoming e-mail and directs it to one of these folders, based on criteria I've set up and saved. Here are a few as examples.

VirgoMan Book: All correspondence between my agent, my editor, and the publisher is immediately directed to this folder.

VM Seminars: This folder contains correspondence from anyone inquiring about my teaching a workshop or their attending a workshop.

Monthly Bills: All billing correspondence, including payment alerts and postings, and all electronic bills and invoices are directed here.

Current Events: These are invitations to events, either from lists I subscribe to or sent to me by friends, family, and colleagues.

Shopping: These are coupons and other notices from online and brick-and-mortar stores that I like. While I don't shop often, and never on impulse, it is nice to see if anything is on sale when I'm in the market for a new whatever. If you are too tempted by these kinds of e-mails, unsubscribe from their lists.

Family: This is correspondence from anyone I'm blood-related to.

Clients: Within the "Clients" folder, I actually have several subfolders: one each for current clients (organized by name) that I'm working with on ongoing projects; one labeled "Casual Clients"; and one labeled "Inactive Clients." That is where any of the named client folders get moved to when I complete a project. If the client becomes active again, his or her folder is moved back into the main "Client" folder. Here's a simplified visual of the folders:

Clients
    Becca & Carol

    Patti & Nina

    Iris

    Etc.

Casual Clients

Inactive Clients
    Amanda Baker

    Mark Hopper

    Richard Nelson

In addition to folders, you can also customize the appearance of incoming mail. For example, bold the subject line and change the color for all e-mails from your clients or boss.

Filters can also play cleanup behind you, automatically moving all read e-mail out of your inbox after twenty-four hours. That way, even if you've forgotten to file them, the computer won't.

Another way to distinguish among e-mails is to flag them. Like the tags for photos mentioned in chapter nine, you can create associated saved searches for each flag. That way you don't need to re-create common searches each time you want to find all e-mails bearing a specific flag.

Finally, using the preview pane at the bottom or the side of your incoming e-mail list allows you to quickly scan through new e-mails that your filters may have missed to then manually redirect them to their proper folder.

THE MORE E-MAILS YOU ANSWER, THE MORE YOU RECEIVE

It doesn't seem logical that as soon as you clear your inbox, it's almost immediately filled again. Like rabbits, e-mails seem to breed at a tremendous velocity and volume. I receive fewer and fewer jokes and hoax e-mails because I don't respond to them. I have a family member who sends me jokes and Web curiosities as expressions of affection. I may not agree, but rather than pick a fight, I open them, chuckle or not, then shuttle them off into the trash folder.

I also don't respond to e-mails that don't require a response. An actual composed thank-you letter is one thing; a simple e-mail that says only "thank you" does not require a reply. They can create an unnecessary volley of e-mails, such as the following, until you're ready to pull your hair out.

"Thank you," "Thanks," or "Thanx"
"Yr welcome"
"No problem"
"Cool"
"Don't mention it"
"I won't"

Someone has to stop volleying. Research e-mail etiquette, establish your own guidelines, and then adhere to them. Leave the above exchange to people who have that much time on their hands.

I also no longer feel compelled to alert people about hoaxes they are unwittingly circulating. Someone else can provide that service. It's enough to know that Bill Gates is not giving away a million dollars to Microsoft users; that so-and-so received this e-mail and ignored it and his dog died, then he forwarded it on to all his friends and won the lottery; or that someone made the grave mistake of answering one's cell phone while it was still plugged in to the wall and it blew the side of his face off.

If you'd like to take on that role, refer your friends and family to one of the following sites to do some due diligence before sending any more of this kind of junk to others:

www.snopes.com
urbanlegends.about.com/od/internet/a/current_netlore.htm
www.hoaxbusters.org

REPLY WHEN NECESSARY

While there are many e-mails that don't require a response, some certainly do. So even if the answer is "no," "no, thank you," or "I can't," do provide some answer if it's clear that someone is waiting for your reply before they plan their next action.

Procrastinating and delaying your reply is not helpful to the sender. If you know when you'll be available to answer, let them know. If you don't have the information requested but know who does, forward it on to the appropriate person and CC the sender. You've facilitated a solution and gotten yourself out of the loop—a double win and the best possible outcome in these kinds of exchanges.

READ THE ENTIRE MESSAGE THREAD BEFORE RESPONDING

Have you ever answered an e-mail only to discover that someone else had previously answered it? Make sure to review all messages in a message thread prior to answering an e-mail. Many e-mail applications offer a way to distinguish and group e-mails related by thread to aid in this process. It will save you time and face.

USE COMPLETE INFORMATION
IN THE SUBJECT LINE

Help the recipient anticipate content and make filing or filtering easy for both of you. Do not use personal shorthand, some private secret language, or overly abbreviated subjects like "Update" (with or without today's date), "Checking In," or "Status"—they are ambiguous and confusing. Be thorough and succinct, to the point and direct. You're sending an e-mail, not laying an ambush. There's no reason to obscure content with a vague subject line. So instead of sending an e-mail in response to a request for a file with the subject line "Your request," send one with this simple yet descriptive subject line: "Volunteer Opportunities File Attached, Per Your Request, 3-30-XX."

AUTOMATE RESPONSES TO
FREQUENTLY ASKED QUESTIONS

Do you often get e-mails asking the same questions? Create standard replies to those frequent questions and fold them into "signature" files in your e-mail program. Then you can select the appropriate "signature" when your reply is sent. There's no need for a personal message when there's no need for a personal message. Here's an example of a signature that does double duty.

> Thank you for requesting more information on upcoming seminars. I am currently scheduling the next few months' appearances, and those dates will be posted on my website. Please check back at www.virgoman.com again soon. Webinars and other online opportunities to participate in events will also be posted there.
>
> In addition, you have been added to the mailing list for your region. But don't worry, we'll never loan, sell, or disseminate your address in any way. I hate spam as much as you do!

Thanks again for your interest. Here's to creating order out of chaos!

> Best,
> Andrew J. Mellen
> President, VirgoMan
> www.virgoman.com

And once you've sent your reply to a frequent question (or really any e-mail that isn't an ongoing correspondence about a project where a paper trail, digital or otherwise, is desired), there is seldom a reason to keep the original message. Delete it.

PUBLISH YOUR PREFERRED METHODS FOR CONTACT

Let people know, either at your website, in your signature, or through some other means, how and when you wish to be contacted. If you prefer text messages to e-mails, let them know. And if you're slow to respond to a mode of communication that you've already indicated is not preferred, the message will start to sink in.

REDUCE YOUR USE OF E-MAIL AS MUCH AS POSSIBLE

Actively seek out alternative ways of communicating. Does a tweet or text message that you broadcast to your network more succinctly get the information out? If you don't need to send an actual e-mail, particularly if there's no response from the other party required, consider publishing things publicly somewhere with a permalink (blog, Twitter, wiki). This will accomplish several things.

- It gets the answer on the Web and away from the need for you to personally answer it.

- It provides a URL that you can supply instead of a personal response when requested.
- It encourages people to exhaust other options before relying on an e-mail for information.

WHEN ALL ELSE FAILS, YOU CAN ALWAYS DECLARE E-MAIL BANKRUPTCY

As more and more people come face-to-face with information overload, there's increasing talk and implementation of "e-mail bankruptcy," a term describing falling so far behind in responding to e-mail messages that it becomes preferable or necessary to delete them all and start over.

The Internet and even print media now feature many opinion pieces on this phenomenon—from the practical nature of how one declares e-mail bankruptcy to the ethical implications of such an act. Like reticent captains going down with the ship, folks have been known to send out one last desperate e-mail informing all recipients that, come tomorrow, this e-mail address will be abandoned and its owner will no longer reply to any past or future correspondence received at it.

As with other forms of bankruptcy, this is really a last-ditch effort. And as many critics have pointed out, while dumping your inbox may bring some temporary relief and buy you some time, if the problem is an ongoing one of the number of e-mails received vs. the time and ability to answer them all, it can't be long, then, before you're back in the same situation.

So consider carefully whether something as drastic as bankruptcy is even going to be the solution you're seeking or whether you need to find the cure to a larger problem. Study the suggestions above and begin to implement them, and start shifting your

> ### Notable Note
>
> Some companies have instituted "zero e-mail Fridays," in hopes of encouraging more face-to-face communication between employees. Experiment with your own mini-hiatus and see how that works for you. Maybe a day free from electronic communication would feel liberating rather than isolating!

relationship to e-mail while examining any internal and external expectations you may have.

Finally, like its financial counterpart, e-mail bankruptcy may bring with it some lasting consequences in the form of others' judgment of and reaction to your technical and time-management competence, so add that into the mix before you press delete.

A corollary to e-mail bankruptcy is simply dumping your e-mail address. Whether as a result of falling too far behind in e-mail responses or because "bots" and other spammers have targeted you, you may choose to simply ditch your current e-mail address and start fresh. You can contact everyone on your e-mail list and update them and then begin using your new e-mail address, enjoying at least a few days of spam-free correspondence.

While less explicit, it may be assumed that with your new address, you're no longer responding to outstanding e-mails from the previous address.

Managing Incoming E-mail

Now that you've established some rules for yourself about using e-mail, take a few minutes to set up your e-mail to better serve you.

Fill in the blanks below.

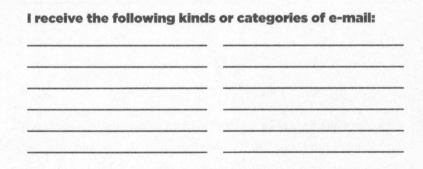

I receive the following kinds or categories of e-mail:

Now create subfolders below your inbox for all of the above categories. Then open either "preferences," "options," or "customize" on the menu of your e-mail program to begin creating your new rules (i.e., filters).

I also use two e-mail addresses—one for personal correspondence, and one for all online subscriptions, banking, and shopping, so I'm not bombarded with nonessential e-mails throughout the day. I can check the second e-mail address once a day—there's never anything that requires my immediate attention coming from any of the following places.

- Banking
- Airlines—promotions and my frequent-flyer accounts
- Travel in general
- Online catalogs, vendors
- Blogs
- News sources
- Software registrations
- Nonprofit organization newsletters and updates
- Social networking sites
- Interests—real estate, home improvement, gardening

Fill in the blanks below.

These are the e-mail lists and services I subscribe to:

_____

_____

_____

_____

_____

_____

Consider which ones arrive and actually annoy you—the ones you thought you'd enjoy but rarely open, or the ones that seem to come more frequently than you remember requesting. If you haven't already deleted them, create a folder now to corral them all and manually drag them into the new folder. Name it "E-mail Subscriptions to Delete." Then set aside fifteen minutes and click on the "unsubscribe" link at the bottom of each message and be finished with them. If you have already deleted the last round of these pesky e-mails, then as each new one comes in, follow the "unsubscribe" link at the bottom of each e-mail and kill them in real time. Either way, it shouldn't take more than a week's time for you to receive one of each and to then eliminate the bulk of them.

If you're feeling at all hesitant right now, if you're thinking, "Yeah, I hate them, but 'someday' there might be one that contains something really important and I'd hate to miss it just because I was impatient," please consider the following. First is that "someday" doesn't actually exist. You can't live in the future and in the moment at the same time. Second (and less philosophical) is that the content or information (if you can call it that) that they are delivering will still be available somewhere—either on their website, somewhere else on the Web, or in actual printed form, either within a book or catalog or magazine. Carefully consider their usefulness. Weigh them against the implicit demand they place on your time simply by arriving. If their content is not information you need for work or life to complete a project or meet a deadline, go ahead and unsubscribe.

Free yourself from the idea that you're missing something important. You're not. You're missing lots of things all the time—a soccer match in South America, a trade show in Dallas, a going-out-of-business sale down the street. It's a given that you can't be everywhere at the same time, so accept it and let that panicky feeling fall away. At the same time, recognize that whatever you actually need to know or find out, you can and will actively pursue. The rest can be recognized for what it is—a possible distraction and some visual noise.

When you finish this exercise, you should be receiving only e-mails from actual people or key companies and organizations you have strong affinity for. If it takes you a few passes to continue to fine-tune this process, that's fine. Don't judge it, just celebrate your expanding freedom from inbox clutter.

E-mail Vampires

Do you have a friend, relative, or client who seems to suck the life out of you with their e-mail correspondence? Do they never reply to an e-mail with answers or statements, only more questions? Do they claim to be interested in clear communication yet refuse to address key points laid out in your letters? Repeatedly? Do they state how confused they are by your e-mails while explaining themselves, defending a point of view that is always about being wronged and misunderstood? Are they frequently pointing out how unfair something is while assiduously avoiding any responsibility for their present circumstances? Are one- or two-sentence e-mails from you answered with novellas? If the answer to more than two of these questions is yes, you've met an e-mail vampire.

Similar to other time vultures, e-mail vampires often experience reality as one big soupy mess of hurt and betrayal. And you have become their latest lifeline. Elaborate, finely detailed excuses are usually offered as reasonable explanations for their circumstances. And your attempt at composing a seemingly foolproof e-mail with clearly laid out instructions and bullets listing action items usually elicits a response in the form of a written tantrum.

Before the Internet, these people would fire off angry letters to the editor of the local paper. Or take hostages at a cocktail party, a PTA meeting, or the grocery store checkout line. Now they simply dominate your inbox. Their relentless campaign to be understood is pathological, and reasoning and rational arguments will prove ineffective in creating an adequate boundary. The more distance you try to gain from their demanding grasp, the more fiercely they fling accusations, desperately trying to keep the dialogue alive.

Unfortunately, like their fictional counterparts, a stake through the heart is the only solution to this problem. Ignoring all communication is the only viable answer as any reply on your part will only re-engage your vampire. As difficult as it may be to cease all written communication with someone, particularly someone who is in genuine need, it is imperative to recognize that the help you have to offer, unless you are a trained therapist or other medical professional, is inadequate in the face of their ills. It is a deep sadness to walk away from suffering. This is where the expression "detaching with love" proves useful for us, if not for them. To them, we become another link in their chain of unbroken misery and disappointment, more proof of how unfeeling the world is in response to their pain.

With perspective we can see that this unhappy conclusion was inevitable. They had already choreographed the entire relationship before we even entered into it. While not puppets, we were cast for our affinity to our written roles. Without guilt or shame, we can recognize the role we played as enablers and find some solace in knowing that our efforts were admirable, if misguided. And start keeping a little garlic near the keyboard.

Online Shopping—A Potential Personal Hell

I have a client, Barbara, who has a shopping problem. She seldom enters brick-and-mortar stores because she doesn't have time. But at two a.m., when she can't sleep, she's online shopping while the Home Shopping Network is on the TV in the background. It's possible that, at this point, one venue for uncontrolled impulse shopping may no longer be sufficient.

She easily receives seventy-five e-mails a day from online vendors, promoting sales and special events. The overwhelming volume of these kinds of messages crowd out important e-mails from her daughter's school, neighbors, friends scheduling social events, and most significantly, correspondence from her work.

Her dining-room table and the entire floors of her entryway, living room, and kitchen are stacked with boxes in various states of examination and return. The hours she spends processing returns is overwhelming—I've spent more than one eight-hour day dispatching thirty to forty packages back through UPS, while ten new boxes arrived on the same day. She tells herself that it's actually efficient to get something in various colors and sizes at the same time, believing that in spite of overwhelming evidence to the contrary, returning things is simple and effortless.

Sadly, this doesn't even account for the many items that linger far past the expiration date for their return because she has trouble making decisions. Those items become gifts for others or are donated to a local charity. While her neighborhood thrift stores may be grateful for her bountiful excess, she carries more than $150,000 in unsecured credit card debt. Even with her six-figure income, she is often delinquent and over the limit on many of her credit cards, receiving dunning letters and collection calls throughout the evening. Her credit is trashed. She's a nervous wreck. She knows it's a terrible way to live, but she is also unwilling to stop. At least not yet.

It is noteworthy that what might seem intolerable to me, and possibly you, may not be sufficiently painful to someone else to motivate them to let go. We are surprisingly strong and resilient creatures, even when apparently dancing on a razor's edge. The ability to sustain prolonged discomfort while hoping to either prove oneself right or prove someone else wrong may not always be a useful attribute. It often comes down to being right or being happy, and many folks, regardless of pain, choose being right.

The willingness to let go is the key to breaking this cycle for Barbara, or for any of us. Willingness. Not strength, not stamina, not cleverness—just being willing to stop doing something that doesn't serve you anymore and becoming willing to do something else. You don't even have to know how or what you will do to break the cycle of this behavior, you just have to be willing to do something different.

And perhaps the most disturbing part of this all is that Barbara already owns a three-bedroom apartment's worth of everything. Plenty of high-quality, well-cared-for clothing, costume and precious jewelry, electronics, artwork, and furniture. She wants for nothing material. So what is that void that she's attempting to fill with this desperate behavior?

If you are also engaged in some form of the above, please pause for a moment. Perhaps you're feeling superior to Barbara and her choices because you get only twenty e-mails a day from online vendors and have a few returns lying around.

Or perhaps you have a sinking feeling in the middle of your stomach that you've just looked into a mirror and actually seen yourself for the first time in a long time. Whatever you're feeling is fine; there's no need to judge. I certainly don't.

If you're starting to hyperventilate, breathe slowly and consciously until you steady your pulse. Count to five as you inhale and five again as you exhale. Identifying with the desperation is a losing proposition. *Identify with the willingness to shift your behavior.* Any effort you exert in the opposite direction from compulsive shopping will break the chains of this kind of bondage. And consistent steps forward will liberate you, perhaps not overnight but certainly over time.

Recognize the crafty ways you may be speaking to yourself about this, either minimizing the negative consequences or justifying your unique position and requirements. Crafty speak is usually just fear wrapped up in a baloney sandwich—fear of not *having* enough, or not *being* enough, or some other fear. That fear and its good pal, desperation, will frantically shove anything they can get their hands on to use as a wedge between you and different behavior.

And surprisingly it is your own, albeit different, behavior that is going to create any change in your life. Experience has shown me that you will seldom successfully modify your actions by waiting to feel better (whatever "better" is) or stronger or ready. Likewise, attempting to change your feelings or suppressing them does little to alter behavior. It is the mechanical shifting of yourself that yields the most consistent and reliable results. As William James so aptly stated, "We don't think our way to right action; we act our way to right thinking."

If you truly want to break the cycle of insanity that compulsive shopping is and recover your financial well-being and your mental health, not to mention the hours wasted aimlessly wandering around the infinite shopping mall we call the Web, the first stop is to immediately remove yourself from online e-mail lists.

Whatever deep discounts or VIP specials that you will no longer be updated on are not important. If and when you are actually in need of something, you may return to any of your preferred sites to purchase that specific item or items. Until then, you can let someone else on their mailing lists benefit from the remarkable "one-day sales" they're advertising. It's nice to share, isn't it?

If you can't seem to stay off shopping sites, and getting rid of your computer is not an option, consider using monitoring software. While originally designed to prevent children from visiting sites with adult content, these virtual nanny programs let you customize them to prevent Internet travel to specified sites. If online vendors are your form of sweet-and-sticky baked goods, this might be an effective tool in denying you access.

Whichever methods you use, and you may employ several to create a comprehensive plan of attack, remember that you are not alone. Shame, frustration, and fear can isolate you, and you may be feeling alone, but chances are there is at least one other person who cares about you and would be willing to help if they knew of your situation. Break the silence, open the door (or a window if the door seems overwhelming), and let someone in. Seek out appropriate help and support from friends, family, and/or professionals.

Just for today, *do not shop*. Whatever it takes. Play some miniature golf, go to a multiplex and see four movies (unless it's attached to a mall!), volunteer at a senior center or animal rescue or hospital, run errands for or with a friend—fill your day with something other than shopping and make the day about someone else. I promise you that for at least that day, you'll be appropriately distracted and the lovely by-product will be a feeling of usefulness and purpose—a feeling that is at best fleeting, if not entirely absent, when shopping.

Organizing Your Bookmarks

Bookmarks (also called Favorites in Internet Explorer) are great tools for getting us to favorite sites on the web, but without some organization, their effectiveness is greatly hindered. If you have just a running list of all your bookmarks in no particular order under the main tab labeled Bookmarks in your browser, your only chances of finding a particular bookmark again would be to scroll until you came across it or to remember when you created it and then looking for it near other sites you marked on or around the same date. Neither option does much to save you time and take advantage of the convenience of actually bookmarking sites in the first place.

To organize your bookmarks, use the same approach outlined for paper filing in chapter four. Identify categories of subjects and interests that groups of bookmarks would fall under and then create corresponding folders to contain your bookmarks. These are some of mine:

Air Travel (general information)

Airlines (specific carriers)

Arts and Culture

Computers

Cooking and Food

Finances

Health and Wellness

News

Sports

Theater

Travel

Weather

And this is an illustration of how bookmarks look inside some of these folders:

Airlines

American Airlines

British Airways

Continental Airlines

Delta Airlines

Cooking and Food

Small Appliances, Equipment & Supplies

Baker's Catalogue

Broadway Panhandler

Chefs Choice.com

Cooking.com

Culinary Parts Unlimited

Professional Cutlery Direct!

Foodies

The 40th Pillsbury Bake-Off Cooking Contest

The Body Gourmet

Bourrez Votre Visage—musings on all things caloric

Chocolate & Zucchini

Cook's Illustrated

eGullet.org

Epicurious

Food Network's FoodTV.Com

The Good Cook

The Grateful Palate

The Kitchen Link

Finances and Money

Credit Bureaus

Equifax

Experian

Transunion

Research Tools

BUYandHOLD.com

Feed the Pig.com

FundAdvice.com

FundAlarm.com

Mortgage Calculators

SaveWealth.com

Your bookmarks toolbar is the place to keep the sites you visit the most frequently. Even more convenient than organized bookmarks in expanding folders, these shortcuts to favorite sites live right in your toolbar so they are displayed in every open browser window, making any site literally one mouse click away.

Every browser offers you the opportunity to customize how windows and tabs are displayed, and that includes customizing your bookmarks and bookmarks toolbar. Take advantage of this convenience to personalize and streamline your Web surfing activities.

Managing Spam—Not the Potted Meat

If you haven't yet been slammed with spam, the following suggestions will help you delay this unpleasant-seeming inevitability. Whether you are just establishing e-mail service for yourself right now or are a seasoned user, carefully consider and choose the right e-mail address.

The following e-mail address prefixes are magnets for spam "bots"—e-mail robots phishing for valid e-mail addresses—and should be avoided: contact@, help@, home@, sales@, support@, webmaster@. Generic e-mail addresses like these are assumed to exist at every domain. For spammers, they're a no-brainer. Here are more suggestions for minimizing your exposure to spam:

- Don't use AOL, Hotmail, Yahoo!, Gmail, and other major Web-based e-mail providers for your primary e-mail address; get a domain name instead. Creating a domain is very easy, and many hosting companies will walk you through the simple process. So instead of being BettyWalker@aol.com, you could be Betty@BettyWalker.com. How about that for customized living? Spammers know that there are almost endless accounts at the big e-mail providers, and they target those accounts with their most aggressive spamming efforts. If you must use one of the major providers, choose an obscure e-mail address that has some combination of letters and numbers.
- Don't list or publish your e-mail address anywhere on the Web. This includes your own website or at news groups, chat rooms, networking sites, or online forums. If you must list it, either break it up with spaces between your user name and the @ symbol and the domain name or write it out like this: "your user name AT your domain name

DOT com." Spammers use bots to surf the Internet and harvest e-mail addresses from Web pages.

- Opt out of e-mail lists, and make sure merchants do not share or sell your e-mail address or other personal data with others. Read the privacy policy of any site before purchasing anything or corresponding with online merchants.
- Never open spam. Never. Simply opening a piece of spam informs the spammer that your e-mail address is valid through embedded graphics or other code within the message.
- Never reply to spam—even to unsubscribe. Spam often offers false "unsubscribe" options as another trick to confirm the validity of your e-mail address. As a result, clicking on the unsubscribe option actually increases the amount of spam they send. In the case of hijacked e-mail addresses used to send out spam, your reply would be sent only to the innocent victim of the hijacking.
- Never purchase anything from an unsolicited e-mail message. Spammers send out spam because it's profitable, either through perpetrating fraud on unsuspecting individuals or through the sale of junk to unsuspecting individuals. If the profits dry up, spammers will find new ways to scam the public but they'd at least give up on spam.

If you are overwhelmed with spam, there are some steps you can take to reduce your inundation. While it's impossible to completely eliminate spam, the following suggestions can alter its grip on your inbox.

- If you don't have spam protection, get some. If you have it and you've yet to employ it, do so.
- Most ISPs (Internet service providers) and Web-based e-mail applications now offer some sort of external spam filter. Log in to your e-mail on their server, which you can do by going to their website and following the links for Web mail. Once there, look for "preferences" or something similar, and look for anything that is labeled "spam

filter" or "spam blocker," or something with the word "spam" in it. Once you find that, you can set the sensitivity level from low (capturing only the most obvious spam) to high (capturing everything from anyone who is not in your address book on your ISP's site—which may be distinct from your address book on your computer). On the highest setting for spam filtering, my ISP generates an e-mail message announcing itself to all incoming e-mails from unknown addresses, encouraging them to request addition to my online address book. Bots can't respond, but real people can—so your correspondents have the opportunity to verify themselves, and you will (only once) have to manually add them to your address book. Captured e-mail that fails to be verified is diverted into a separate folder on the ISP's server and is deleted daily.

- Most e-mail programs also offer some form of spam filter. They may be called "filters" or "rules." The program filters e-mails based on parameters you set in a preferences area, which instructs the program to handle certain e-mail in certain ways. You can set it to block e-mails with certain key words or from specific senders. Those key words may be further isolated to the subject line or body of the e-mail, or both. For example, any e-mails that contain "Viagra" or "get rich now" anywhere could be sent straight to the trash. As you recognize patterns or trends in your incoming e-mail, edit the filters or rules to keep current with any shifts in content.

- The last option for controlling spam is third-party spam-filtering software. As software design changes daily, I offer no specific recommendations of particular products. At any time there are probably a few free choices out there, along with others that you'd have to purchase. Any software you select should be easy to use, easy to customize, and powerful enough to do whatever it claims to do. With that in mind, I suggest you do some research online, talk to friends and anyone who has stronger computing skills than you do for their suggestions and recommendations, and then take your choice for a test-drive.

If none of the above is successful at significantly slowing down the volume of incoming spam, your last resort may be to abandon the e-mail address that's being swamped. Before you panic or grow resistant, remember that what I'm suggesting is not that you sell your home and move to a remote island with no indoor plumbing. No matter how fond you are of your e-mail address, you are not your e-mail address, so keep that in mind. If breaking free from spam's grip means you have to send one e-mail to everyone in your address book alerting them to your address change, it's a small price to pay for even temporary freedom from spam. And it reinforces the temporal nature of all things, even e-mail addresses.

Organizing Your Computer

FOLDER NAMES

While it may seem that computers are really just expensive e-mail management boxes or online shopping boxes, they are powerful tools that can save us time and process information quicker than whole teams of people could previously do manually. Which doesn't prevent them from also becoming labyrinths of files and folders that seem impossible for us to find our way through.

If you think of your computer as a virtual filing cabinet, you'll have a useful image to guide your work in getting and staying digitally organized. The fact that the files and folders are all data and not paper is the only distinction of note—otherwise, a file is a file is a file, to paraphrase Gertrude Stein.

It is possible that you have not read or worked through chapter four yet. It's also possible that you do not have a physical filing cabinet, or that if you do, that you are underutilizing it. You may not own a single file folder, and you may be surrounded by stacks and piles of papers in an order that makes sense only to you. If that is the case, when we are finished with this chapter, your computer's organizational structure will become the blueprint for any future filing you'll do of actual paper.

To begin organizing your computer's files, please go to your computer now. Make sure it's on and that you're at your desktop. You should already have a folder called either "Documents" or "My Documents" on your hard drive. Please find it now. If you don't have a "Documents" or "My Documents" folder on your computer for some reason, create a new folder now and name it "Documents."

This will now become your root, or base, folder for all your documents and personal files. By personal files, I mean all data or documents that you have the ability to download, create, modify, and store on your computer. Remember, we're not altering stand-alone software applications or programs—these too are stored in folders on your hard drive, typically inside a folder that shares the name of the application it contains, such as Quicken or Intuit or Microsoft Office. Unless you are a computer programmer, you should probably never be inside an application's folder altering or moving or deleting any files. Files with seemingly innocuous names could be pivotal pieces of code that will irreparably impair an application's ability to run on your computer. When it comes to folders containing applications or other pieces of software, remember this adage: when in doubt, stay out.

Whether you have a physical file cabinet or not, you want to imagine your "Documents" folder as your virtual file cabinet. Unlike a real file cabinet, there are no drawers to provide structure, only folders. So we will create master folders that define the first or broadest level of category that we're trying to contain, such as "Finances," or "Correspondence," or "Home Improvement." Then within these folders we will create more specific folders to further define the contents of each folder. For example: within "Correspondence," we may have folders called "Creditors," "Family," "Friends," and so on.

The rule for creating and naming file folders is to always make their names specific enough to be recognized by someone other than you but not so specific that they would contain only one thing.

Here's a list of some of the master folders on my computer, laid out to illustrate their relationship to each other within the hierarachy of folders.

Documents

VirgoMan

Current Writing

Medical and Health

Correspondence, Personal

Correspondence, Professional

Finances

Gardening

Grad School

Office Supplies

Owner's Manuals

Photos

Recipes

Travel

Two things to note here: First, you'll notice that several master folders are not in alphabetical order. That's because I've inserted a space (or several) before the names of several of these master folders' names to force the computer to put those folders at the top of the list. Because the computer strictly alphabetizes the folders' names, those names beginning with empty spaces automatically rise to the top of the list. This is useful for me because my company's name begins with a "V" and I want to be able to access those folders quickly and often, so having them at the top of the list means less scrolling down. This tip may also help you to "force" folders you use frequently to rise to the top of a list.

Second, many of these master folders contain subfolders that further separate the contents into more specific groupings. Consider these subfolders within the master folders.

Documents (Root Folder)

VirgoMan (Master Folder)

    Client Files (Subfolders)

    VM Artwork

VM Bios, Résumés, and Head Shots

VM Contracts

VM Gift Certificates

VM Public Relations

VM Workshops and Seminars

If we drill down one more level, this is how the folders look.

Documents

VirgoMan

Client Files

Becca and Carol

Patti and Nina

Iris

Inactive Clients

And one more level looks like this.

Documents

VirgoMan

Client Files

Becca and Carol

Patti and Nina

Iris

Inactive Clients

Amanda Baker

Mark Hopper

Richard Nelson

Using the above illustration as a guideline, begin to list the names of the master folders you already have or will create within your Documents folder, either in the spaces below or in your notebook.

Documents

_____

_____

_____

_____

_____

_____

Great. Now for all of those master folders, begin to outline the folders that would live inside them.

_____ *(Master Folder from above)*

_____

_____

_____

_____

_____

You can either photocopy the above list and use it as a worksheet or, after completing this list, use it as a template to actually create these folders on your computer. Ultimately, that's what you're going to want to do anyway. This exercise should get you thinking in these terms (folders and subfolders) and give you a visual map you can play with and alter without any consequences.

Continue to go down as many levels deep as you need to in creating subfolders, so you can accurately and thoroughly corral each of your documents into an appropriate folder. In your attempts at specificity, pay attention to whether you have created folders that still will contain too many loosely related documents, or folders that are so specific they will contain only one document. In most cases, careful consideration will find that one document somewhere else to live. But if that is not the case, stick to your guns and maintain the folder with only one document.

Note at this point that we have yet to actually do anything on your computer. This is all prep work for the actual sorting and organizing.

FILE NAMES

Gone are those DOS days when file names could be only eight characters long and not contain any symbols. Today's computers, both Macs and PCs, allow you to name files almost anything you want, so take advantage of this advance. Name each file in a way that you will remember it, that will allow you to search for it, and that will distinguish it from its many brothers and sisters. That said, you should still endeavor to keep file names as brief as possible, while avoiding too many abbreviations. Long file names require larger windows to see the full title. To avoid guessing or misidentifying files, keep their names comfortably snug. So rather than having a file named "229 West 138th Street HVAC Renovation Project, Summer 20XX, Smith Contracting," try this instead:

Folder: 229 West 138th Street
   Folder: Summer 20XX Renovations
      Folder: HVAC
         Folder: Smith Contracting
            File: Smith Bid Proposal, 6-28-XX

Adopt a consistent language, style, or method for file and folder naming. Develop this naming system, and create a style sheet outlining the rules you use in naming files. Share this with anyone who uses your computer and adds files to it. Consistency in naming files is the best way to ensure that you will be able to find files you haven't looked at in months or years.

Use common names that make sense to you and, when appropriate, include applicable model numbers, project names, or the names of key people in the file name. Also always add a date to the title of each document. Update the date each time you edit the document. If you have multiple revisions on the same day, also include the time as well. You can't rely on the modification date of the file to tip you off to the most current version of any file.

So rather than using "My Card List" as the name for my holiday card list, instead I've named it "20XX Holiday Card List, 11-7-20XX." This way we know that it's the 20XX version of this list. It's clearly named as the holiday list, in case I have other lists of addresses or contacts. It's further defined by the date it was last modified, 11-7-20XX. Now if I search for either "20XX" or "holiday," the files are sure to show up in the search. And when I review all possible documents, the date will further direct me to the most current draft.

SAVING AND CUSTOMIZING FILES

When you save documents to any drive, external or internal, make sure to select the *correct* location when prompted to—this "files" your new (or edited) document in its appropriate folder.

Likewise, when installing new programs, make sure you always direct the computer to put them in the program files or applications folder. Pay special attention to *never* save files that you're working on, files that contain text or information or data that you are altering and using, in the same folder as any software application. That means do not save your Microsoft Word documents in any folder labeled Microsoft Word that contains the actual program or application named Microsoft Word. By always keeping document files separate from program files, you reduce the risk of accidentally deleting your documents when you install or upgrade programs.

Don't save unnecessary files—be selective. You don't need to save every draft of a document once you've arrived at your final version. Lift any key sentences or ideas out of previous drafts and save them in their own file to source for future projects. Then delete the working drafts, retaining your final version. Be sure to label it "Final" or "Published" or something that identifies it as the last edited version.

Instead of saving multiple copies of the same document in various locations, use shortcuts and shortcut links instead. *This is not to be confused with making multiple backup copies.* But if you need to get to the same file from multiple locations, don't just create duplicate copies of the file. You run the risk of making competing edits in each version and losing valuable work. Instead, create as many shortcuts in as many locations as you need, all pointing back to the one actual original document. On all computers (even Macs now support two-button mice), a right-click on your mouse while selecting the file will offer you the option to create a shortcut. For Macs, shortcuts are called "aliases." These can then be dragged and dropped in as many other locations as needed.

There are several third-party programs (some free and some for a fee) which allow you to color-code the names of your folders and files. This is useful for folders and files you use frequently. Finance or money files could be colored green, etc. This is another way to recognize and access files and folders quickly.

Thumbnails are little images you can apply (think 2-D electronic decoupage) right on top of a folder. Searching through folders in the thumbnail view (usually listed under the "view" tab in your toolbar) allows you to find things visually as well as by name. I've applied thumbnails to several folders—they're fun and help me distinguish particular folders from their neighbors with just a glance. You can apply pictures or clip art or icons right onto the folder. I've attached Quicken's dollar-sign icon to my "Quicken Files" folder and a picture of a water meter to my folder named "Utilities." They amuse me and make the folders stand out. To apply an image to a folder, right-click the folder and click "Properties." In the properties dialogue box, click the "Customize" tab. In the folder pictures area, click "Choose picture." For Macs, you do this under "Get info." You'll see an icon on the top next to the file name—just paste the icon or image over the generic image of a file folder and you're done.

ORGANIZING YOUR FILES AND FOLDERS

Now that we've gone over how to create folders, properly name them, and even have a little fun decorating them, it's time to actually organize them.

If you've left your computer, please return to it now. If you're still there, make sure it's up and running and not sleeping. Get your timer as well. I suggest no more than two hours at a sitting when it comes to this kind of comprehensive organizing. And even so, every fifteen minutes you should shift your focus and change your physical position. The eye and body strain of prolonged uninterrupted computer use is debilitating. If you need to, pause your timer, get up, get a quick drink or snack (keeping food and drink *away* from your computer—you must know someone who's spilled a beverage on their keyboard by now), and resume working.

Begin by finding and opening up your documents folder. Create a new
folder within the documents folder and call this "Temporary Dumping
Ground" (we'll refer to this going forward simply as TDG). Derive slight
amusement from this name. Open this new folder and set it aside.

Don't minimize the folder down to your dock or toolbar, just size it small
enough that you can have another window open beside it. You can do this on
a PC by pointing your mouse at any corner of the window until you see a short
diagonal line with double arrows appear. Click and drag on this line and you
can resize your window in any direction, making it wider, taller, or wider *and*
taller. On a Mac, there are three diagonal lines in the lower right-hand corner
of every window. Simply place your mouse over these lines and click and drag
to accomplish the same resizing.

Now you may minimize the documents folder. Great. We now have one
open folder on our desktop named TDG.

Now open up your hard drive, labeled "My Computer" on a PC and
"Macintosh HD" on a Mac. Size this window large enough to view several

levels of the file hierarchy without having to keep adjusting the window's dimensions.

With this window open, begin searching for all files and folders that may be currently located anywhere *besides* inside the documents folder. As you find these files and folders, drag them to TDG. And keep repeating this exercise until you are as certain as you can be that you've found everything and relocated it.

Now, close the window showing you "My Computer" and expand the documents folder. The documents folder and TDG should now be side by side.

Inside the documents folder, we're going to begin creating all your subfolders. Refer to your worksheet above or notebook for the comprehensive list of your file and folder names. Compare the names of the files and folders you've just found with your written list and see what you already have. Create any missing folders now. Once these folders are in place, begin to open each existing folder in TDG and examine its contents. If there are files that you know you can toss just by looking at their names, do so now. For all others, open each file and confirm if it's a keeper or a tosser. Once you've examined a folder's contents, drag that newly edited folder from TDG into one of the folders you've created in your documents folder. This is another "rinse and repeat" activity. You'll do this for each folder and file until the TDG folder is empty and everything has been reassembled within the folders you've created in your documents folder. Depending on the volume of files and folders on your computer, this exercise may take fifteen minutes and it may also take many hours and multiple sessions. Whatever it takes to complete this task, the goal is to properly name every file, place each file inside a folder with its brothers and sisters, and properly name that folder so it accurately reflects its contents.

When you have sorted and organized all your files, you may now empty the trash or recycle bin and delete all the extraneous files you've discarded. Congratulations, you're computer is perfectly organized. For today.

A FEW MORE THINGS ABOUT KEEPING YOUR COMPUTER ORGANIZED

I am strongly opposed to your desktop serving as a catchall for files and folders. If you are working on a few projects, it's fine to create shortcuts on your desktop to those folders or files. Under no circumstance should you be creating new files or folders and defaulting to leaving them on your desktop. One Home for Everything means the folders need to be created as subfolders within your documents folder from the very beginning, not "later" or "someday."

The way to keep your computer crisp and neat is obviously to move slowly and deliberately when creating files and folders. Always name things accurately at the time of their creation and store them in their proper home. Like with Like ensures that you'll keep similar files and folders together. If you don't make a mess, you won't have a mess—keep that in mind when you're inclined to rush or feel so pressed for time that you tell yourself, just this once, you'll cut a corner and that you promise to come back soon and clean it up. Bad habits breed more bad habits. Take the time to do it right the first time and you won't need to make a promise that begs to be broken down the line.

Backing Up!

Along with burning disks of important information and storing them in a file and/or a safe-deposit box at the bank, consider getting an external hard drive that attaches to your computer through either a FireWire or a USB port. These drives can be used manually—you can just drag and drop key files and folders onto the drive, and many of them come with software that allows you to establish routine backups of your files. You set the parameters for which files, when, and how often they get backed up, and the drive (and its software) does the rest. I like to set them to back everything up once a week after midnight—I'm unlikely to be on the computer that late, and I just leave the machine running and it takes care of everything by morning.

Likewise, there are online backup services available. Some offer a limited amount of space for free and charge a fee for greater amounts of storage, while others charge for any access to their servers. Either way, these sites can be configured to automatically back up your computer at an interval of your choosing. Investigate them online and make sure they have enough room and drives to ensure at least triple backing up so you'll be sure to not lose any data should one leg of their system fail.

Thumb drives are far too unstable to be reliable backup sources. One too many drops on the floor or accidentally stepping on it can render it unusable—they're fine as portable transfer devices, but I wouldn't rely on one as the repository of important data.

As the saying goes, "Back up early; back up often." Having lived through my own and clients' computer hard-drive failures and multiple-thousand-dollar data retrievals, I insist on multiple backups in multiple forms—external drives and several copies of CDs and DVDs burned with key data. Do not put all your eggs—or in this case, files—in one basket. Every few months I burn new disks and place them in a safe, along with a copy or two dropped in a file folder in my file cabinet, aptly labeled "Backups." Learn from others' misfortunes and avoid unnecessary heartache. It's an awful feeling when a computer fails before you've had a chance to save your personal files.

As long as you retain the original software installation disks, there's no reason to ever back up applications. In the event of a computer failure, you'll want to install any programs cleanly and from either a downloaded file or an original disk, anyway. Copying software and trying to reinstall it from those copies is tricky at best—you can never be sure that every piece of code for a particular application has been successfully backed up. It takes only one missing piece of code to render a complete application useless.

Social Networking Sites— What's in It for Me?

A social networking site is a website that creates a virtual community online, either for people who share a common interest or are looking for a place to gather online with no geographic limitations. Each site requires you to become a member to take advantage of their full suite of features, and membership is typically free. Each member creates an online profile with biographical data, which could be as spare as your name and birth date but could also include pictures, likes and dislikes, and just about any other piece of information you'd care to share. Members often restrict access to their profile to friends, and each site provides a way of contacting and accepting friends into your network. Members can communicate with one another by voice, chat, instant message, videoconference, and blogs, and each hosting site typically provides a way for members to contact and introduce themselves to people in one's extended network, or friends of friends.

Social networking sites allow you to meet new people, establish or join groups of folks interested in particular subjects, and span both professional and recreational networks. Still others use them to find old friends. I've recently heard from several folks from my childhood who found me through a social networking site. Sites may also serve as a vehicle for ultimately meeting in person. There are dating sites, friendship sites, employment sites, and sites that cater to particular industries or businesses, as well as hybrids that offer combinations of any of the above. More and more sites are being created that serve a particular niche of the larger community. There are niche networking sites for everything from learning a new language to sharing recipes to recovering from addiction. And while the history of social networking sites is fascinating, I'll leave that for folks to research on their own. For now, I'd like to address how they can prove useful as a communication tool.

By now, many of us have heard of potential employers using social networking sites to learn more about prospective employees. Googling possible hires and reading their online profiles has become standard research for human resources departments at some companies. Keep this in mind before you post the pictures of you and your friends celebrating a birthday by getting rowdy at some neighborhood watering hole. Your future job prospects could be compromised by seemingly innocent information that is now publicly available.

Mobile phones are still in the beginning stages of developing applications that expand the social networking experience beyond the home computer. Uploading photos, video, and GPS tracking to facilitate real-time rendezvous are just a few of the ways that mobile phones are exploiting these online networks.

Some of you may be thinking that this stuff is for kids. You'd be mistaken. While no doubt many teens and twentysomethings are all over these sites, there are many of us over thirty who use these sites for everything from planning events and broadcasting invitations to completing projects, whether personal or work-related. Social networking sites are here to stay for the foreseeable future, and there's no reason to miss out on the many opportunities they present. Like anything, you can get lost wandering through them; the scale of many of them is vast, but also like many things, you may soon tire of aimless wandering and figure out the particular uses each site offers you and home in on them, exploiting the site for its full utility.

Support, friendship, and community are all possible online. You can find contractors and other tradefolk, plan a party, or share information on a health condition you may have. You'll find and meet people who have common interests and goals, or common dislikes and aversions. For some of us, social networking sites will never replace face-to-face contact. But for others of us, some of whom may be limited by mobility or geography, the possibility for connection and resource sharing is as real as meeting at the general store on a Sunday morning for coffee and the latest gossip.

Finding people is one of the most interesting features these sites offer. Most of the larger sites suggest people you may know based on people you already have in common, e-mails you've sent, and lists you subscribe to. It's quite amazing the threads some of these sites pick up on to link us to people from our past, our recent past, and our present. It's almost always a pleasant surprise when you get a message from someone you haven't seen in more than twenty years—and in the few cases when it's not, you needn't fear. As the person being contacted, you retain full control and can simply refuse to accept them as a friend. So much for the cheerleader who snubbed you in seventh grade. Revenge can be sweet, even if it takes thirty years to happen.

Instant Messaging? I'm Just Getting Used to Instant Pudding . . .

Instant messaging (IM), also referred to as "chat," is the exchange of text messages in real time between two or more people logged in to a particular instant-messaging service or via mobile telephones. What separates chat and instant messaging from technologies such as e-mail is the perceived synchronicity of the communication by the user—chat happens in real time. E-mail messages can often be queued up on a mail server for seconds, minutes, or even hours at a time. IM allows effective and efficient communication featuring immediate receipt of acknowledgment or reply.

While there are no page-layout options offered with instant messaging, meaning the text remains unadorned and font choices are limited, IM increasingly offers expanded options for videoconferencing, picture and video uploading, and file sharing. It's also possible to save a conversation for later reference. With that in mind, remember that once you send something, whatever it is (a picture, your phone number, your unpublished manuscript), it's beyond your reach and no longer under your control. Be mindful of new technologies and assumed privacy—Detroit's mayor Kwame Kilpatrick was finally done in by a trail of instant messages between him and his chief of staff. Just because you want or assume that something is going to be private, doesn't mean it's going to stay that way.

Users sometimes utilize Internet slang, or "text speak," abbreviating common words and expressions to quicken conversations and minimize typing. This slang has crossed over into the common vernacular with well-known expressions such as TMI (too much information) and LOL (laughing out loud), which are now peppered into spoken language. Others, such as BTW (by the way), BRB (be right back), IMHO (in my humble opinion), and TTYL (talk to you later), continue to infiltrate popular communication. This evolving language has entire websites dedicated to it, offering definitions of these abbreviations, as well as corresponding diagrams of emoticons, those punctuation-based symbols for various feelings (for example, :), :(, etc.).

Like social networking sites, IM has both social and practical applications. IM conversations tend toward brevity and typically cover one topic at a time. Media-switching and multitasking are common among users, employing e-mail, file sharing, and phone or Skype communication alongside the IM as the shape and needs of the chat shifts. In professional applications in particular, IM is often used by colleagues for more sustained but intermittent conversations—often including hyperlinks to external websites, pertinent work files, and other additions as a way to track progress or collaboration on a project.

The seemingly impersonal nature of IM makes it a preferred means of communication for the rapid sharing of information that doesn't require a conversation. That said, more people continue to explore its use as a twenty-first-century way of expressing passing affection, even the sending of love notes. IM is best used when the subject of the communication is one of the following.

- Quick questions and clarifications
- Coordinating and scheduling tasks and events
- Coordinating impromptu social meetings
- Keeping in touch with friends and family

IMing between mobile phones requires only that you know the other mobile number and the other phone has texting capabilities. On a computer using IM software, buddy lists serve as contact lists or abbreviated address books, listing the "handles" of friends, family, and colleagues. Not unlike CB radio users in the 1970s, each IM participant has a user name of their own choosing that is unique to them. This is how you will contact them. When you log on with your IM software, you are immediately alerted to who is online, who is unavailable, and so on. As the people on your buddy list change their status, it's instantly reflected in a display window on your screen. As is your status for them. If you leave the computer for any length of time or wish to be undisturbed, you may update your status at will. Through preferences, you may also limit access to anyone, for any reason, at any time. These settings as well may be updated at will. The flexibility these programs afford the user allow you to always remain in control of who contacts you when. Unfortunately, they haven't yet figured out a way to limit access based on content—so once you've accepted a chat, you'll need to excuse yourself if the conversation takes a turn you are unhappy with. The modern equivalent of hanging up the telephone!

In Conclusion

These modern computing machines—desktop and laptop computers, notepads, smart and not-so-smart phones—offer us many clever, fun, streamlined, and complex ways of interacting with information and with one another. The key to successful use and enjoyment is to embrace advances in technology while holding the awareness that these machines exist to serve us and not the other way around. And not in a science-fiction way, where they take over your life and literally imprison you, but in much subtler ways, where their demands on your time and energy, their constant tugs to keep up, no longer offer convenience and support but rather begin to exhaust and drain you of your focus and enthusiasm.

Just because you can send an e-mail or IM, just because you can surf the Net and spend hours skipping from site to site on those nights you can't sleep, doesn't mean that you need to. You can remain calm, unhurried, and proactive in determining exactly when and how you use any of these tools. Others may disagree, but I offer you my certainty that the choice remains yours.

11 New Things and the Rest of Your Life

Before we set our hearts too much upon anything, let us examine how happy those are who already possess it.

FRANÇOIS DE LA ROCHEFOUCAULD

It is through creating, not possessing, that life is revealed.

VIDA D. SCUDDER

Don't cry because it's over. Smile because it happened.

ATTRIBUTED TO DR. SEUSS AND WALT DISNEY

n the words of Robert C. Hunter, "What a long, strange trip it's been." We've made it from your front door out into cyberspace and back in one piece. Congratulations. In some ways, it's now that the real work begins. You have some awesome new habits. Having touched everything you own or are the steward of, you should now know where everything lives. And just as you may enjoy a night out on the town but then return safely home for a good night's sleep, so should your possessions. Take them out, use them, share them, be prepared for them to occasionally break (and then to let them go), and in the meantime, always put them back where they came from—One Home for Everything and Like with Like have become your new mantras.

Your computer is a microcosm of your home or office, also neat and tidy, with things in their proper place. And you finally know where that proper place is. You should now be starting to spend more of your time doing things that are important and meaningful to you, rather than scrambling around looking for things that have been misplaced, or distracting yourself with unconscious shopping or other, subtler forms of consumption. You're on a path of consciously living each day. Perhaps you'll find yourself smiling at strangers, unless they're stealing your parking place—and then after a momentary scowl, you'll find ways to smile about something else.

If this works for you, don't keep it a secret. If your friends, family, or colleagues comment on these shifts, in large or small ways, let them know what's changing for you. Allow your enthusiasm and newfound freedom to be a twinkling power of example. Celebrate your successes while of course remaining mindful of boasting or lording your progress over your friends, even innocently. Few people like a know-it-all or unsolicited feedback. They may appreciate the message, but they will invariably resent the messenger.

What We're Going to Cover in This Chapter

- ☐ New Things
- ☐ Impulse Shopping and Kicking the Habit
- ☐ Something In, Something Out
- ☐ One Home for Everything and Like with Like
- ☐ It's Christmas/Chanukah/Kwanzaa . . . Where Will I Put All the New Stuff?
- ☐ The Value of Stuff
- ☐ Time: The Commodity Not Traded on the NY Stock Exchange
- ☐ Needs vs. Wants
- ☐ Spiritual Materialism
- ☐ Belief as Definition
- ☐ "VirgoMan, I Think I'll Miss You Most of All. . . ."

New Things

New things, shiny things, pretty things—who doesn't love new stuff? Even as we resent the shrink wrap that slows us down, as we tear through plastic shells that resist most attempts at opening, we giddily celebrate the glossy unblemished yummy freshness of "the good stuff" we're about to make our own.

I want to say that new things are great. Really. I'm not suggesting anyone other than a monk actually live like a monk. Have enough of anything and everything that serves you, and have nothing that doesn't. The core of my philosophy is based on reaching "stuff equilibrium." And this book has been laid out to lead you through a process for gaining that equilibrium. A curated and well-edited life is what I'm advocating, where thoughtfulness and mindfulness guide your consumption, and where experiences are valued over things.

If having fewer things allows you to have nicer things (i.e., nicer to you), that doesn't sound like an unpleasant compromise. Luxury is not inherently bad. The opposite of extravagant consumption may be some form of puritanical asceticism, but we're not seeking the opposite. We're seeking an antidote, and the antidote to extravagant consumption is modest (in terms of volume), tasteful consumption. If you can afford them, or if someone really loves you and gives them to you, enjoy Frette or Anichini linens—they're fabulous—but you don't need twelve sets of them any more than you'd need twelve sets of any other designer's linens. Even if you can afford them. You can sleep on only one set at a time. (See chapter five to learn more about linen closets and how many sets of sheets are appropriate.)

Particularly in the United States, it's often assumed that the solution to whatever ails you is to buy something. The idea of simplifying your life doesn't call for renouncing all purchases, just an insistence that each purchase be selective and carefully considered. Focus on quality, not quantity. And not from a status point of view but from a practicality point of view. We don't want to make choices about consumption based on fear, and certainly not a fear of keeping up with the Joneses. We want to make our choices based on what we feel is sustainable, responsible, practical, enduring, and aesthetically pleasing, whether that's food or art or countertops. The rest doesn't matter.

Impulse Shopping and Kicking the Habit

Seldom are the criteria detailed above—sustainability, responsibility, and durability—considered when impulse shopping. One of the root causes of tremendous amounts of clutter, most impulse shopping is the perfect collision of nonessential items running into ill-considered snap decisions.

Money can certainly be a powerful motivator in kicking the impulse-shopping habit. Regardless of your financial situation, whether you "could" afford to buy whatever you want whenever you want or you need to monitor each purchase's effect on your bottom line, one end result is the same—more clutter and things that you don't necessarily need. For those of us more closely watching that bottom line, the loss of useful resources that could be better applied elsewhere should be additional inspiration. Unfortunately, sometimes rather than providing that extra motivation, fear around debt and declining resources provokes instead a spiral of shame that threatens to drag us down into depression and additional self-destructive behaviors. So let's interrupt that pattern before it becomes entrenched.

Here are some tips and tricks to avoid impulse shopping.

SHOP FROM A LIST

And stick to it. Everyone agrees—from building supplies to groceries, you don't walk into a store without a list. And don't get sidetracked. If you actually, really need something that didn't make the list, complete the rest of your shopping first, *then* go back to collect the forgotten item.

DON'T ZONE OUT WHILE SHOPPING

Stay alert—shop mindfully and deliberately every single time you venture into a store, real or virtual. Don't multitask while shopping. No chatting, checking e-mail, or texting with a cart in front of you. Each item should be vetted before it enters your cart—is it on your list? Does it serve a real and immediate purpose, or are you stocking up for "someday"?

AVOID SHOPPING CARTS

Use a handheld basket or just your hands. If you've run into the store for milk, grab the milk and go—don't then grab a bag of chips, some ice cream, and some chicken that's on sale. Likewise, if you've run into the office-supply store for paper, don't then grab a new printer, stapler, and folders just because you can.

START AT THE REAR OF THE STORE

Go deep and then head for the exit. The faster you're in and out, the less likely you'll be to head back in for something random.

BUY IT NEXT TIME

This is the only time I think "someday" is a good idea. When you come across some groovy gadget that you must have but that isn't on your list, jot it down on the bottom of your list for "next time." Then check at home to see if this is a valid purchase or an impulse buy. If you determine that it's an appropriate purchase, add it to your new list.

TAKE A PICTURE

Instead of actually buying something that isn't on your list, take a photo of the item with your camera or your phone and carry it around with you. Live with it for a week or two and see if, after the initial blush has faded, you think you still need to purchase it.

GET A SHOPPING BUDDY

Set up a mini support group with a good and reliable friend who's available. Your best friend the flight attendant who's often on a jet is not a viable candidate. Make a pact to do the same for your friend. And then actually pick up the phone. Call first and purchase only *after* you've had a complete conversation. You can't say, "Oh, just a few things," when your arms are overloaded with stuff. Be honest and then listen when your friend asks pointed questions, such as, "Do you absolutely have to buy this now?"

SEND SOMEONE ELSE

It may feel like cheating, but it's a surefire way to get the errand done and avoid temptation. Wait in the car or outside the store, or better yet, at home while a child, friend, or partner runs out to the store. Temper whatever disappointment you feel at not shopping with acknowledging the surplus cash that's still in your wallet.

PICK YOUR CHECKOUT AISLE

Do a little study of the checkout lines where you shop. Find the one in each store, usually toward the end of the row, that has fewer displays and make this "your" line. Self-serve lines seem to have the fewest promotional items of all. If you're a magazine buyer, carry something to read in your bag so you resist the urge to pull one off the rack and start reading it while waiting in line. Likewise, if you're a snacker, carry a protein bar, some nuts, or string cheese with you to avoid grabbing a last-minute candy bar.

SHOP WITH CASH—ONLY

More and more people are using only cash to pay for things. Bringing a limited amount of money with you accomplishes two things: it keeps you within your budget, and it prevents you from running up the balances on your credit cards.

The key to this technique is leaving your checkbook and credit and debit cards at home. Try leaving the house with just the amount of money you've budgeted for your shopping. When you run out of money, return home. This forces you to pay closer attention to each purchase as you spend your cash.

STOP READING CATALOGS, SALES FLYERS, AND E-MAIL SOLICITATIONS

Stop "rehearsal" shopping. Read a book or magazine instead. Go for a walk. Go to the movies. Volunteer somewhere. If you know you need a new laundry basket, start the search then. At the back of this book, in the Resources section, you'll find websites listed where you can remove yourself from catalogs, junk mail, and junk e-mail lists.

DON'T SHOP AS ENTERTAINMENT

You're not actually shopping for windows, are you? Aimlessly wandering down Fifth Avenue or through your local shopping mall is not an appropriate pastime. Remember that you can't keep stepping into a barbershop without eventually getting your hair cut.

EAT BEFORE SHOPPING

Eat a full meal before heading out to the store, whether grocery shopping or running errands. People who shop while hungry are more easily distracted and tend to shop emotionally—see below.

DO NOT USE SHOPPING AS THERAPY, "RETAIL" OR OTHERWISE

Many people shop the same way they eat: emotionally. Take the time to get to know yourself. You may not need to spend long hours studying your navel to discover why you buy what you buy.

Perhaps shopping distracts you from feelings you don't want to deal with. Many people buy something because it feels good to buy things—while you may have felt overly passive in a recent encounter, you're now engaged in an activity, making choices, exercising your will, taking control.

Rather than automatically shopping as a way to get some relief, take a few moments and write about your feelings. You don't need to write a book, but sit still long enough to jot down, "I'm angry with my girlfriend/husband/partner, she or he's lately been . . ." or "At work I've been feeling . . ."

Making a list of the things on your mind and noting what's bothering you interrupts the loop of things racing around inside your head. Write until you've exhausted all the things you've been thinking or possibly obsessing about. Of the things you've written down, what has an easy fix and what involves time and another person? Take on the easiest things first, and build up some momentum to address the more complex issues you've identified.

If you often feel isolated, and shopping facilitates a fantasy life in which you're entertaining or going out and showing off your new purchases, consider having people over to enjoy your home as it is. Look through your wardrobe and find a flattering outfit and dress up in it and head out on the town, even to the library or for a walk.

If you find that the intensity of your feelings intimidates or concerns you, consider seeking out a support group or therapeutic setting where you can work through those feelings with peers or professional support. Just like anything else we know little about, there's no shame in seeking guidance and skills in areas where we find ourselves lacking knowledge.

TRACK YOUR SPENDING

Figure out exactly where your money is going. Create a log or spreadsheet, or use software, such as Quicken or Microsoft Money, to record all your transactions. Flag all the purchases that weren't absolutely necessary, and total them up. Look at other areas of your spending that have been limited because of these purchases, and see how you could shift these impulse buys into either more immediate needs or saving for big-ticket items, such as a vacation or a major purchase.

OWN YOUR BEHAVIOR

You may be adept at arguing your case for choices you make, but even if you're an attorney by trade, no one besides you really cares why you did something. There is no better reason for a choice than because you wanted to. So make choices you can stand behind without excuses or explanations. You can't fall back on "the devil made me do it."

Nor are you punishing someone or teaching anyone a lesson (besides yourself) by shopping impulsively. Shopping is not a form of revenge.

In all instances, as soon as an excuse, explanation, or justification starts rumbling around, pause and reflect. See if you can then say, "I did it because I did it. I can see now that I may want to make a different choice. In the moment, I wasn't considering the consequences."

Something In, Something Out

Along with curbing impulse shopping, whenever something new comes into our lives, it's important to ask why. And what for. Whether the item was mindfully purchased by you, found on a curb somewhere, swapped at a friend's house, or lovingly gift-wrapped (with or without a gift receipt enclosed), always ask yourself the following questions even as you're doing your happy dance:

- Do I absolutely need to have this?
- Do I absolutely need to have this now?
- What purpose does this serve?
- Where will this live and do I have the room for it?
- If it's something that was previously owned and in need of refurbishment, will I actually do the work necessary to restore it to full functionality (or get it to someone who will)? When?
- What is it replacing?
- Am I willing to replace _____ with it?
- Can I see myself owning this for many years to come?

These are not trick questions, and they are not intended to shame you or to pry something lovely out of your hands. They are here to ground you and keep you responsibly present. These questions are designed to slow you down, so when something new enters your life it's carefully considered. Not only in the moment, but so the long-term implications are also weighed. We don't want to jettison the hard work already done in exchange for a quick rush over something shiny. To call these diversions deadly would be hyperbolic, and yet calling them counterproductive is an understatement.

A little side trip into acquisition euphoria may feel innocent enough and fun in the first flush of excitement, but not if it means undermining your progress and recently established patterns for living. Just like not flossing for one night will not cause your teeth to fall out but prolonged procrastination will lead to gum disease, so too one quick dance with unfettered consumerism and unconscious grasping is not going to create chaos. But it does reopen the door to "later" and "someday," and that becomes harder to undo with each step they take back into the room. Add to that our concerns about environmental responsibility and proper disposal of things already in our possession, and you can see how a moment's diversion can have lasting repercussions and consequences far outweighing that breathless bubble of bliss.

Once you are present and settled within the knowledge that you have enough, that you have useful tools and functional machines, a wardrobe that flatters you, and pretty things to look at and enjoy, you should be able to begin shifting your thinking from accumulating to swapping out.

Enter Something In, Something Out. This is the surest way to maintain stuff equilibrium. And very simply, it means that whenever something new comes in (as opposed to "arrives," since some things may just be passing through), something that's already here leaves.

Unless you are setting up a new home, you already have things. And I hope those things are useful and increase your comfort and ease of living. If they don't, replace a lumpy uncomfortable mattress when you can. Eliminate non-stick coated cookware from your kitchen when the finish begins to flake off into your food. If a friend gives you her patio furniture, pass yours along to someone else. When the need arises or the opportunity presents itself, replace, update, upgrade. Just don't make it a sport. We didn't create this opening of time for you to fill it with fretting about stuff.

If you have enough of everything, you're either replacing things when they fail or swapping something that still works for a newer version of it that you like better—whether that's a microwave oven or a new blouse. Retail therapy may be amusing on sitcoms and talk shows but not when it creates chaos in your home and credit card debt at the bank. There are other more practical, powerful, and effective forms of therapy. Pursue them instead.

Something In, Something Out now joins One Home for Everything and Like with Like to complete our organizational triangle.

One Home for Everything and Like with Like

New stuff doesn't have a home when it arrives, so if it looks as though it's staying, find it someplace to live. Someplace comfy and cozy and not too crowded. In any instance where something new is *not* replacing something existing, find the new item a home alongside its sisters and brothers. Whenever new things are replacing existing things, the old item should be recycled or discarded and the new one put in its place. Equilibrium remains.

It's Christmas/Chanukah/Kwanzaa . . . Where Will I Put All the New Stuff?

The year-end holidays provide a particular challenge to stuff equilibrium. Madison Avenue's aggressive marketing aside, the gathering of friends and family and the ensuing gift giving, grab bags, Secret Santas, and other exchanges of items at this time of year are meaningful and important to many people. Chances are you'll end the season with more things in front of you than you started it with. Or you could.

Once the wrapping paper is off and the flush of excitement quiets down, when you're alone and feeling steady, refer to the list of questions above and apply them to your new things. Things that do not improve the quality of your life are not required to stay in your life. They're allowed to just pass through.

Nor should you weight something's value with additional significance solely because of who brought it into your life. Meaning a scarf delivered by your grandmother is not somehow more valuable *as a scarf* than a scarf from your kid's second-grade teacher. In both cases, it's the gesture that carries the value, not the scarf itself. Even if one came from Saks Fifth Avenue and the other from a discounted retailer. The scarf might *mean* more having come from your grandmother, but as a neck-warming garment their value is equivalent. In both cases someone thought enough of you to honor you rather than do any other thing at that moment in time—that's what matters. It's about the act, not the object.

You can acknowledge and derive pleasure and satisfaction from each individual act of kindness, each demonstration of affection that's expressed through a gift, regardless of whether the gift remains in your life. And as lopsided as it may sound on first hearing, this applies with whatever arrives, whether it's a plate of cookies or a new BMW. You may never know how much time and care went into the making of those cookies, and the car might have taken all of ten minutes and a credit card to obtain. Or vice versa. Someone might have mortgaged their home to buy you that car, and someone else may have opened a package of Pepperidge Farm cookies and plated them on a paper doily. Instead of judging a thing by someone else's formula for value, evaluate each object on how it arrived, who delivered it, and what it potentially brings to your life.

Any conversation about the "value" of a thing must bring us back to its actual practical value to you. In usefulness. Unless we're speaking of fine antiques, fine art, or precious stones or metals, once something has been purchased, it has no value *beyond* its use. And the above exceptions are exceptions only because enough people have agreed that these things retain some value beyond their functionality. If everyone decided tomorrow that all a diamond was good for was etching glass and refracting light, the market in diamonds would shift and they'd be no more valuable than a crystal prism or a glass cutter. So pay attention to conversations you might have with yourself about how much something is "worth" when trying to determine something's place in your life. When I'm trying to read a newspaper, my dime-store reading glasses are worth a lot more to me than a Rolex wristwatch.

The system we've created—or rather the system that has been created for us—that overvalues certain stuff and undervalues other stuff does not need to make our decisions about stuff. Likewise, just because something arrived at a particular time of year in a particular kind of wrapping does not suddenly change the rules, either. 'Tis the season? Maybe and maybe not.

The Value of Stuff

The value of some new thing is not its retail or wholesale price, nor is it the *difference between* its retail price and what was paid for it. Some people might call that number a bargain, but it's not a bargain if you don't need it.

Stuff's only value is the value you derive from its use because, with the exceptions mentioned above, most stuff is an illiquid asset. Unless you're a dealer of stuff—be it antiques, art, etc.—or have some other outlet for resell-ing some valuable thing for more than you paid for it, its worth is actually unquantifiable. That frees up any further calculating and returns us back to: "Can I use it, and if I can't, what's the best thing to happen to it next?"

As an exercise, rather than reinforcing the idea that stuff is inherently valuable, let's experiment with shifting our view to one in which stuff is basi-cally worthless. Perhaps even a liability. If that seems too "out there" or crazy to you, consider this: recall all the time you've spent in the past carting stuff around, sorting through stuff to find other stuff, being responsible for stuff. Have you ever made decisions about where to live or how to relocate based on the amount of stuff you owned? Have you spent time and resented it while maintaining your stuff? Have you ever ruled out certain homes because they couldn't house all your stuff? Have you avoided certain neighborhoods that otherwise seemed appealing only because you feared for the safety of your stuff, not necessarily your person? Have you ever fantasized about chucking it all and heading out with just a backpack and some cash, but then stopped—not because of people's potential reaction but because of some attachment to your stuff? So maybe stuff really owns us rather than the other way around.

Time: The Commodity Not Traded on the NY Stock Exchange

In previous chapters we've talked about living deeply and being present for experiences rather than simply accumulating objects to either symbolize the experience or substitute for the experience. Previous chapters also offered detailed instructions, tips, and guidance on how to accomplish certain tasks. It's time to expand the conversation. Now that we know where things live in your home (or office), let's focus on where things live in your life.

We want to avoid any situation where maintaining stuff equilibrium is an unpleasant chore or where monitoring things occupies too much of your time—that is not the point of this work. We don't want to replace disorgani-zation with obsessive organization. While you may no longer be drowning in clutter, simply managing your things is the least desirable outcome of the previous chapters' efforts. All the work to get your possessions down to a manageable number and into consistent locations, and establishing habits of using and returning those possessions back to their homes, *was to free up your time to do and pursue the things that you love.*

So don't sell yourself short. Don't settle for just knowing that the knives are now always in the knife drawer. That achievement is not insignificant, so feel appropriately proud of your accomplishment. But compared to the tremendous amount of time spent hunting for things, maintaining this system should require much less energy.

All that time saved is what this work is about. The time you would have spent hunting for the knife that is now free for other pursuits is the one thing you can't buy or accumulate. The clock is always ticking, and since the only thing we can truly be certain of is this breath, and by extension this day, let's not waste a minute of it hunting for knives. Let's spend every minute we can doing the things we love, whether that's curing cancer or baking a cake or weeding in the garden or drawing a picture with a child. Or sitting on a glider, looking at the sunrise. How much nicer to do any of the above without the nagging thought that you have something else to be doing . . . such as finding the knife. Because you know exactly where the knife is.

Let's also shy away from imperatives such as "spend it wisely," as that implies if you're not hyper-vigilant you may end up spending it foolishly. Rather, let's spend it mindfully. Let's make some conscious and active choices, and then let's not take the evaluating and judging any further.

If watering the garden typically takes twenty minutes and you're still at it two hours later, we may say that you've not been efficiently watering the garden. But perhaps this day you were observing a swarm of butterflies travel from flower to flower, and then you were drawn to the sight of a mother bird feeding some chicks in a nest. And suddenly two hours had passed. I'm not comfortable labeling that time as time spent foolishly. All we know is that it took you two hours to do something that usually takes twenty minutes. That's the fact. The rest is a story.

Likewise, when my father died, I watched a lot of movies—particularly old westerns, which he loved—and napped a lot and ate a fair amount of chicken egg foo yong, his favorite dish. And cried a lot. I was not very productive in a "producing a product" kind of way during that month or so that I took off from work. I wouldn't say that I didn't spend that time wisely. The key element in both of these examples is choice. I chose to spend as long as I needed mourning my father's death and celebrating his life. The fictional person in the garden chose to linger and observe nature. In both cases, we were the agents of decision, not reacting to fear or some looming unformed worry that something else should have been happening. Many other things could have been happening, but none were more important than what we had chosen to do at that time. And that's what I wish for you. Enough time to make choices that satisfy you in the short term, leaving you with no regrets in the long term.

We want to get the business of running your home and your life down to a mechanical, easily maintained system so the bulk of your day, when you're not trading your time for money at work, is filled with things that feed your spirit. Things that make the world a better place for you and those you love and even those you may never meet. So that the only time you're racing for something is when you have a number on your chest and someone else is timing your finish.

Needs vs. Wants

It may be useful to distinguish between these two words, as often people plead for something they desire with a plaintive "I really need it."

Need (noun):
Anything that is necessary but lacking.

Want (noun):
A specific feeling of desire.

One is required and missing; the other is all about longing for. So now, when you evaluate something new by running through those questions on page 360 you'll understand that what you're asking yourself about is need—not want, not desire. I'm all for some good desire, but not at the expense of sanity. I've chased after plenty of things that I was very confused about when it came to distinguishing between need and want. And while I may have enjoyed some of those pursuits, cleaning up the mess left in the wake of those pursuits was never fun. And every cleaning up lasted so much longer than even the most delicious pursuit ever did.

Language is important. How we talk about things is important. We, as well as other people, are actually listening very carefully to the words we use, and if in some hazy moment we mistakenly refer to a want as a need, it will be heard. If only by our subconscious minds. And we'll be off and running after something that we no more *need* than I "needed" five-inch platform shoes in 1974. I really, *really* wanted them, but nobody could ever be persuaded into thinking that I needed them. Except me.

And that is the point. We will deceive ourselves if we deceive no one else.

No one really *loves* a fast-food hamburger. You're not going to marry it and settle down and raise a family with it. You're very fond of it; you find it tasty (when it's fresh—those things have a fifteen-minute shelf life). So while it may seem silly to stress this point, I believe strongly that how we think about stuff and how we talk about stuff significantly informs how we relate to stuff.

Try this exercise. Get your notebook, and write the following sentence in it. Take a few minutes and repeat completing the sentence until you've run out of things to write down. And remember that we're talking about something that is necessary and currently lacking. Think in terms of antibiotics if you have a bacterial infection, or enough money to pay the rent or tuition.

Right now, I need _____.

Once that's finished, let's look at the things we desire that are not essential. On a separate page, write down this sentence and complete it as well. Again, continue writing until you've exhausted the list of things you desire.

Right now, I want _____.

Were you able to list fifteen things that you need, that are actual necessities that are lacking from your life? Were you able to list more? I'm concerned if you are that lacking in basic needs and strongly encourage you to seek assistance in getting those needs met promptly. Clean water, adequate nutritious food, heat in the winter, and clean clothes are available, and there are websites for agencies that will help you to obtain them listed in the Resources section at the back of this book. Be diligent in their pursuit and do not give up until you receive them.

What about wants? Did you fill the page? Did you find yourself writing on several pages because there were so many things to list? That's great. Desire them. Just don't fool yourself into thinking that you need them. In six months, come back and review these lists and see how many of your needs have been met and how many of your wants have either been satisfied or replaced with new things you now desire instead. If you're like most people, your needs will be few and your wants will be a merry-go-round of ever-changing items.

Spiritual Materialism

You are not going to buy your way into heaven. Led Zeppelin wrote that song already. Nor are you going to buy your way into serenity. Surrounding yourself with crystals and Buddhas or other icons and inspirational sayings can bring you only so far. Lighting candles and hoping that somehow by burning enough paraffin something will shift without your moving another muscle is perhaps overly optimistic and possibly misguided. You can lay the groundwork for change this way, you can create an environment that is peaceful and calm and pretty, but then you actually have to take some action, some peaceful, calm, and pretty action, if you want to see those characteristics reflected in your life as well.

You might think you're "in the zone" when you're shopping, you might feel at one with the universe, but the act of shopping is not the same as sitting and meditating. If it were, you'd see shopping malls filled with Buddhist monks and monasteries filled with shopping bags.

So be mindful of what the actual goal is. If you want a calm and peaceful and pretty life, make choices that support that outcome. Simplifying your life will bring you closer to calm and peaceful than will any amount of crystals or incense or robes you surround yourself with. Like most things of significance, this too is an inside job. Don't worry so much about dressing up the outside; keep the drawer tidy and clean—the outside will take care of itself.

Regardless of how serene the photo spreads in shelter magazines or catalogs of simple, elegant environments appear, we don't have a clue as to how people actually live in those spaces. If you've ever opened the spare-room door and thrown every nonessential item lying around the house in that room and then slammed the door before company arrived, you too may have presented a calm and so-called Zen environment to your guests. At least for one night. So let's not judge a book by its cover. If what you want is a clean, crisp, uncluttered home, create one. If you want a clean, crisp, efficient, and uncluttered life, create one of those. Less stuff, rather than different stuff, is probably going to bring you closer to gentle restful stillness. It has for me.

Belief as Definition

What do we believe about ourselves, and how does that define what we feel, what we think, what we do? Are there things we don't attempt because of a particular belief? Are there things we continue to do, even if the results are less than desirable, because of a particular belief?

We can know certain things definitively. For me: I'm 6'1", my eyes are brown, my hair is brown, and I weigh 170 pounds. Those are facts.

I believed at one time that I was going to work in the theater for the rest of my life. I loved my work, was good at it, and while many other things came and went over the years, the theater remained constant. I had no reason to doubt that would ever change. I genuinely felt called to be an artist.

Flash forward to 1996. I was laid off from a theater I was running in Seattle. I spent six more months there, acting and directing and looking for administrative work, before I decided to head back to the East Coast. Almost immediately, I got a gig coproducing an awards ceremony at the Kennedy Center in Washington, D.C. One of the awardees was a prominent author and Nobel Peace Prize winner. I went to New York to collect some photos from his office, and what I found was a mess. The photos were in complete disarray—some were mislabeled and some had been lent out and never returned, others missing entirely. After a few hours in the office there, the Nobel Peace Prize winner's wife asked me into their apartment for a soda. We talked about life and what I had been doing most recently and my plans to move back to New York after the awards presentation. She asked me if I wanted a job organizing their photographs. I started to tear up, I was so moved by her offer and at the thought of coming to work for such a remarkable humanitarian. We made arrangements for me to start in late December, once I had returned to the city. I took the photos I needed and headed back to D.C., giddy with possibility and excitement.

Well, I never went to work for them. Over three months, we had scheduled as many start dates, and three times their assistant phoned me to reschedule, the last time with no new start date. When another month passed and I still hadn't heard back from them, I let it go. I couldn't bring myself to call them a fourth time—it just seemed too desperate. I figured if they knew how to reach me to cancel, they knew how to reach me to reschedule.

But in the meantime I had told everyone I talked to that I had this great gig creating a comprehensive photographic archive for this Nobel laureate. I mean, what an honor! And I was thinking big. After I got all the missing photos back, after I found the misfiled and mislaid photos from around the office and everything was all together, I was imagining publishing a coffee-table photo book. From the few images I had seen, I thought that book would be a slam dunk.

My enthusiasm must have been infectious, because a friend referred me to her accountant, who needed a filing system created. And when that work was completed, I started getting calls from several of the accountant's clients, who showed up with duffel bags full of receipts. They hadn't filed taxes in four or more years, were overwhelmed, were now being pursued by the IRS, and were so frightened and tardy that they didn't know where to begin. I organized the receipts, entered them into the computer, and created reports for the accountant. And this kind of word-of-mouth momentum continued to spread. Each new client led to three more.

In addition to organizing folks, I was still freelancing as a director and a producer. I even had a play that I wrote presented off-Broadway during this time. But as busy as I was with theater work, it felt to me as though my life was shifting in some way. The work I was doing with clients was immediate and powerful, and I could see the impact my efforts had on their lives instantly. There was no metaphor between us, just clear communication, direction, and results.

In 1998, I made a decision to pursue this work full-time. It was as if there was a huge neon YES in the sky right in front of my face and I couldn't look away. It felt wrong somehow to turn away from that yes—simply because I had this historical belief and expansive résumé that said I was a theater artist. Because what I knew, what I had come to know after many years, was that, more than anything, I was supposed to be of use to my fellows. And I had also discovered that I couldn't always know the best way to be of use, that it was often revealed to me in small increments, without warning or a recognizable pattern.

My work in the theater had been in alignment with that sense of service for many years, and I'm certain that I did positively affect people's lives through my work as an artist—they've told me so in restaurants, on street corners, and in shopping malls. And yet here was this new opportunity. Was I going to hold fast to a belief that seemed to be growing obsolete but had been with me, had comforted me and guided me, for so many years previously? Or was I willing to lay down that belief in service of something else? Something where the outcome was unpredictable but that felt so appropriately seated in my body and my heart that it would have felt like a betrayal to ignore. I think by now you can sense how not "woo-woo" I am. So when I tell you that this decision to open my hands and let fall the one thing that had defined me for more than twenty years had nothing to do with my analytical abilities and everything to do with my feelings, I'm as awed by it today as I was when it first happened.

This was not a decision for which I could make a pro-and-con list and calculate my risk. And thinking back to that time, I can tell you that I wasn't frightened. I was uncertain, I was confused, I was curious, but I was not afraid. It just felt like the next thing I should be doing.

And while this story is about a large-scale belief shifting, regardless of the scale of the belief, the point is still the same—that space for something new requires letting go.

So if you began reading this book believing that stuff brings you happiness, would you consider reconsidering that belief now? After working your way through this book, after experiencing some relief as a result of letting things go, of finding things the first time you looked for them, of walking into a room and not wanting to turn around and run out because it was so suffocating, could it be possible that in fact stuff does not bring you happiness? Or maybe not in the way you thought? Is it possible that something else does instead? Wouldn't it be great to find out what that is? And imagine if what that is doesn't even cost any money? Wow!

I'm not suggesting that you discard everything you've ever believed in. I am suggesting that anytime you see yourself about to turn away from something that holds out a promise you desire, and the only thing standing between you and the pursuit of that desire is a belief, that you spend enough time examining that belief to be sure that what you believe in is solid and grounded in your belly. Not superstition or something you read in a book or overheard in a café, or, like me, something you believed in and relied on successfully for twenty years and came to take for granted. Make sure that belief is as valid today as it was when you first adopted it. Then you'll never have regrets over choices made or paths not taken.

"VirgoMan, I Think I'll Miss You Most of All. . . ."

We've come to the end of our time together, at least for now.

I feel you strong and capable, thoughtful and alert, and ready for the challenges ahead of you. I am confident you'll find your way through whatever adventures lie before you, known and yet to come. You have the skills, you have the knowledge, and if you also possess the willingness, you truly are a triple threat.

Remember the things we've discussed, hold on to and honor the things you value that are not objects, and hold lightly in the palm of your hand the objects that you value. Figuratively, of course, if you're thinking of your hot tub right now. . . .

Do not expect or demand perfection from yourself. What you can expect is that if you are diligent about this work, if you are mindful and patient and kind and steady, you will always find whatever you are looking for, whether that's inside the knife drawer or inside your heart.

In peace and in simplicity, I wish you success and happiness in all you attempt, and thank you for spending this time with me. It's been an honor.

Here's to kicking the clutter habit once and for all!

Namaste.

Thank-Yous and Acknowledgments

While I did all of the initial typing and plenty of thinking, this book was not a solo effort. I'd like to recognize the following people for their contributions.

Thanks to Dr. James Rapport and the rest of the folks from Northern Michigan University's Theater Department, for the love and care they showed me in years past in that oft-frozen landscape we affectionately call the UP (that's Upper Peninsula for those not in the know). In addition, two professors at NMU, Tom Hruska and Phil Legler, taught me the craft of writing from very different perspectives, not surprisingly both leading to the same place.

That time in northern Michigan powerfully shaped part of who I've become today.

For personal and/or professional reasons I'd like to thank: Andrew Baron Cohen, Andrew Wendt, Anna Carafelli, Beth Godley, Betty Rogers, Bob and Donna Wright, Carolyn and David March, Carolyne Landon, Chip and Caren Dingman, Chuck London, Cookie Schamroth, Craig Manzino, Daigan Vincent Gaither, Dan Sullivan, Darrin Bodner, David Stewart, Dean Western, DeAnna and John Margiore, the folks at RIVR Media (especially Dee, Rob, Craig, and Leigh), Desmond Rutherford, Dody DiSanto, Dyana Robenalt, Edith Wolff, Eleuthera Lisch, Ellen and Mike Shaler, Eric Schwartz, Francis Donnelley, George Fulginiti-Shakar, George Kimmerling, Gillian Caldwell, Gordon Brode, Herb White, Ileana Gomez, Jason Oxreider, Jerry Beaver, Jim McCarthy, Jim Zarchin, John Breitweiser, John Coleman, John Dillon, John Dreyfuss, John Troyan, Johnny Caruso, Joyce Ellen Weinstein, Karen Kraig, Keith Aldred, Keith Curran, Keith Weber, Kevin Berrill, Kevin Scullin, Larry Fuller, Larry Vrba, Laura Yost Manthey, Lee Fox, Linda Heller Kamm, Lisa Acocella, Lisa Lapides Sawicki, Lisa Lerner, Liz Dolan,

Lynne McGinty, Lynnie Raybuck, Marion and Elie Wiesel, Mark and Jill Chafetz, Mark Epstein, Martha Sturgeon, Mary Mitchener, Maryellen Hurwitz, Michael Kunnari, Michael Lassell, Michael Polscer, Michael MacLennan, Morris Ardoin, Nancy O'Hara, Natasha Reatig, Park Borchert, Peggy Thorp, Peter Edlund, Peter Walsh, Phil Rossiello, Ray "Skip" Sheetz and Michael Perry, Reid Williams, Richard de Long, Richard Eagan and Elizabeth Ostrow Eagan, Robert "Bobby" Efros, Robert Thurman, Roberta Rockwell, Sarah Stebbins, Seiko Susan Morningstar, Sheila Layo, Shellye Arnold, Stephanie Kelly, Stephanie Winston, Stewart Hopkins and Nancy Werner, Susan Protter, Tabitha Vevers, Tamar Getter, Tammy Newmark, Tee Sullivan, Tim Whiteside, Tom Lucidore, Tonen Sara O'Connor, Virginia Kennedy, Virginia Vitzthum, Vito Russo, Vivien Labaton and Nicholas Arons, William and Deborah Boyer, and William Harrop.

Gita Drury and Nicole "Jade" Ullmann are so much more than walking testimonials, although their willingness and ability to spread the gospel of VirgoMan amazes me. They are good friends, ardent supporters, and true believers in the power of transformation and I appreciate and celebrate their constancy.

My family have been great and steadfast cheerleaders. They've expressed their pride and love in small and large ways. My mother and father have encouraged me in my endeavors, even when they couldn't see what I was up to or where it was leading. I'm grateful for the independence I've experienced that has allowed me to always find my own way. Other kin I'd like to thank individually include: my "better than aunts" Lois Chafetz and Sandy Efros, Sara Jones, Elyse Kaps, Irene Krinsky, Scott Krinsky, Leslye Page, Betty, David and Erinn Mellen, Burton Osborne, Neil Osborne, Ethel and Gary Rosenblatt, Leslie Rosenblatt, Marc Rosenblatt, Lauren Turetsky, Susan and Maurice Turetsky, Andrea Wilber Marcus, and Stuart Wilber. Special thanks to my talented cousin Lauren Turetsky, who designed the VirgoMan logo over bagels in Santa Fe and perfected it in her design studio.

Rosalind Wiseman offered advice at various junctures and more than that, introduced me to my agent, James Levine. Twice.

Sharon Salzberg and Molly O'Neill each have taught me much—about writing and sitting still and writing some more. They are both deeply talented, prolific, and remarkably kind. Their counsel has been consistently practical and sage.

Good friends who are also very smart people read this book in various forms and offered excellent feedback and encouragement (and laughs). They are: Linda Badami, Jaime Grant, Judith Helfand, Linda Lippner, Michael Mark, and Tina Sabuco. A special thank-you to Linda Badami, who christened me VirgoMan one morning in her DC storeroom. Who knew then where it would lead . . .

Thanks to Amy Gross, Gayle King, Pat Towers, Sudie Redmond, Liz Brody, Suzan Colon, and the folks at *O, The Oprah Magazine*. That lunch was something special and the piece was, too. And Amy Gross read these pages and offered her strong encouragement and frank feedback, which helped carry me through more than a few questioning days.

My many clients have informed my work and the information in this book—to protect their privacy, I'll simply acknowledge them here without naming names. They know who they are. Their kindness, willingness, and receptivity have taught me much—as have their reticence and resistance. It's all grist for the mill. Together we've pushed and pulled in all directions, seeking and discovering many universal and some very personal solutions to clutter and organization. They like to say they don't know what they'd do without me. Without them and their generosity, I don't know if I would have connected these dots in quite this way. Thanks to them, we don't have to wonder.

Laurie Brown, Sarah Byam, Nancy Stern, and Jennifer White provided a perfect blend of cheerleading and critical vision. Their astute, spot-on feedback consistently guided me to write better, smarter, and cleaner. They are all over these pages, in the best ways.

Gaylord Neely served as midwife to this book—or to me—it's sometimes hard to discern the difference. I know this is a better book, I'm a better writer, and certainly I'm a better person for her friendship, love, and support.

My agent, James Levine, took my energy, enthusiasm, and vision and helped me shape the proposal that brought us here. He was my steward in navigating the world of publishing and he did it with skill, generosity, and wit. What a gift.

Publisher Megan Newman extended a warm welcome to me from our first meeting, and that has remained throughout the amazing process of turning words and ideas into something slightly more concrete. She has guided this book through Avery's halls (and computers) with great acumen and ease, setting the tone for the entire collaboration. And all the folks at Avery have been a delight to work with. My editor, Lucia Watson, has brought her deep enthusiasm, sharp mind, and light touch to the process. Talk about gifts—an editor who gets it and gives it and loves it. And her assistant, Miriam Rich, brought similar heart, discipline, and efficiency to the project. Thanks to her, I always felt supported and these pages actually made it into the book.

Finally, I thank the countless strangers and friends, named and unnamed, who have shown me a better way to be. Through their examples, I strive to pass on what I have gleaned as I stumble and dance my way along the path. It's not always been pretty, but I do seem to keep moving . . . and miraculously, there's always been a hand out to steady me at just the right moment.

I'm humbled and grateful for the opportunity to grow that each day presents, and hope I adequately treasure that gift for the jewel it is, even when lurching forward, consumed with utter humanness. It is grace that has brought me this far, and grace that helps me to know it. Thank you for allowing me to share it with you.

Appendix: What to Save

HOW LONG SHOULD I KEEP THIS?

When does stuff become clutter? When it ceases to serve you. And paper that no longer serves you presents unique storage challenges and potential hazards. From the need to securely store sensitive documents to possible losses (late and missed payments, identity theft), the consequences of improper filing and record keeping may be devastating.

Items you'll keep indefinitely should be stored in a safe-deposit box at your financial institution or in a fireproof container at home. These storage spaces should also contain a list and photocopies of all current ATM debit cards, credit cards, contracts, and agreements, as well as your valid driver's license and passport.

Laws and circumstances will change and it's always better to be safe than sorry when you have access to a shredder, so please confirm the following information with appropriate legal or financial advisers before disposing of anything.

Finally, this is what we know today: the current tax code allows the IRS three years from the filing date to examine your return for errors. They have up to six years to audit your return if they suspect underreported gross income of 25 percent or more. There is no statute of limitations on an audit when deliberate fraud is suspected.

THE "SHOULD I STAY OR SHOULD I GO?" CHART

If you are self-employed or have been advised to retain records to support your tax return filings, retain all records for seven years.

Toss After One Month

- ATM and bank deposit/withdrawal slips. Retain until your monthly statement is received and reconciled.

RECEIPTS, CASH

Enter these into your checkbook or computer software if you track expenses.

- Major purchase with warranty. Staple to the owner's manual and retain for the duration of the warranty.
- Major purchase without warranty. Retain if the replacement cost exceeds the deductible on your insurance policy.
- Minor purchase without warranty. Shred.

RECEIPTS, CREDIT/DEBIT

Retain these until your monthly statement is received and reconciled.

- Major purchase with warranty. Staple to the owner's manual and retain for the duration of the warranty.
- Major purchase without warranty. Retain if the replacement cost exceeds the deductible on your insurance policy.
- Minor purchase without warranty. Shred.

Toss After One Year

- Bank/financial institution statements (monthly)
- Brokerage/mutual fund statements (monthly/quarterly statements after reconciled with annual statement)
- Credit card statements (monthly statements)
- Credit reports. You are entitled to free reports from all credit bureaus each year. Review for errors and update as needed.
- Mortgage statements (monthly statements after compared with annual statement/Form 1098)
- Telephone/utility bills (monthly statements)

Keep for Three Years

- Correspondence (general—not sentimental)
- Insurance policies (expired)
- Pay stubs. Reconcile annually with your W-2 or 1099.
- Unemployment income stubs. Reconcile annually with your W-2 or 1099.

Keep for Seven Years

- Contracts and leases (expired)
- Mortgage statements (annual)
- Options records (expired)
- Tax return backup paperwork (cancelled checks/receipts/statements), including but not limited to:
  - Alimony/child support paid or received
  - Charitable donations (monetary and in-kind)
  - Child-care receipts
  - Credit card year-end statements
  - Disability records
  - Medical expenses
  - Mortgage interest 1098 forms
  - Retirement account contributions
  - Utility and Teledata company year-end statements
  - W-2 or 1099 forms

Keep for the Duration of Ownership or Expiration Date

- Auto insurance card and registration
- Bank account registers and debit cards
- Canceled checks (for real estate purchases, major purchases, capital improvements)
- Contracts and leases still in effect (expiration date plus seven years)
- Credit card account information and rates
- Insurance policies: auto/home/life/medical/renters (current)
- Leases (current)
- Motor vehicle titles, purchase receipts, and licenses, records of auto service/repair
- Passport
- Pension and retirement plans
- Real property deeds, titles, purchase contracts, bills of sale, abstracts, appraisals, construction documents
- Receipts for major home improvements and renovations (capital improvements)
- Sales receipts for major purchases (until warranty expires or return/exchange period expires)
- Savings certificates
- Stocks, bonds, and other securities

Keep Indefinitely

- Accident reports/claims (including related medical records)
- Adoption and custody records
- Advance directives (living will/durable power of attorney for health care or health care proxy)
- Audit reports prepared by accountants
- Birth certificates
- Burial lot deed
- Canceled checks (for tax payments)
- Citizenship papers
- Correspondence (legal or important)
- Death certificate
- Divorce agreement and decree
- Education records (diplomas, transcripts, tuition records, school correspondence—for yourself and your children)
- Employment records
- Insurance records of claims made and paid
- Inventory of household goods and appraisals, updated as needed (including rental property)
- Inventory of valuable papers, their location, and contact information for all advisers
- Investment records clearly showing beneficiary information (purchase/sale/transfer records)
- IRS audits
- Jewelry and other valuable items
- Licenses
- Loan documents and notes (loans you've made)
- Marriage certificate/license
- Medical records, updated as needed (including immunization records for children)
- Military records
- Mortgages (letters of satisfaction), other lien documents (for home and any rental property)
- Powers of attorney
- Religious records
- Settlement agreements, claims and litigation documents
- Social Security card
- Tax assessment notices
- Tax returns
- Will

Resources

While it may go without saying, I'll say it anyway: the Internet and its contents are in a constant state of evolution, with new sites coming online and favorite sites disappearing or changing their URLs with equal suddenness. We'll use this as another valuable lesson in the impermanence of all things, while acknowledging the potential frustration that happens when searching for something familiar or desired that can't be found.

When we went to press, all these sites were live and valid. If they are no longer, I humbly ask your forgiveness and encourage you to seek comparable sites and tools using any number of search engines and key words. As with most things, cleverness and diligence will yield a bounty of results—most of them even desired!

Alas, I must also report that none of these sites have provided any sort of consideration for inclusion here. To avoid partisanship, I am also not endorsing any products or services offered at these sites—please use caution and your best judgment when visiting and contacting any of them.

A quick Internet search, at home or in the public library, may yield a bounty of local services available in your area to help with recycling, repurposing, and disposing of your excess belongings. Do not be discouraged in your pursuit of proper placement for your surplus stuff—a little stamina and tenacity will go far in finding the best home possible.

I've refrained from listing commercial sites where you can purchase things and products for getting organized. There are many out there—shop smartly, and remember that *you* will get yourself organized, not any amount of tubs or containers or gorgeous shiny gadgets, even if they are on sale!

BASIC HUMAN NEEDS RESOURCES

- HUD's Housing and Rental Assistance: http://portal.hud.gov/portal/page/portal/HUD/topics/rental_assistance
- The National Domestic Violence Hotline: http://www.ndvh.org/
- USDA's Nutrition Assistance Programs: http://www.fns.usda.gov/fns/

RECYCLING

Appliances

- American Council for an Energy-Efficient Economy: http://www.aceee.org/Consumerguide/disposal.htm
- Appliance Recycling Centers of America, Inc.: http://www.arcainc.com/home.html

Books

- Adopt a Library: http://www.adoptalibrary.org/
- The Daily Green's "Ten Helpful Ways to Recycle Used Books" (good resource for more than just books): http://www.thedailygreen.com/going-green/community-tips/recycle-used-books-460808

Clothing

- Dress for Success: http://www.dressforsuccess.org/
- The Good Human (another multipurpose site): http://www.thegoodhuman.com/2008/04/06/earthtalk-recycling-worn-out-clothing/
- GreenStrides: http://www.greenstrides.com/2010/01/06/recycle-non-wearable-clothing-and-shoes/
- Wearable Collections (NYC area only): http://wearablecollections.com/locations.php

Computer • Electronic Devices • Toxic Materials (Mercury, Batteries, Cell Phones, Etc.)

- Battery Solutions: http://www.batteryrecycling.com/?src=google
- Call 2 Recycle: http://www.call2recycle.org/home.php?c=1&w=1&r=Y
- Cell Phones for Soldiers: http://www.cellphonesforsoldiers.com/
- Computer Hope: http://www.computerhope.com/disposal.htm
- Computer Recycling Center: http://www.crc.org/
- Earth911: http://earth911.com/
- The Green PC: http://www.thegreenpc.com/

- Recycle My Cell Phone: http://recyclemycellphone.org/
- U.S. Environmental Protection Agency: http://www.epa.gov/waste/conserve/materials/ecycling/donate.htm
- World Environmental Organization: http://www.world.org/weo/recycle

Shredding Options
- Cintas: http://www.cintas.com/DocumentManagement/DocumentShredding.aspx
- Code Shred: http://www.codeshred.com/
- Shred-it: http://www.shredit.com/index_v2.asp

ANNOYANCES

Catalog Opt-Out Options
- Catalog Choice: http://www.catalogchoice.org/

Credit Card Offers
- Maintained by all three credit bureaus: 1-888-5-OPTOUT (1-888-567-8688)

E-mail Opt-Out Lists
- Direct Marketing Association Choice: http://www.ims-dm.com/cgi/optoutemps.php

Junk Mail Opt-Out Lists
- The Consumerist: http://consumerist.com/2008/03/8-ways-to-opt-out-of-junk-mail-lists.html
- Direct Marketing Association Choice: https://www.dmachoice.org/
- Do-It-Yourself: http://www.obviously.com/junkmail/
- Do Not Mail: http://www.donotmail.org/?gclid=CPSetLjrs58CFQk65Qodo39I0w
- Federal Trade Commission: http://www.ftc.gov/privacy/protect.shtm
- 41 Pounds: http://www.41pounds.org/
- The Privacy Council: http://privacycouncil.org
- Privacy Rights Clearinghouse: http://www.privacyrights.org/fs/fs4-junk.htm

National "Do Not Call" Phone Registry
- https://www.donotcall.gov/

Index